HABERMAS, MODERNITY, and PUBLIC THEOLOGY

HABERMAS, MODERNITY, and PUBLIC THEOLOGY

Edited by

Don S. Browning

and

Francis Schüssler Fiorenza

CROSSROAD • NEW YORK

1992

The Crossroad Publishing Company
370 Lexington Avenue, New York, NY 10017

Printed in the United States of America
Typesetting output: T_EXSource, Houston

Library of Congress Cataloging-in-Publication Data

Habermas, modernity, and public theology / edited by Don S. Browning
and Francis Schüssler Fiorenza.
    p.   cm.
    Chiefly papers first delivered at a conference held at the
Divinity School of the University of Chicago, Oct. 7–9, 1988, titled
"Critical Theory, its Promise and Limitations for a Theology of the
Public Realm."
    Includes bibliographical references.
    ISBN 0-8245-1107-7
    1. Habermas, Jürgen—Congresses.   2. Critical theory—Congresses.
3. Theology—20th century—Congresses.   I. Browning, Don S.
II. Fiorenza, Francis Schüssler.
B3258.H324H34   1992
230'.01—dc20   91-23283
                                           CIP

Contents

Preface

Most of the papers in this volume were first delivered at a conference held at the Divinity School of the University of Chicago on October 7–9, 1988. The conference was organized by Phil Devenish and me and was titled "Critical Theory: Its Promise and Limitations for a Theology of the Public Realm." The costs of the conference were covered by a grant from the Lilly Endowment, Inc. On behalf of the Divinity School, I want to express our deep appreciation to Robert Lynn, then vice-president and in charge of the religion division of the Lilly Endowment, for financial assistance with this conference.

There were other participants in the Chicago conference whose written and oral responses to some of these papers cannot be included here. These include Robert Bertram, Mary Knutsen, Paul Lakeland, Joseph Prabhu, and Robert Schreiter. I want to express my deep appreciation for their important contributions.

Finally, my assistant, Ian Evison, not only helped organize the original conference but also helped pull together this volume. His energy and good spirit make every project go more smoothly. I greatly appreciate all that he has done.

DON S. BROWNING

Introduction:
A Critical Reception
for a Practical Public Theology

Francis Schüssler Fiorenza

Jürgen Habermas is by far the most pre-eminent and influential philosopher in Germany. The breath and depth of his writings are remarkable. Their influence extends over a broad range of disciplines that include philosophy, social theory, hermeneutics, anthropology, linguistics, ethics, educational theory, and public policy. The impact of Habermas's writings upon theology extends across its diverse disciplines, from fundamental to political theology, and from moral to practical theology.

This influence of Habermas's work upon theology has led to innumerable monographs and articles in which theologians have either commented on Habermas's work or have drawn out its implications for theology.[1] In entering into dialogue with Habermas this collection of essays makes a unique contribution in two significant ways.

First of all, it focuses on his most recent work, especially, Habermas's interpretation of modernity, his theory of communicative action, and his development of a discourse ethic. Much of the theological interest in Habermas has concentrated on his early writings, especially the relation between theory and practice, the delineation of three cognitive interests (technological, communicative, and emancipatory), and the analysis of the legitimation crisis of modern capitalist society. By focusing on Habermas's more recent work, the essays eliminate some of the prevalent misreadings of Habermas's work within theological literature — misreadings that have simplistically emphasized practice without attending to the more theoretical component and nuances of Habermas's critical theory.

1

Second, these essays advance a dialogue between theology and Habermas's work. Despite the widespread theological interest in Habermas, a serious and sustained dialogue between Habermas and theologians has not taken place. While theologians might have appealed to Habermas's work, he himself has not responded and entered into the theological discussion. This volume is exceptional insofar as it provides such a dialogue and response.

The occasion for such a dialogue has been provided by Don Browning. With his inspiration and planning, the Divinity School of the University of Chicago sponsored a conference entitled "Critical Theory: Its Promise and Limitations for a Theology of the Public Realm," on October 7–9, 1989. At this conference a large number of papers and responses explored the significance of critical theory for public theology. The contributors dealt specifically with Habermas's most recent work; as a participant in the conference, he responded to many of the papers during the course of the conference, and at the end of the conference developed a typology of the diverse theological positions. He thereby has elaborated his views on the theological reception of his work as well as on the relation between theology and critical theory.

This volume includes the papers and some of the responses from the Chicago conference. In addition, though Charles Davis and Gary Simpson were not at the Chicago conference, we have included essays of theirs in this volume. These deal directly with the relation between Habermas's critical theory and public theology. Whereas Charles Davis's essay stems from his book *Theology and Political Society,* one of the first English treatments of the relation between critical theory and theology, Gary Simpson's essay, a widely read contribution from the *Journal of the American Academy of Religion,* represents a distinctive theological approach.[2] Habermas has expanded his response in order to take them into account.

In examining the relation between critical theory and a public and practical theology, the contributors to the present volume mark both the promise and limitations of Habermas's basic arguments and categories. They appropriate his insights, although not uncritically. The contributors do not simply take over Habermas's categories or proposals in order to apply them to theology. Instead they enter into a genuine conversation with Habermas. They challenge Habermas as much as they learn from him. The result is theology both critical and practical. A theology for the public realm is not merely the application of a theory to practice, with critical theory replacing traditional theory. Instead it is the entering into the public arena of discussion and dialogue whereby theology is as much challenged as it challenges.

Through such mutual challenge and critical dialogue, these essays constitute prime examples of what Don Browning has advocated as practical theology.[3] Such a practical theology "involves the highly philosophical turns of fundamental theology and the hermeneutical turns of systematic theology."[4] It explores the theoretical interpretation of contemporary praxis in social theory with a method of mutually critical correlation. Such practical theology does not apply theory to practice, be it social theory or Christian faith, but is itself constituted by the critical interaction between theory and practice as well as between social theory and theology.

The majority of the contributors are theologians. In fact, even the two nontheologians, Robert Wuthnow, a sociologist of religion, and Fred R. Dallmayr, a political philosopher, are conversant with religious themes and their theological explication. The theologians here share the conviction that religious traditions contain resources necessary for interpreting human nature and society. Consequently, theological reflection on the meaning of religious traditions can significantly contribute to an understanding not only of human nature and society, but also of rationality and modernity. On the basis of this shared conviction, they argue that if Habermas would attend more to the role of religion within human life and society, he would more closely realize his project for a communicative rationality under the conditions of modernity and would offer a more comprehensive understanding of rationality, society, and modernity.

The contributors maintain that religious traditions and theological reflection point to a dimension of public and private life that ultimately supports the overcoming of the reduction of rationality to technocratic and strategic reasoning — the very goal of Habermas's communicative rationality. They argue that Habermas's very insights and goals can be more consistently developed and achieved if one draws out the implications not only of a critical theory for religion and theology, but also of religion and theology for critical theory.

Habermas's work is complex, covering a wide range of topics. A reader unfamiliar with his work is best advised to first read one of the excellent English introductions to it.[5] Moreover, since the essays presuppose some basic knowledge of the principal arguments of Habermas's *Theory of Communicative Action*, some acquaintance with it would be helpful.[6] These essays do not provide such a general introduction, but instead concentrate on several specific themes that are central to the interrelation of religion and the modern public realm.

The first of these themes, the relation between rationality and the public realm, is inherent in Habermas's communicative conception of rationality. Habermas elaborates this conception through a speech-act theory of language, a classification of validity claims, and a discourse theory of ethics. The second theme, the interpretation of modernity, is developed by Habermas through the categories of life-world and system and by means of the thesis of the colonization of the lifeworld through monetarization and bureaucratization. These two themes are unfolded in diverse variations throughout the essays in their exposition of the promise and limitations of Habermas's critical theory for a theology of the public realm.

In reading the various essays from the perspective of these two themes, it is helpful to attend to what the various authors consider to be the promise of Habermas's work for an understanding of the interrelation between rationality and the public realm and for an interpretation of modernity. Then one can examine what they view as Habermas's limitations with regard to the interpretation of modernity and the relation between system and lifeworld within modernity. In this way, the basic issues in the conversation between the authors and Habermas will come to the fore. It will then become apparent why many argue that a critical reflection upon the religious dimension of human experience is as constructive for critical theory as critical theory is for theology.

THE PUBLIC REALM AND RATIONALITY

From the beginning of his academic career, Habermas has focused on the nature of the public realm. His investigations of the historical, societal, and political preconditions of the institutionalization of practical public discourse have linked rationality with public discourse. In his first published work, *The Structural Transformation of the Public Sphere: An Inquiry into a Category of Bourgeois Society*,[7] Habermas argued that in the eighteenth and nineteenth centuries modern societies contained a democratic public sphere in which political and social issues were discussed. Consensus and opinion on public affairs were formed by debate in the public sphere.

The public sphere is broadly defined by Habermas as a "realm of social life in which something approaching public opinion can be formed."[8] Indeed, "a portion of the public sphere comes into being in every conversation in which private individuals assemble to form a public opinion."[9] In this public sphere, in which dialogue and conversation form opinion and consent, practical political rationality is formed. Through his elaboration of the significance of the public sphere, Habermas provides a basic framework for his conception of discourse ethics and practical political reasoning.[10]

The importance of the public realm lies in the link between

rationality and public dialogue. Habermas endeavors to develop a conception of rationality that avoids the dual pitfalls of either an instrumental or a monological conception of rationality. Whereas an instrumental or technocratic rationality limits rationality to the choice of means rather than to a decision about substantial ends, a monological conception of rationality bases rationality on an individual's self-reflection. Against both the technocratic and monological conceptions of rationality, Habermas associates rationality with the raising of validity claims in communication and consequently seeks to elaborate the communicative nature of rationality. Such a conception of rationality as communicative underlies Habermas's critical theory of public discourse and provides the basis for its promise.

In many respects David Tracy's essay sets the agenda for the volume, for it touches on all the significant issues raised herein. Tracy shows that a communicative understanding of rationality is significant for the public nature of theology. It compels theology to recognize that the public with which theology is in dialogue is neither an abstract universal public nor a monological reason but rather a public constituted by open conversations, plural discourses, and diverse communities.[11] Theology becomes public insofar as it enters into dialogue with many voices and diverse communities within society. The appeal to the public nature of theology within the context of a communicative understanding of rationality does not deny the existence of particularity, as the critics of theological correlation imply. On the contrary, it acknowledges particularity, for it takes contemporary pluralism so seriously that it surrenders the idea that theology represents a privileged cultural and linguistic form of life. And it understands theology as a communicative undertaking that becomes public precisely through its openness to conversation and dialogue.

My own essay constitutes a similar argument in regard to ethical discourse. Habermas views ethical discourse as a type of practical reasoning that seeks to adjudicate conflicting moral points of view about how we ought to live. For Habermas, however, moral reasoning does not adjudicate different moral points behind a "veil of ignorance" (as in Rawls's original position), but rather in concrete discourse with others. Habermas replaces Kant's monological reflecting moral subject with a community of subjects engaging in moral discourse.

Habermas's discourse ethic provides a model for understanding the role of the tradition of moral discourse and the public task of political theology. A communicative conception of rationality impels a political theology to base its political and moral appeals not simply upon the authority of a religious tradition, but rather upon open discourse within the community and in relation to the discourses of other communities within the public realm. Habermas's communicative conception of reason should inhibit political and liberation theologies from basing their ethical political judgments upon abstract appeals to natural law, divine command, eschatological proviso, or apocalyptic interruption. A political and liberation theology sensitive to a communicative conception of rationality must be willing to submit its religious claims and their political implications to the challenge of public discourse.

Likewise, Charles Davis argues that by widening the concept of rationality beyond an instrumental one, Habermas provides theologians with a framework in which to explore the rational underpinning of the distinctive validity claims of religious hope. In a quasi-transcendental fashion, he examines the validity claims of hope with reference to an unconstrained discourse within a particular religious community, in particular the Christian community. Davis concludes that Habermas's approach to rationality undercuts theological reasoning and interpretations that omit both rational critique and the voices of other traditions. The communicative notion of rationality, therefore, serves a critical function within the theological articulation of Christian hope. Davis thereby attempts to develop a distinctive political theology that links praxis, free discourse, and critical reflection.[12]

In exploring the relation between the communicative nature of rationality and the process of the linguistification of the sacred, Simpson suggests that Habermas's most significant contribution consists in making communicative argumentation through language the basis of community. Since communication brings about rationally motivated agreement, it serves not simply to transmit traditions or agreements, but to bring about agreement and thereby to constitute community. Communicative argumentation forms the basis of a community's solidarity.

In short, the above four theologians illustrate the promise of Habermas's critical theory by exploring how his communicative conception of rationality expands previous conceptions of rationality and how such an expansion affects the understanding of theology. Though they argue from diverse theological perspectives, the authors respectively suggest the significance of communicative rationality for the public nature of theology, the discursive character of political theological affirmations, the nature of hope, and the relation between a communicative conception of rationality and community.

MODERNITY AND ITS INTERPRETATION

Habermas develops his communicative notion of rationality and the importance of the public realm for ethical, practical, and political discourse in combination with an analysis of the transformation of the public realm within modernity.[13] His analysis of this transformation has, therefore, not just a historical, but also a systemic relevance. In *The Structural Transformation of the Public Sphere* Habermas argued that the emergence of the mass media and the culture industries has led to the decline of the public sphere within modern democracies. In *The Theory of Communicative Action*, he explicates this transformation through the categories of system and lifeworld and with the thesis of the colonization of the lifeworld. Interpretations of modernity are often simplifications, and modernity has its critics as well as its defenders. Habermas intends to offer a theoretical framework that enables one to comprehend the achievements of modernity (in particular the significance of the Enlightenment project) and at the same time to grasp both its crises and pathologies.[14]

Robert Wuthnow approaches Habermas from a perspective known as "interpretive sociology," which, as used by Wuthnow, embraces a broad diversity of approaches.[15] He proposes that Habermas contributes to the understanding of modernity through his analysis of the two dominant tendencies of modernity, namely, capital accumulation and state bureaucratization. In this way Habermas goes beyond neo-Marxist and Weberian analyses of advanced capitalism and state socialism. His categories of lifeworld and system as well as his analysis of how money and power function to steer the system of society provide a concrete analysis of modern society — more concrete than the general categories of "public square" or "civil religion." Moreover, Habermas's categories have the distinct advantage that they enable a diagnosis of the ills of capitalist as well as of socialist societies.

Habermas's interpretation of modernity is profiled against the backdrop of the views of the Enlightenment formulated by the early members of the Frankfurt School.[16] Helmut Peukert notes that the first generation of critical theorists sought to diagnose the pathologies of modernity. They viewed these pathologies as stemming from a positivistic scientific view that reduces reason to instrumental and technocratic rationality — a reduction that Peukert has clearly traced and documented in his dissertation, *Science, Action, and Fundamental Theology*.[17] Peukert also traces countermoves to this reductionism and Habermas's attempt to counter this positivism. Modern theories of science and social theories gradually move from positivistic and monological conception of action to ones that are linguistic and social. Habermas's communicative conception of rationality is a further move in this direction; it represents an extension of Peirce's community of scientists and a development of Mead's ideal communication community.

Yet the pathologies of modernity go beyond the reduction of reason to instrumental rationality. They also and especially include such authoritarian political movements as Fascism and Stalinism. Marx's theory of capitalism and Weber's interpretation of modernity as the expansion of bureaucratic administrative power do not suffice to explain these modern pathologies. Habermas's interpretation of modernity and his specific view of the colonization of the life-world provide a better grasp of the dominative power of modernity than Marx's or Weber's. His work, consequently, provides a significantly more precise conceptual framework for understanding both the positive and negative aspects of modernity.

In pointing to the ambiguity of modernity, Helmut Peukert has set the stage for Matthew Lamb's critique of modernity. Lamb argues that modern rationality does not display a linear progression as modernists would have us believe. Instead it exhibits the dogmatism of instrumental rationality as well as the domination of its technological rationality. Lamb suggests that Habermas's analysis of the ambiguity of the rationalization process of modernity provides a significant resource for modern theology. In contrast to the global postmodern criticisms of modernity, Habermas criticizes the modern Enlightenment yet does not abandon the project of the Enlightenment. His dialectical interpretation of modernity steers the middle path between a modern dogmatism and a postmodern nihilism. Following Peukert's interpretation that the critique of reason belongs to the tradition of the Enlightenment, Lamb underscores the point that rationality entails a learning and self-correcting process. Communicative action is, therefore, not simply a new model that replaces an old one. Rather, it involves an ongoing and critical process so that we can and must interpret modernity in a way that makes us aware of its ambiguity, that is, of its potential for domination as well as emancipation.

Though these contributors differ in their assessment of modernity, they point to Habermas's theory as a significant framework for interpreting the ambiguities of modernity, especially the ambiguities of its rationality and power structures. Habermas's categories provide a conceptual framework that is superior to Karl Marx's categories of structure and superstructure and to Max Weber's thesis of privatization. Nevertheless such a positive assessment of Habermas's conceptual framework is coupled with some basic disagreements. These disagreements revolve around the nature and role of religion and they affect the interpretation of modernity and the public-private distinction, insofar as human religiosity relates to human dignity and self-fulfillment.

RELIGION AND THE PUBLIC REALM

A central issue of disagreement is Habermas's interpretation of the historical evolution of religion and the current role of religion within society. The contributors take issue either with Habermas's explicit treatment of religion or, more significantly, with his failure to analyze and to explore the resources of religion for the public sphere.

David Tracy argues that Habermas's insistence that there are three kinds and only three kinds of autonomous validity claims (scientific, social, and aesthetic) does not do justice to the aesthetic and religious dimensions of human life. This division reduces the aesthetic to the expressive and leaves out of consideration the specific validity claims of modern religious thought. Such a neglect leads Habermas to disregard the significance of religion within contemporary social and political movements that are religiously inspired. Examples of such are the involvement of the churches in the civil rights movement and the liberation movements inspired by various theologies. The examples of Martin Luther King, Jr., and Mahatma Gandhi exemplify this connection between religious and political movements.

In several constructive proposals Tracy seeks to articulate the public significance of religion and religious symbols with reference to a post-Kantian process metaphysics and the hermeneutical retrieval of aesthetic and utopian thought. Habermas's awareness of the relation between the beliefs of the world religions and the emergence of a universal formal ethics within the world religions should have prompted him to examine more thoroughly the resources present within religions. Instead, by reducing the claims of art to personal authenticity and by neglecting the claims of religion, Habermas ignores powerful resources that can help work against the very colonization of the lifeworld that he wants to overcome.

Whereas David Tracy aims to articulate the distinctive validity claims of classic religious texts and symbols, Robert Wuthnow crafts the issue in terms not of distinctive rationality claims, but of zones of the lifeworld that are marked off from rationality claims. He is, thereby, questioning whether Habermas's point of departure from thematized validity claims is adequate for understanding and impeding the growing rationalization of the lifeworld. Wuthnow argues that Habermas ought to attend more to the expressive forms of communication that constitute the lifeworld as a means of saving the lifeworld from being increasingly dominated by money and bureaucracy. This argument enables Wuthnow to give a different valence and interpretation to contemporary protest movements, especially the environmental movement. It is based in part on Wuthnow's previous argument that a "dramaturgic" approach to social order broadens the relevant categories of social conditions affecting the meaningfulness of symbolic social actions.[18] In this respect, his argument parallels David Tracy's that the entire breath of symbolic forms, actions, and images needs to be explicated as forms of resistance to colonialization and alienation

Following a line of argument that is similar to Tracy's appeal for a dialogical and conversational public theology, my own essay traces the relation between the tradition of religious and moral discourse and a communicative discourse ethics. Since Habermas distinguishes sharply between issues about the good and the right, he casts his discourse ethics as constituting principles of justification for the question of the right. Though the pluralism of modern societies leads to a focus on the right rather than the good, assumptions about the good are not completely eliminated, as I argue. Instead, there emerges a "thin conception of the public good" within the public sphere. Consequently public practical discourse is impoverished to the extent that it presupposes conceptions of the good that it does not articulate. Since Christian churches, as communities of discourse, seek to interpret the practical potential of their moral and religious traditions, insofar as they enter into discourse with the society, they bring their substantial traditions of the good into discourse with the formal conceptions of the right. Such a discourse has consequences for theology and its relation to public ethical discourse. The ethical discourse within modern theology is not one based exclusively on authority. Rather, it seeks to relate the visions of the religious tradition, as moral and utopian visions of the good, to public discourse about justice.

At the Chicago conference, Sheila Briggs in her lecture raised similar issues from a feminist perspective. (Unfortunately, she was not able to turn the draft of her lecture into a publishable manuscript, and she decided not to publish the draft. Since the lecture referred to an important feminist debate about Habermas's work, it is worth noting this debate as well as Habermas's written response to it.) Her lecture refers to the work of Carol Gilligan, Sharon Welch, and especially Seyla Benhabib.[19] The question is whether Habermas has too sharply divided ethical motivation and application from the cognitive justification of moral principles. In regard to moral practical decisions, Habermas appeals to a principle of universality that justifies these decisions, but appeals to personal and individual cases to apply them. Habermas's distinction pertains to a method of argumentation rather than a social location. These questions, however, suggest that Habermas's conception of communicative reality is thereby caught in a tension between a conception of reason as historical and a conception of reason as formal and abstract. The issue is whether Habermas has sufficiently attended to historical conditioning of moral reasoning and the role of concrete needs and imagination as elements of a discourse ethics.

RELIGION AND THE INTERPRETATION OF MODERNITY

Several contributors caution against the social evolutionary framework in which Habermas has expressed his interpretation of history and modernity. Some point to the transformation of religion within modernity (Tracy, Peukert, Fiorenza). Others echo Metz's theological appeal to "non-contemporaneous religion" as a resource for modifying Habermas's understanding of modernity, and they challenge the modernism of the framework (Peukert, Lamb, Simpson, and Dallmayr). In general, Habermas's interpretation of modernity is challenged in two ways.

First, the experience of massive suffering within modernity pushes us to an interpretation of modernity beyond the colonization of the lifeworld. It ignites the issue of the meaning of suffering. Such an issue appears to reformulate the classic question of theodicy, which is transformed into a question of the meaning of modernity. Second, Habermas's distinction between lifeworld and system resolves in a somewhat ambiguous fashion the relation between the private and the public within modernity. His resolution correlates with his expressive interpretation of religion and art, his specification of the relation between the right and the good or between principles and application, and his understanding of the role that emancipatory groups have within modernity.

Theodicy and Modernity

Several theological contributors (Peukert, Lamb, Simpson) make the theodicy question the context for assessing Habermas's interpretation of modernity. The excess of suffering within modernity is everywhere. The Holocaust has become a symbol of this suffering and evil. Today it continues in the experience of hunger and misery in poor countries, the bloodshed of the Killing Fields of Cambodia, and the countless murders by death squads in Latin America — to name just a few examples. Yet these examples raise the theodicy question, not only as a religious question about the justification of God in the face of suffering, but also as a religious question about the possibility of meaning in the face of such suffering and the possibility of solidarity with the victims of such suffering. Viewing modernity through the lenses of the theodicy question provides theologians the opportunity to examine various interpretations of modernity.

Peukert

Peukert's theological argument borrows the notion of an "unfinished past" from Walter Benjamin and Max Horkheimer and draws upon apocalyptic motifs from the Jewish religious tradition. If our collective historical experience is to have any meaning, then the suffering of those who have been denied their voices in the collective conversation suggest that our search for universal solidarity must include these victims. The experience of Auschwitz and Nazism affects the meaning not only of modernity, but also of justice and of universal solidarity. The traditional theodicy question becomes transformed into one of solidarity and justice within a world of suffering, especially our solidarity with the victims of suffering. When we interpret modernity as a process of rationalization, monetarization, and bureaucratization, then we do not go far enough. When Habermas calls for unlimited conversation, then he does not go far enough unless he takes into account past victims. The colonization of the lifeworld does indeed describe an essential dynamic of the societal process of modernity; the limit question of suffering and of our solidarity with its victims, however, still remains. It is this limit question, raised in religion, that pushes us to the limit question about the solidarity inherent in a communicative rationality.[20]

Lamb, Simpson

The theodicy question, articulated by Peukert, is also raised and developed in diverse fashion in the contributions by Lamb, Simpson, and Davis. Lamb argues that the massive poverty and misery within the Third and Fourth Worlds bears a radical critique of the culture of modernity. The history of massive suffering in modernity challenges not only interpretations of modernity, but also theoretical answers to such suffering. Taking up a line of argumentation first raised by Peukert, Lamb appeals to both Jewish and Christian traditions — both mystical and prophetic — with their faith in the Other. Simpson explicates the theodicy issue as a forensic one of justice. Indebted to the political theology of Jürgen Moltmann, he seeks to explicate the significance of a theology of the cross for the interpretation of a forensically fraught world.[21]

Dallmayr

In differing with Habermas, Peukert and Lamb appeal to motifs and ideals that the earlier members of the Frankfurt School (especially Benjamin, Horkheimer, and Adorno) have developed. Fred Dallmayr follows a similar line of argument, but he differs in perspective and direction. Peukert and Lamb, as former students of Johann Baptist Metz, seek to advance political theology. They attempt to integrate a left-Hegelian emphasis on emancipatory praxis with a theological understanding of redemption. Dallmayr, steeped in the philosophical tradition of phenomenology and one of its foremost expositors in the United States, takes a different track.[22] He seeks to retrieve the commitment of the early Frankfurt School to a reconciliation with nature. He does not do so in order to advance a left-Hegelian revolutionary praxis, but rather to vindicate Hegel and to justify a notion of reconciliation that is more indebted to Hegel than to Marx. Therefore, whereas Peukert and Lamb underscore religious eschatology over against Habermas's notion of unlimited community, Dallmayr suggests that language today can claim the absoluteness or the role that Hegel's Spirit played earlier. In place of Habermas's communicative understanding of language and rationality, Dallmayr emphasizes the listening dimension of language, and in a more Derridean and deconstructive fashion, he underscores the centrality of play and playfulness and explicates the importance of mimesis for an understanding of reconciliation.

In this conversation with Habermas concerning religion, the differences are considerable. Whereas some theologians underscore the fact that religion has become transformed within modernity and consequently disagree with Habermas's characterization of religion, others point to the significance of religion precisely as "noncontemporaneous" to modernity and, therefore, capable of providing a resource for a critique of the distortions of modernity.[23] The theological appeal to a communicative conception of action toward a critical future praxis that emerges in Christian hope differs from the appeal to the playfulness of language. The interpretation of modernity displays disagreements not only with Habermas, but also among the authors themselves.

The Public and Private Split

The contributors also disagree with Habermas on the concrete question of the relation between the public and private spheres within modernity. Two of the authors (Fiorenza and Tracy) appeal to the work of Seyla Benhabib, a student of Habermas, in their criticisms of Habermas.[24] Benhabib brings both a feminist analysis and a knowledge of the early generation of the Frankfurt School to bear upon Habermas's interpretation of the public-private distinction. This analysis affects several aspects of Habermas's position, especially his understanding of the role of needs and interests within discourse ethics and his distinction between application and justification within moral reasoning.[25] It bears upon the relation between the expressive need for self-fulfillment and principles of justice. And, as the theologians in this volume have stressed, it influences Habermas's conception of the role of religion within society.

Seyla Benhabib and other feminist theorists have noted that Habermas's categories of system and lifeworld and his thesis of the colonization of the lifeworld place the "private/public" distinction in a dual location. On the one hand, the public belongs to the institutional system, and yet on the other hand, it also belongs to the lifeworld. The feminist challenge to Habermas points out that the private/public distinction needs to be analyzed with regard to both the relegation of women to the private sphere and the exploitation of women in the private sphere not only in terms of system (monetarization and bureaucratization), but also in terms of the oppressive prejudices of the lifeworld itself.

BASIC DISAGREEMENTS

Though Habermas's response is receptive and appreciative, it shows that significant disagreements still remain. On the one hand, he accepts criticism in regard to some individual points. For example, he acknowledges the validity of David Tracy's criticism that the aesthetic is more than the expressive. He also concedes that a significant development of religion has taken place in modernity (Tracy, Fiorenza, and Peukert) and that one cannot simply subsume the public role of religion under the Weberian label of privatization. On the other hand, he challenges individual readings of his work. For example, since Dallmayr is the most critical, Habermas takes strongest issue with his objections. Since Habermas strongly disagrees with Dallmayr's interpretation of his critical theory as a type of humanism, he offers alternative readings of his pragmatic and communicative understanding of language. Another disagreement is with the interpretation Sheila Briggs gave in her lecture. Whereas Briggs associated Benhabib's critique of Habermas's discourse ethic with Carol Gilligan's plea for an ethics of care as complementary to an ethics of justice, Habermas observes that Benhabib ultimately agrees more with his universalistic conception of justice than with Gilligan's ethics of care. Moreover, his distinction between issues of justice and those of the good life should not be equated with a distinct social location, that is, with the difference between the public and private life.

Beyond these individual points, a fundamental difference exists in regard to the interpretation of religion. This difference comes to the fore in Habermas's typological division of theological options within modernity into three major directions within contemporary theology. One direction, represented by modern Protestant kerygmatic theology, follows the tradition of Kierkegaard and insists on the independence of faith from reason and roots religious insight in the kerygma. Another direction, which he calls Enlightened Catholicism, links faith and reason. Hence it enters into dialogue with diverse nontheological disciplines, so much so that it does not sufficiently elaborate the distinctive contribution of religion. A third type is methodic atheism, with its radical program of demythologization, that extends from Hegel's philosophical reconstruction of religion to Jens Glebe-Möller's political interpretation.[26]

Habermas does not explicitly associate any one of these directions with individual contributors; indeed, he is aware that they might reject such characterizations. Nevertheless the typology is important, because it shapes the contours of his response. He poses the question of the distinctiveness of the religious contribution to the public realm to those contributors who emphasize the public and self-critical nature of theology's discourse. Habermas does indeed acknowledge the ethical, political, and utopian potential of the religious tradition and its classic symbols. Nevertheless when theologians urge that these traditions and symbols be subject to a mutually critical dialogue and seek to communicate these traditions in the public realm, Habermas suggests that theology is losing its distinctiveness. He interprets such communication as a translation from one language to another — a view the theologians themselves do not share. Though Habermas envisions reason as constituted through communication, he does not envision theology as communicative. Such a theology instead appears to Habermas as one that goes beyond its distinctive religious basis and experience in its move into public discourse. His theological conversation partners, however, argue that theology as a critical practical and public theology is self-confidently theology when it is not authoritarian but open to other sources of knowledge, when it is not sectarian but engaged in discursive deliberation about its ethical content, and when it advocates a method of critical correlation or broad reflective equilibrium on diverse principles and criteria.

To the more specifically religious appeal to the belief in a transcendent solidarity, as raised by the limit question of suffering and meaning, Habermas responds that the appeal to such a belief does not necessarily justify it. The authors offer a indirect rather than a direct apologetic, for they point to the *aporia* and impasses of his position rather than attempt to justify their own. The limit question posed by the unrequited suffering of past victims of injustice and raised by the need for a more universal solidarity does not demonstrate the existence of an absolute. The postulate remains a postulate and one that is in Habermas's view not one "we are unable to think." Consequently, a solidarity with victims and a consciousness of guilt remains and must be transformed into an active struggle against injustice and its conditions.

CONCLUSION

The relations among critical theory, theology, and the public realm involve crucial issues. These essays constitute an emerging theological discussion about them. First, they represent both a beginning and a further step on the path to a continuing dialogue between theology and critical theory, especially as exemplified in the work of Jürgen Habermas. Second, the essays exemplify a critical practical theology in the way in which they engage critical theory and Habermas. They do so in distinct ways. Taking up Habermas's insights, the essays expand, modify, and challenge them in relating religion and theological reflection to the public realm. Others point to dimensions not adequately addressed within Habermas's constructive proposals and thus point to the limits of critical theory and to the ways in which religious faith points beyond those limits.

Third, the essays represent a contribution to critical practical theology concerned with the public realm insofar as they struggle to clarify the meaning of such basic categories as rationality, modernity, and the public/private distinction and insofar as they argue that religion provides a source of cultural political change and represents a force against the colonization of the lifeworld.

NOTES

1. See the bibliographical survey of the recent theological reception, Joachim vom Soosten, "Zur theologischen Rezeption von Jürgen Habermas's 'Theorie des kommunikativen Handelns,'" *Zeitschrift für Evangelische Ethik* 34 (1990): 129–43; see also Edmund Arens, "Theologie nach Habermas. Eine Einführung," in *Habermas und die Theologie,* ed. Edmund Arens (Düsseldorf: Patmos, 1989), 9–38.

2. Charles Davis, "Pluralism, Privacy, and the Interior Self," in *Theology and Political Science: The Hulsean Lectures in the University of Cambridge, 1978*

(Cambridge: Cambridge University Press, 1980), 158–85; in this volume 152–172. Gary M. Simpson, *"Theologia Crucis* and the Forensically Fraught World: Engaging Helmut Peukert and Jürgen Habermas," *Journal of the American Academy of Religion* 57 (1989): 509–41; in this volume 173–205.

3. See Don S. Browning, *Practical Theology: The Emerging Field in Theology, Church, and World* (New York: Harper & Row, 1971), 1–18.

4. Ibid, 13.

5. See Thomas A. McCarthy, *The Critical Theory of Jürgen Habermas* (Cambridge, Mass.: MIT, 1978); Stephen White, *The Recent Work of Jürgen Habermas* (New York: Cambridge University Press, 1988).

6. Two helpful commentaries are David Ingram, *Habermas and the Dialectic of Reason* (New Haven: Yale University Press, 1987), and Arie Brand, *The Force of Reason: An Introduction to Habermas's Theory of Communicative Action* (Boston: Allen & Unwin, 1990).

7. Jürgen Habermas, *The Structural Transformation of the Public Sphere: An Inquiry into a Category of Bourgeois Society* (Cambridge, Mass.: MIT Press, 1989).

8. "The Public Sphere: An Encyclopedia Article (1964)," *New German Critique* 1, no. 3 (Fall 1974): 49. Also published as "The Public Sphere," in *Jürgen Habermas on Society and Politics: A Reader* (Boston: Beacon Press, 1989), 231–36.

9. Ibid.

10. Jürgen Habermas, *Moral Consciousness and Communicative Action* (Cambridge, Mass.: MIT Press, 1990).

11. One of Tracy's most significant contributions to theology has been his explanation of the diverse publics of theology; see *The Analogical Imagination* (New York: Crossroad, 1986).

12. Charles Davis, *Theology and Political Society*, 51–74. A more recent and excellent appropriation of critical theory is Paul Lakeland's *Theology and Critical Theory: The Discourse of the Church* (Nashville: Abingdon Press, 1990).

13. Bernstein, Richard, ed. *Habermas and Modernity.* Cambridge, Mass.: MIT Press, 1985.

14. Although Habermas's *The Philosophical Discourse of Modernity: Twelve Lectures* (Cambridge, Mass.: MIT Press, 1987) deals explicitly with the issue of modernity and postmodernity, the systematic framework for these lectures is provided in his *Theory of Communicative Action.*

15. See Robert Wuthnow's *Meaning and Moral Order: Explorations in Cultural Analysis* (Berkeley: University of California Press, 1987), where he illustrates the use of subjective, structural, dramaturgic, and institutional approaches to the analysis of culture.

16. Max Horkheimer and Theodor Adorno, *Dialectic of the Enlightenment* (New York: Seabury, 1972).

17. Helmut Peukert, *Science, Action, and Fundamental Theology* (Cambridge, Mass.: MIT Press, 1984).

18. See Wuthnow, *Meaning and Moral Order*, 344.

19. Though as Habermas's response notes, Benhabib's position on justice

adheres more closely to Habermas's universalistic conception of justice than to Gilligan's conception.

20. Peukert's response to Habermas has not gone without criticism; see Peter Hodgson, *God in History: Shapes of Freedom* (Nashville: Abingdon Press, 1989), 224–28.

21. For complementary treatments of the same issue by Simpson, see his "The Linguistification (and Liquefaction?) of the Sacred: A Theological Consideration of Jürgen Habermas's Theory of Religion," *Exploration* 7:21–35 (published in German in *Habermas und die Theologie*, ed. Edmund Arens), and his "Wither Wolfhart Pannenberg? Reciprocity and Political Theory," *Journal of Religion* 67 (1987): 33–49.

22. Dallmayr's publications on European trends of philosophy, linguistics, and hermeneutics in their relation to political philosophy have contributed greatly to awareness of the interconnection of diverse developments. See especially his *Language and Politics* (Notre Dame, Ind.: University of Notre Dame Press, 1984), *Polis and Praxis: Exercises in Contemporary Political Theory* (Cambridge, Mass.: MIT Press, 1984), *Critical Encounters: Between Philosophy and Politics* (Notre Dame, Ind.: University of Notre Dame Press, 1989).

23. See Johann Baptist Metz, "Von der produktiven Ungleichzeitigkeit der Religion. Eine Antwort an Jürgen Habermas," in his *Unterbrechungen. Theologisch-politische Perspektiven und Profile* (Gütersloh: Gerd Mohn, 1981), 11–19.

24. Seyla Benhabib, *Critique, Norm, and Utopia: A Study of the Foundations of Critical Theory* (New York: Columbia University Press, 1986).

25. See the more recent essay by Seyla Benhabib, "Afterword: Communicative Ethics in Practical Philosophy," in Seyla Benhabib and Fred Dallmayr, *The Communicative Ethics Controversy* (Cambridge, Mass.: MIT Press, 1990), 330–69.

26. See Jens Glebe-Möller, *A Political Dogmatic* (Philadelphia: Fortress, 1987).

1

Theology, Critical Social Theory, and the Public Realm

David Tracy

INTRODUCTION: THE PUBLIC REALM — RATIONALITY AND MODERNITY

A public realm, by definition, is dependent on a shared concept of reason. The debates across the disciplines on the nature of rationality can seem to affect all hope for an authentically public realm. A public realm is that shared rational space where all participants, whatever their other particular differences, can meet to discuss any claim that is rationally redeemable. Any strictly relativist reading of the nature of reason cannot inform a public realm as public. Indeed, even a rigorous contextualist like Richard Rorty must logically insist that no philosophical defense of the public realm is possible, but only a historical defense: namely, that a public realm is necessary (as a kind of heuristic fiction) for any modern democratic society.

In spite of his appeal to Dewey, Rorty's construal of the reason for the public realm is the exact opposite of Dewey's. For Dewey, reason properly construed logically entails the equality and liberty of all conversation partners and thereby implies a democratic polity. For Rorty, democracy properly construed logically entails the equality and liberty of all citizens and thereby implies some shared notion of reason that, however indefensible on strictly philosophical grounds, is necessary on historical and cultural grounds. Dewey, with the mainline pragmatic tradition, believes that democracy can be rationally defended. Rorty believes that the shared rationality necessary for a public realm can be defended, if at all, only historically.

Some "postmodern" thinkers, such as Jean-François Lyotard, go a step further than Rorty: the history of Western democracies and the notions of rationality entailed by those histories are the last gasp of a failed Enlightenment project. In this view, the Enlightenment notion of universal reason has caused the oppression in bourgeois culture and the inability of any bourgeois reason that claims for itself universal rationality to allow for genuine difference despite much self-deceptive pluralistic rhetoric. Some forms of critical theory — most notably that of Theodor Adorno in *Negative Dialectics* and Horkheimer and Adorno in *Dialectic of Enlightenment* — approximate, without embracing, the claims of Lyotard. Adorno argues with Weber's sociological reading of the rationalization (and thereby bureaucratization and technicization) of all modern culture and argues philosophically that an "identity-logic" in the Enlightenment claim to universal reason has trapped modernity into a false universalism. Adorno's form of critical theory is also akin to Lyotard's portrait of "postmodernity" in that both appeal to avant-garde art and to an aesthetic discourse modeled on avant-garde principles as the sole hope for a modern Western culture caught in the vise of Weber's all-pervasive "iron cage."

The difference between Adorno and Lyotard, however, is also clear: Adorno still believes, however despairingly, in some forms of classical reason. He refuses, therefore, a completely aestheticized model for contemporary rationality. Adorno's "immanent critique" and his purely "negative dialectics" are greatly chastened expressions of the Hegelian-Marxist hope of reason; nevertheless, they remain expressions of it. Adorno's contemporaries, Ernst Bloch and Walter Benjamin, found other resources for hope — mainly utopian for Bloch and often mystical for Benjamin. These resources served Bloch and Benjamin as strategies of both hope and resistance. Their critical theories freed them from a purely aesthetic reading of the rational possibilities embedded in both avant-garde art and in the eschatological and mystical strands of the religions.

Paradoxically, many neoconservative critics of modernity share several crucial presuppositions of the postmoderns. Some neoconservatives either argue philosophically like Leo Strauss that the project "modernity," as initiated by Hobbes and Machiavelli and as culminating in Weber, Nietzsche, and Heidegger, has been proven a failure by its historicist self-contradictions. They argue further that modernity has also betrayed the Western tradition's concept of reason — the concept defended in Straussian readings of Plato and Aristotle. Alternatively, some sociological rather than philosophical neoconservative critics (like Daniel Bell) insist that avant-garde art is anything but a resource for resolving our dilemmas. Rather, the "avant-garde" released an "adversary culture" as a model for culture itself and thereby helped assure the privatization of the entire realm of culture and the further encroachment of the techno-economic realm into the realm of the polity. Many neoconservative thinkers also rethought the rejection of religion by modern intellectuals and the privatization of religion by modern society. But, unlike Benjamin and Bloch, the neoconservative thinkers, on the whole, do not want religion to play a prophetic or utopian role, whether Marxist or Weberian. Rather, neoconservatives assert that religion should play a conserving, stabilizing, Durkheimian role. Hence they appeal to either the "Judeo-Christian" ethos or, more expansively and amorphously, to the "sacred" and its alleged ability to provide a "sacred canopy" (Berger) of shared values for our "naked public square" (Neuhaus).

In Christian theology itself, the same kind of scenario has developed. There are many appeals to theologians to withdraw from a concern with the public realm save as witnesses to an alternative community of beliefs and virtues (Hauerwas and possibly MacIntyre). At most, theologians should engage in occasional ad hoc apologetics and ad hoc alliances with other communities in the pluralistic public realm. In a final step, those theologians (like myself) who have been concerned with both the dilemmas of the public realm and the character of a modern correlational theology are advised to acknowledge the emptiness of the concept of modern rationality and embrace the later Wittgenstein's defense of plural language games and plural forms of life. We are also advised that modern theology's very attempt to establish mutually critical correlations between interpretations of the modern situation and interpretations of the Christian tradition is thoroughly mistaken. For modern correlational theology, despite its best intentions, has been trapped in either a foundationalism or an aesthetic experiential-expressive model of Romantic and idealistic origin. The only hope for theology, or any discipline, is to embrace a cultural-linguistic model (like that of Clifford Geertz or some Wittgensteinians). Thereby theology will serve its proper role: to clarify its own narratives, virtues, and community, while abandoning any claims to a common rationality — including that idea of rationality present in traditional notions of a public realm.

In these now familiar debates, it is interesting that both the concept of rationality and the concept of modernity are at stake — and indeed, at stake together. Hence my first thesis: what modern correlational theologies can best learn from critical theory is the need for a critical *social* theory, that is, one where "rationality" and "modernity" are analyzed together and where the materialist and intellectual links between the two categories are clarified. For me, this aim is what makes Jürgen Habermas's ambitious and complex attempt to develop a new critical social theory as a theory of communicative action so promising for any theology concerned with the public realm. As I will suggest, I have important disagreements with some of Habermas's claims. But with his basic aim I am in full accord.

Before interpreting Habermas, a self-criticism is in order: I, like most theologians who have been struggling with the issues of theology and the public realm, have given almost all my attention to the debate on rationality rather than the debate on modernity. This, I am now persuaded, is a mistake. I continue to believe, with Habermas, that only a defense of communicative rationality will resolve the issue philosophically. I also continue to believe in contrast to Habermas that conversation rather than argument is the most encompassing category for an analysis of communicative rationality. This internal debate in communication theory is a debate whose basic terms were set not only in the famous exchange between Gadamer and Habermas, but at the time of the Greek origins of Western notions of reason in the implicit differences between Plato's development of the model of the dialogue and Aristotle's clarification of the nature of argument. Yet, however important this implicit generic disagreement between Plato on dialogue and Aristotle on argument, it is secondary to the agreement of Plato and Aristotle, and of both Gadamer and Habermas on the need for, the basic character of, and the limits to communicative reason.

For, whether one claims that conversation or argument is the more inclusive (and, therefore, more fundamental) exercise of communicative reason, there is need, in either case, to defend the character and limits of reason (with the ancients) and of rationality (with the moderns). In modernity, this defense has led to several *aporias* that a theory of communicative action (that is, action involving mutual recognition and understanding) is designed to address.

Some models of modern rationality cannot account for rationality as communicative action. Positivism is now acknowledged to be unable to account for the hermeneutic character of science itself. Positivism is unwilling to consider other exercises of reason (for example, the practical-moral) on other than emotivist terms. The defeat of positivism in the last thirty years, however, has not made traditional forms of modern philosophies of consciousness more persuasive. Modern philosophy of consciousness (including the transcendental, especially neo-Kantian and Husserlian, versions) are monological, not dialogical. They cannot account, therefore, for either intersubjectivity (witness Husserl) or communicative action. Nor do philosophies of consciousness ordinarily understand language other than instrumentally (that is, as an instrument employed by the conscious thinker to articulate for oneself and to communicate to others the results of one's conscious reflections).

The dual failure of positivism's narrowing of the range of rationality and philosophy of consciousness's inability to defend reason on other than monological terms has encouraged the developments listed above. Some thinkers either abandon strong claims for rationality altogether in favor of a "contextualism" so strong that it finally seems indistinguishable from relativism. Others argue for an aestheticization of reason like that which informed the original artistic avant-garde and now informs some postmodern philosophical accounts of rationality. There is, as I shall suggest, more to be learned from an aesthetic postmodernity and from some contextualist accounts of reason than Habermas characteristically allows. But — and here one must stand with Habermas — two lessons should *not* be drawn from the failure of positivist and philosophy of consciousness accounts of reason: first, that philosophical accounts of rationality other than a purely contextual or purely aestheticized ones cannot redeem themselves; second, that the logic of modernity has proven, through a kind of inevitability, a triumph of merely technical reason resulting either in Weber's "iron cage" or Lukács's total reification of all culture. In many circles, the words "rationality" and "modernity" have, like the word "liberal" in contemporary American political discourse, become words that no one dares to speak. Here, surely, a critical social theory can help: at least one, like Habermas's, informed by both a modest but persuasive defense of reason as communicative and a modest but persuasive defense of modernity as not inevitably an iron cage.

The major paradigm shift in modern philosophy is away from the turn to the subject's consciousness and toward the linguistic turn. The linguistic turn in modern philosophy, to be sure, has taken many detours, possesses many internal conflicts, and has reached some dead ends. But, insofar as one can show that in every communicative action, whatever the other particularities of its context, there is an exercise of self-transcending dialogical reason with language as the necessary medium of that self-transcendence, there remains hope for the kind of reflective reason demanded by all critical theory. If language is not a mere instrument of consciousness but the basic medium of all human understanding, then every act of understanding is intrinsically intersubjective, never purely subjective; every communicative action is dialogical, not monological. If understanding is dialogical, it is also, as hermeneutics and critical theory alike attest, both historical and contextual. But, insofar as reason is genuinely dialogical or communicative in any historical context, it is not, in principle, limited to that context. Any act of understanding implicitly puts forward a claim to more than subjective understanding. Any act of understanding addresses all others with a claim to its validity — a validity that, in principle, the inquirer is obliged to redeem if challenged.

HABERMAS AND THE PUBLIC REALM: CONTRIBUTION

The need of the public realm, therefore, is twofold: first, to clarify the character of rationality so that the genuinely *public* nature of the public realm may be defended; second, to clarify the sociological realities that have weakened the public realm in societies like our own, in advanced industrial and postindustrial Western democracies. Most theologians who have concentrated their attention on theology's possible contributions to our damaged public realm have adopted one of three strategies. First, many European and some North American political theologians have used categories like Marxist "alienation" to interpret our situation, as well as classic Christian eschatological (especially apocalyptic) symbols to enrich our possibilities. Second, most liberation and African-American theologians as well as prophetically oriented feminist and womanist theologians have appealed to the counterexperience and counterideologies of oppressed peoples whose discourse has been marginalized by the dominant groups. Thus do liberation theologians clarify the nature and the interrelationships of various systemic forms of oppression (racism, sexism, classism, elitism), even as they demonstrate the promise of liberation in the praxis of marginalized groups. Third, in most "public theologies" in North America and Europe, there have been arguments about modern rationality (for example, hermeneutics and pragmatism) as well as a development of revisionary correlational theological methods to address the new situation of the damaged public realm.

These brief observations on these three different theological models for dealing with the problems of the public realm must remain ideal types. Any actual theology (like my own) is likely to employ resources from the other two models. Nevertheless, each of these three models for theology and the public realm possesses distinct methodological and substantive characteristics. Each model can, at times, learn from the others. Each model is also, at other times, in serious conflict with the others. Each begins with a characteristic set of hypotheses about both the situation and the tradition. All three types, moreover, are clearly distinct from all those other forms of theology that characteristically consider any major theological attention to the modern situation as, at best, secondary to the properly theological task.

For the moment I will avoid these inner-theological conflicts in order to clarify how the third model (public theology) can learn from Habermas's critical social theory. What is distinctive about Habermas's theory of communicative action is its effort to rethink familiar philosophical discussions of rationality in direct relationship to sociological discussions of modernity. Public theologies have often learned from and contributed to philosophical discussions of rationality. They have been thus engaged in order to account for the nature both of the public realm as public and of theology as a modern discipline that clarifies and defends its implicit validity claims. This dual insistence has occasioned whatever limited success public theology may have had in clarifying the nature of the public realm, the nature of modern theology as intrinsically correlational, and the discussion of religious symbolic resources for the public realm. As a single example of the latter kind of enterprise, I may, perhaps, cite my own previous attempts to develop the notion of the "classic" as a resource for the public realm. Any classic, although highly particular in origin and expression, is public in effect. The use of the category "classic" may, therefore, clarify how one may employ in the public realm the symbolic resources of different traditions: of Judaism and Christianity or the cosmological symbols of such religious traditions as Buddhism. All such classics may be used as public, utopian symbols worthy of serious reflection, dialogue, and argument by all inquirers. These classic resources then can inform such issues as human rights, the relationship of justice and love, or the ecological crisis.

All these models of political and public theology are challenged by Habermas's recent theory. European political theologians are challenged to rethink their possible overcommitment to Hegelian-Marxist categories and their occasional Weber-like and Adorno-like full-scale cultural pessimism about the damaged institutions and practices of modern bourgeois democracies. Liberation theologians, by their social location amid oppressed peoples and groups, are spared this first dilemma. Indeed, they challenge both Habermas and public and political theologies by developing new theological resources (centered on the symbol of liberation) from groups and movements too often marginalized by critical theorists and public theologians. With some notable exceptions, however, the various forms of liberation theology still seem relatively unconcerned with the debates on rationality and the debates on modernity and postmodernity. Without such explicit and systematic analysis it is difficult to see how the crucial contributions and challenges of liberation theologies can be redeemed fully in a pluralistic public realm. There is no good empirical evidence that such pluralism will decrease. Indeed, Clifford Geertz insists rightly that we live in an age where no one will leave

anyone else alone — ever again.[1] There is no good theological reason, moreover, why publicness (which entails a willingness to defend
all implicit validity claims and implies a democratic polity) should
be ignored by any form of theology. Insofar as any form of theology is theology, it is, in theological terms, a work and not the gift
(grace) of faith. It is not only witness but critical reflection on that
witness. In the modern period, theology has become a critical mode
of inquiry willing to give reasons for any of its claims. Many forms
of liberation theology (even, indeed especially, when they challenge
dominant notions of rationality) engage in such distinctly modern
theological inquiry. At least some among them could, without loss of
their challenge, enter more explicitly into the debates on rationality and modernity rather than dismiss them, as some do, as merely
"bourgeois" or "liberal" concerns.

Otherwise, even the liberation theologians could be driven, despite their clear intentions, to those enforced "reservations of the
spirit" where a reigning technical rationality wishes to place all
countermovements. The dialogue of communicative action in the
public realm is the exact counterpart of the solidarity-in-action that
these new movements and new theologies justly foster. Or, as Jesse
Jackson recently put it, we must all collaborate, for any one of us
alone finds that our patch is too small! Coalition and, when necessary, reasonable compromise on concrete actions within the dialogue
of communicative action and solidarity on concrete actions remain
the hope of reason and action alike.

My principal concern, however, is not to argue that political
theologians or liberation theologians should accept Habermas's challenge. Indeed, far more detailed intra-theological arguments would
be needed with, for example, Metz or Moltmann, Segundo or Cone,
Radford Ruether or Elisabeth Schüssler Fiorenza, beyond the very
general observations made above. My principal concern is rather to
clarify the challenge of Habermas's proposal to attempts like mine
at public theology.

The problems I have had over the last fifteen years in clarifying the nature of public theology as fundamental, systematic, and
practical are shared, as far as I can see, by many theologians who
employ some form of a revised correlational method when address-
ing theology's role in the public realm. To put the problem in its
starkest terms: there is no lack of critical theory in most forms of
public theology but there is a real lack of critical *social* theory. To
put the problem in more categorial terms: without a critical *social*
theory, the link between the debates on rationality and the debates
on modernity (and postmodernity) are difficult if not impossible to
clarify. That methodological failure has important substantive conse-

quences: first, the correlational category "situation" (as with Tillich in the *Systematics* or most of my own work) has the strength of allowing for good cultural analysis. Yet most "situational" analysis is also in danger of becoming trapped in purely "culturalist" or even "idealist" categories unless the correlational theologian can show the links between the cultural resources of our situation and the materialist (economic, social, political) conditions of our society. Public theology, at its best, has shown how to employ critically the symbolic resources of the traditions and the cultural situation for the public realm. But most public theologians pay too little attention to the materialist embedding of all symbolic resources in the kind of society within which we actually find ourselves: one constituted by a democratic polity, a capitalist economy, and an ever more bureaucratized political administration. A research program that would demand empirical testing of all claims to publicness in relationship to a particular society would necessarily be a social theory. A research program that would allow for, indeed demand, reflective reason would necessarily be a *critical* social theory. Today such a theory must be informed by a dialogical, linguistic understanding of reflection rather than a monological philosophy of consciousness. Habermas's research program includes both crucial elements and becomes, therefore, a natural conversation partner for public theology.

His critical social theory helps analyze and test the social systems of our society: the economy and political administration and their media of money and power; their necessary use of purposive, technical rationality; and their invasion, if unchecked, of the communicative rationality necessary to the social action in the lifeworld of the society, especially the public realm. Indeed, to understand why the "public realm" has become impoverished in our society and why the lifeworld has been "colonized" by the systems of the economy and political administration demands a social analysis that can show how the communicative rationality of the "citizen" can gradually be affected by the purposive rationality of the client and the consumer in developed modern societies. At the same time, Habermas's critical social theory shows the existence of the vestiges of communicative rationality in the various realms (ethical, political, and aesthetic) of the lifeworld as well as in the "new movements" of resistance to the colonization of the lifeworld. Without such empirical, testable hypotheses about both system and lifeworld and their complex interactions in our society, the public philosopher and theologian is left with either purely culturalist modes of analysis or merely impressionistic sketches of the dilemma of the public realm in our society.

All the familiar cultural and implicitly sociological themes of modern philosophy and theology — the "possessive individualism" of Bellah et al., the "Dialectic of Enlightenment" of Adorno and Horkheimer, the "iron cage" of Max Weber, the triumph of "calculative reason" of Heidegger, and the "postmodernity" of Lyotard — are, one and all, not merely general (and often valuable) cultural insights but proposals for understanding our complex society. As such they must be as open to empirical testing as are all other sociological proposals. But these proposals can be tested properly only by a theory that combines empirical testing with critical reflection — more exactly, a mode of dialogical reflection that can enlighten us on the limits and possibilities of reason and thereby help emancipate us from systemic illusions.

As critical theory, Habermas's theory challenges both positivism and empiricism by insisting (with hermeneutics, language philosophy, and pragmatism) that human action is intrinsically interactive and communicative and thereby reflective. As social theory, Habermas's theory challenges any purely culturalist or idealist mode of inquiry (including many forms of hermeneutics and public theology) with the call to test all cultural theories sociologically. As critical social theory, therefore, any theory on the nature of the public realm in our society must be, in Habermas's phrase, "reconstructive": that is, one that can defend philosophically a theory of rationality and link that philosophical theory to a reconstructive, empirical, testable, sociological hypothesis about the nature of modernity as modernity has been institutionalized in the distinct rationalization processes of both the social systems (purposive rationality) and the lifeworld of social action (communicative rationality) of our society. The problem of the public realm as we find it in our society can only be solved by showing how both the economic and administrative systems and the lifeworld have been, in all their principal institutions and disciplines, rationalized in and by modernity.

On the philosophical side, the temptation of most modern philosophy has been to defend rationality from the viewpoint of a philosophy of consciousness. From Descartes through Kant to Husserl to most forms of contemporary transcendental philosophy, this "turn to the subject" has been the great hope of modern reason. But here — as Plato with his model of reflection-through-dialogue and Aristotle with his analyses of forms of argument would have known — the turn to the subject's consciousness does not suffice. No philosophy of consciousness seems able to account for the interactive, dialogical character of our actual uses of reason in linguistic, communicative exchange. It cannot avoid monological defenses of reason or even account adequately for intersubjectivity (witness Husserl).

As with communicative reason, so with social action: social action is, by definition, interactive; if communicative at all, social action can be construed as dialogical interaction. Both hermeneutics and pragmatism see this insight with clarity. For that reason, for example, in my own work in theology and the public realm, I have consistently turned to the notion of dialogue and have attempted to clarify its conditions of possibility as the surest rational way to clarify what "publicness" (as rational social action) means. Habermas's work over the years — from his initial formulation of knowledge (constitutive interest), through his theory of the ideal speech situation, to his recent theory of communicative action — has focused on this same interactive, dialogical, and linguistic character of reason.

By his critical use of Austin, Searle, and Strawson, moreover, Habermas also uses analytical philosophy to clarify the conditions of possibility for all communicative action (namely, comprehensibility, truth, rightness, and sincerity). By his reformulations of Weber on "rationalization-processes" and of Lukács and Adorno-Horkheimer on reification, Habermas has also managed to free both the early Frankfurt School and Weber from their own implicitly monological philosophy of consciousness categories. Thereby he retrieves the dialogical, interactive character of the Hegelian-Marxist tradition. At the same time, Habermas's reconstruction of both Weber's "rationalization" hypothesis and Adorno-Horkheimer's formulation of "the Dialectic of Enlightenment" has emancipated these positions from their temptations to full-scale cultural pessimism, by showing how, on the basis of their own analyses, there is no "inevitability" to the "iron cage" of modernity. In sum, Habermas by his reconstruction of sociological theory (on both social system and social action) presents a plausible and testable critical social theory. The heart of this theory is the claim that the problem of modernity is not a problem of the inevitability of the triumph of technical reason but a problem of "selective rationality," that is, attention to the purposive-technical rationality in the social systems of modernity has provided a selective, one-sided account of rationality that ignores the character of that communicative rationality necessary to all social reason.

This one-sided, selective development of purposive rationality in the social systems of our society accounts for the perilous dilemmas in the public realm in our society as distinct from, for example, the eighteenth-century situation of the American Founders. In our society, the entire lifeworld (including the public realm) has been subject to an "internal colonization" as the systems of both late-capitalist economics and political bureaucratic administration have increasingly (but not completely) colonized the lifeworld; hence, the "citizen" (who, by definition, must be involved in communicative action) becomes a mere "producer," a "client," and a "consumer."

The only plausible defense of the kind of rationality appropriate to the public realm is a defense not of purposive rationality but of communicative action (action directed to mutual understanding and demanding reciprocity). The importance of the linguistic turn over the earlier modern philosophical paradigm of the subject's consciousness can scarcely be overemphasized here. For, if the only philosophical defense of communicative rationality is one provided by a transcendental philosophy of consciousness, then the problem of the privatization of all the resources of communicative action in the public realm (ethics, politics, aesthetics, and theology) is increased.

The solitary conscious thinker may be under the illusion that language is only an instrument for expressing her/his conscious insights. The speaker-listener of dialogue can be under no such illusion. Language is not an instrument of an a-linguistic consciousness, but the necessary medium for all interactive understanding (including the speaker's own personal, but not private, reflections). Habermas, therefore, has learned from the linguistic turn of hermeneutics, analytical philosophy, and Peircean pragmatism alike, in his development of a theory of communicative rationality. His fundamental argument is a familiar and, in my judgment, a sound one: anyone who communicates with the purpose of establishing mutual understanding implicitly affirms the validity of the claims put forward. These claims may be empirical-factual or moral or aesthetic. In every case, it is necessary to understand the kind of argument needed to redeem any particular claim and to be willing to redeem the claim, if challenged.

Like Aristotle, Habermas is chiefly concerned to clarify the nature of argumentation and thereby the distinct kinds of argument needed for the principal spheres of modern inquiry. Like the earlier critical theorists of the Frankfurt School, Habermas is concerned to clarify how reason, as reflective, is both enlightening and emancipatory. In his model, reason functions *as* reason only through the persuasive force of the best argument. All critical theory is designed to unmask coercive use of power, whether externally imposed (as in totalitarian states) or internally imposed (as in the neuroses and psychoses unmasked by psychoanalytical theory). Like any social theorist, Habermas must also show how different notions of rationality are embedded in different practices and institutions of society: especially of one as complex as any modern society constituted by both internally regulated social systems (the economy and administration) and a communicatively rational lifeworld constituted by social action. Hence, there is need, as in all social theory, to show the exact relationships of social system and social action in our society. Here Habermas attempts to demonstrate how a theory of communicative action can account for the gains in social theory provided by systems-theory (Parsons and Luhmann) without reducing social actions (as communicative action) to purely systemic (and hence purposively rational) action.

This is undoubtedly an ambitious, complex, and impressive research project. With its basic philosophical arguments on communicative rationality I am, as I state above and argue in my own work on dialogue, in fundamental agreement. Habermas argues persuasively for the four criteria (comprehensibility, truth, rightness, and sincerity) entailed in every act of communicative rationality. He argues just as persuasively for the democratic implications of all communicative rationality (equality and mutual reciprocity demanding individual dignity). For his reconstructive social theory on the relationships of social system and social action in modern society, I can only state my necessarily tentative agreement with its general hypothesis — that the problem of the public realm today demands both a social theory attentive and appropriate to the systems-analysis of modern social systems and an analysis of the communicative action entailed by all social action in the lifeworld. His central social theory seems to me to clarify how the problem of modernity (including the problem of the public realm in modernity) is one of a selective and one-sided use of a purposive rationality appropriate to social systems, but inappropriate to, indeed devastating to, the communicative rationality necessary for all social action in the "lifeworld." Insofar as the public realm is public and not, paradoxically, another private "reservation of the spirit" for the publicly spirited, only a critical social theory like Habermas's could free any public theology or public philosophy from purely culturalist and, at the limit, idealist analyses or merely impressionistic commentaries on the problems of the public realm.

Habermas's critical social theory also frees analysts from the dual temptations of cultural optimism and cultural pessimism by showing the nature of the problem of reason in our society as one of selectivity, not inevitability. He also analyzes the vestiges of reason in the practices and institutions of the lifeworld. There is evidence that the lifeworld, although often devastatingly colonized by the demands of the kind of purposive rationality appropriate to social systems, is not simply an "iron cage" nor Henry Miller's "air-conditioned nightmare." At the same time, Habermas's central social theory helps to clarify the reasons for and promise of various "new movements" of our time: for example, the nuclear protest movements, various liberation movements, and the ecological movement. All these movements provide hope by resisting the increasing colonization of the lifeworld as well as by implicitly affirming the need for communicative action. As an empirical social theory, Habermas's theory meets the critical standards of empirical testability. As critical theory, Habermas's social theory departs from any lingering positivism or empiricism of much social theory to defend (along with analytical philosophy, hermeneutics, and pragmatism) the fundamentally dialogical character of all reflective rationality.

CRITICAL QUESTIONS ON HABERMAS'S THEORY FOR THEOLOGY AND THE PUBLIC REALM

Habermas's philosophical defense of communicative rationality and his sociological analysis of social systems and social action unite to provide his basic defense of modernity as well as his critique of the selective rationality of modern society and the colonization of the lifeworld. These central claims are the heart of his fuller theory of communicative action and, as argued in his recent work, are indeed philosophically persuasive and sociologically plausible. Thus far, however, I have refrained from commenting on certain subsidiary theorems in his theory of communicative action. As far as I can see, one can agree with Habermas's basic theory (as I do above), even if one is doubtful about other, subsidiary theorems in his complex research project. Whether that agreement with the heart of the matter amid serious disagreements on other theorems in the wider research project is possible remains, for me, the central question of the usefulness of Habermas's critical social theory for a theology of the public realm. I shall concentrate most of my critical attention on what I claim to be the confusion and inadequacy of Habermas's account of both the aesthetic realm and the religious-theological realm. First, however, I will list some related issues that deserve further critical attention.

(1) How strictly integral is Habermas's "theory of social evolution" to his reconstructive theory? As far as I can see, one can agree with the basic proposals I outlined above without accepting Habermas's theory of social evolution. That distinct cognitive spheres (science, morality, art) possess distinct validity-confirming modes of argument is philosophically true. There is also strong sociological evidence that these distinct cognitive spheres have come to possess relative *sociological* autonomy in modernity. That each autonomous sphere has developed its own "learning processes" (Piaget, Kohlberg) is also clear. That these three Weberian sociological autonomous spheres parallel the distinct cognitive interests of Kant's three critiques is true.

But the exhibit of this fit between Kant and Weber seems all too neat a response to the disturbing contrary hypotheses of modern anthropology, history of religions, and philosophical hermeneutics. The almost Comtean unfolding of Habermas's theory of social evolution in its movement from myth to metaphysics to communicative rationality is troubling and unnecessary for his general theory. Habermas needs to give far more attention than he has given to modern discussions of myth (Eliade), symbol (Ricoeur and even part of Kant!), metaphysics (especially post-Kantian neoclassical metaphysics), modern theologies (and their distinct validity claims), cross-cultural dialogical possibilities (Geertz), and interreligious dialogue (Panikkar). I do not raise these issues as if a mere citation of them defeats Habermas's theory of social evolution. Indeed, each issue (myth, symbol, metaphysics, intercultural and interreligious dialogue) would clearly demand detailed examination to see whether Habermas's social theory works in spite of these counterclaims. One can agree with Habermas's basic sociological account of modernity and agree, philosophically, with his account of communicative action without using an evolutionary schema in other than a very weak, heuristic sense. Indeed, as the issues and thinkers cited above testify, there are good reasons to doubt theories of social evolution like Habermas's. Both cultural anthropology and history of religions, moreover, have shown, by their own abandonment of earlier evolutionary schemata, that we need not embrace relativism or abandon Western communicative rationality to deny the usefulness of social evolutionary models. One can defend both communicative rationality and the "vestiges" of that rationality in Western modernity without embracing a full-fledged theory of social evolution to account for those realities.

All social evolutionary theories are tempted to silence certain debates that have been present in Western modernity since at least the time of Kant: the cognitive nature of symbol in the *Third Critique*, and the possibility of a neoclassical metaphysics and a rational philosophical and theological account of the central validity claims of the religions. Further, as contemporary debates on pluralism suggest, it is important not to reduce a plurality of differences to an implicit identity of meaning by overemphasizing similarity or commonality. In the extreme case, differences are accorded the status of mere particularities and, at the limit, even regarded as cultural retrogressions in too many social evolutionary models. As Habermas's own formal account of morality itself shows, there is great room for further contextual arguments about different substantive proposals for the "good life" and "happiness." In his recent work, moreover, he makes more substantive use of utopian theory for further rational suggestions for the "good" society.

This suggests both that some vision of the good was already present in his ethics of rights and that the utopian core of his Hegelian-Marxist vision of the good does not accord well with his revised Piagetian and Kohlbergian theory of social and moral development. The first question recurs: does Habermas need a theory of social evolution to defend his basic claims? Habermas gives no argument to demonstrate that he needs that subsidiary theory, though he clearly desires one to buttress his basic argument about communicative rationality and Western modernity.

(2) A second issue suggests itself: Habermas has not thus far developed an other than purely objectivist account of the scientific and technological attitude to "nature." Many other traditions, especially East Asian and African, show how an interactive relationship between nature and humankind is possible without rejecting science and technology and without returning (as Habermas fears) to Romantic cosmologies like that of Schelling. Indeed, the emergence of interactive rather than dominating attitudes to nature in Western science itself (under the rubric of postmodern science by Toulmin and Ferri) as well as the non-Romantic critique of Habermas's position by Thomas McCarthy and others suggest that, on both natural scientific and ethical-practical grounds, our modern Western "dominating" attitude to nature should be questioned with the same kind of clarity with which Habermas unmasks the colonization of the human lifeworld by the purposive demands of social systems.

(3) As feminist critics have noted, Habermas's theory needs to account for the gender-specific nature of many realities in Western modernity. For example, "client" and "consumer" are gender-specific roles in our society. Moreover, our social institutions (both systemic ones like the economic and political administrative orders and lifeworld ones like the family) possess, in Western modernity, gender-specific actualities that are partly but not fully illuminated by general appeals to the equality and mutual reciprocity of communicative action. Gilligan's critique of Kohlberg's rational formal ethics is particularly appropriate here, as is Fraser's critique of Habermas.

(4) Habermas's formulation of the kind of validity claims for the scientific and ethical realms have considerable persuasive power with certain corrigible exceptions. First, as suggested above, there is need to revise Habermas's understanding of science to allow for such new and important (both scientifically and ethically) disciplines as ecological science. Second, there is further need to see how ethical discussions of the "good" (the good life and happiness) might be related to (because already implied by) Habermas's formal analysis of the validity claims entailed by a morality of "right." These proposed developments would cohere, however, with the more formal analysis

of the kinds of validity claims to scientific truth and ethical rightness proposed in Habermas's theory. His basic theory does allow him to revise Kant's monological philosophy of consciousness position into a linguistic, dialogical theory of different validity claims. That same general theory of communicative action and its clarification of three kinds of claims (truth, rightness, sincerity) allow Habermas to accept Weber's analysis of how modernity produces autonomous spheres without yielding to Weber's decisionism on ethical issues or to Weber's total cultural pessimism on the implications of technical reason for the entire lifeworld.

On science and ethics, Habermas's theory could be developed in the manner suggested above — with relatively minor revision. However, in two other validity-spheres, religion and aesthetics, only major revisions would really help.

(5) On religion and theology, Habermas's theory of social evolution (on which I have expressed my serious reservations above) allied to his insistence on three — and three only — modern kinds of autonomous claims (scientific, social, aesthetic) may account for his relative lack of attention to religious thought and practice in modernity. This must be considered unfortunate, both intellectually and sociologically. Sociologically, religiously inspired movements (for instance, Martin Luther King, Jr., and the civil rights movement in the United States, some of the Greens in Germany, and theological liberation movements throughout the world) have substantially influenced some central modern developments (for example, the struggle for justice and ecological consciousness). Their religious validity claims (and not only their status as new social movements) demand further attention in any full theory of modernity. Intellectually, Habermas's rigorous division of the modern intellectual world into three strictly autonomous spheres (scientific, ethical, and aesthetic) seems to ignore the validity claims of the religions in ways that even Kant, if not Weber, would have found puzzling.

One must surely insist, with Habermas, that the implicit or explicit validity claims of the religions demand, in modernity, the kind of critical reflection, dialogue, and argument on their claims that are accorded all other claims. But unless one assumes, rather than argues, that no religious or theological claims are argumentatively redeemable, a modern critical social theory should also account for and argue over just these claims.

Modern philosophy of religion (since Kant's *Religion within the Limits of Reason*) and modern theology (since Hegel and Schleiermacher) have demanded the same kind of critical reflection as other modern disciplines. Of course, the peculiar logic of religious claims renders them far more difficult in principle and debatable in fact than the claims implicit in science, ethics, and aesthetics. Indeed, the basic character of religious claims (namely, to speak validly of the "whole" of reality) renders them exceptionally difficult to analyze in modern critical terms. Furthermore, the fact that any religion's claim to construe the nature of ultimate reality (and not any one part of it) makes it logically impossible to fit religion as simply another autonomous sphere alongside science, ethics, and aesthetics.

The problems are real but not insoluble. Indeed, both the discipline of philosophy of religion (which was invented by modernity) and the discipline of modern theology (from classical modern liberal and modernist theologies to contemporary "public correlational theology" models) are, at their best, fully modern critical disciplines. Both philosophy of religion and modern theology should be acknowledged as modern critical disciplines that, in a sociological sense, may attend to the "autonomous" sphere of religious validity claims.

In a more properly philosophical sense, however, the logical peculiarity of the kind of claims implied by the religions logically demands a distinct form of argumentation and renders the sociological autonomous "spheres" language of Habermas intellectually inappropriate. That distinct form of argumentation can logically only be construed as metaphysical — not in the pre-Kantian and premodern sense but in neoclassical sense advanced, for example, by Charles Hartshorne. I acknowledge, with Habermas, that any transcendental analysis dependent on a philosophy of consciousness demands reformulation into explicitly linguistic and dialogical terms, if the earlier monological impasse is not to recur. I suggest, furthermore, that even process thought, however distanced from a philosophy of consciousness, needs to be rendered in terms that give more explicit attention to the linguistic turn and its dialogical implications. Nor do I mean, by these brief suggestions, to claim that the issue of the validity claims of the religions has been resolved by the various (and often conflicting) modern philosophies of religion and modern theologies. I make, rather, a more modest but, in relationship to Habermas's theory, a more crucial claim: namely, that, short of assessing whatever arguments he may have against the metaphysical arguments of philosophers and theologians on the central claims of the religions (in Western religion, especially the nature and reality of God), modern theologians and philosophers of religion will remain unpersuaded by Habermas's occasional (and usually sociological and social evolutionary rather than strictly philosophical) comments on the validity claims of religion and theology.

Even in Habermas's own intellectual tradition, it is somewhat strange to find him silent on the role of religious questions as limit-questions in Kant. Kant's position has been refined, moreover, by contemporary philosophical reflections on religious questions as questions raised by any reflective person on the limits to science (why any intelligibility or order at all?) or on the limit-questions of morality (why be moral at all?). Moreover, Kant's analysis of symbol in the *Third Critique* has been developed not only by the Romantics Habermas so fears but in modern hermeneutical and communicative terms by such philosophers as Paul Ricoeur, such theologians as Paul Tillich, and such historians of religion as Mircea Eliade. To ignore these discussions impoverishes Habermas's analysis of the actual character and disclosure possibilities of the classic religious symbols (and, indeed, of aesthetic symbols as well, as we shall see below). Sociologically, moreover, Habermas's agreement with Weber's interpretation of the role of the world religions in aiding the emergence of a universal, formal ethic also suggests that, short of imposing a model of three autonomous spheres, the validity claims of the religions need serious philosophical attention in modernity.

I do not claim that I have provided here the complex philosophical arguments needed for proving the validity claims of the religions. I have only recalled familiar arguments that have already been developed by many philosophers and theologians. Yet this seems appropriate for my present more modest but crucial claim: namely, that there is no *argument* in Habermas that disallows these questions and these validity claims. There is, therefore, no good reason, either philosophically or sociologically, for a modern critical social theorist to so confine his analysis to three and three only cognitive spheres as to stop short of even asking the questions of validity claims of the religions as they have been analyzed by both philosophers of religion and theologians.

(6) The same kind of problem with equally serious implications for the study of religious and aesthetic symbols emerges from Habermas's comments on aesthetic discourse. Here the problem is not a relative silence (as on religion and theology) but a relative confusion. The confusion is this: sometimes Habermas accords the aesthetic realm the power of disclosing new possibilities for communicative action (for example, utopian possibilities). More characteristically, however, he interprets aesthetic discourse as purely expressive, that is, as expressive of internal, subjective states and, therefore, as determined by the validity claims of "sincerity" or "authenticity."

This mixed discourse on aesthetics must be considered. If aesthetic validity claims are *only* claims to personal sincerity or authenticity, then they cannot also serve as resources for the disclosure possibility of meaning and truth for dialogue by the whole community concerned with discussing possibilities for the good (and not only the right).

As Habermas argues in his more recent writings, the need for a utopian ethics of the good society demands resources beyond his earlier purely formal and autonomous ethics. One reason Habermas may have difficulty in using his theory of communicative action to analyze the validity claims of the utopian resources for the good he clearly favors is the relatively narrow reading he usually accords aesthetic discourse (namely, the establishment of validity claims of sincerity). However, as his other occasional remarks on aesthetics and disclosure possibility suggest (but do not argue), there is no good philosophical reason to so narrow the range of the aesthetic. In Kantian terms, Habermas's expressive aesthetics is an aesthetics of the beautiful and the free play of the imagination. Such an aesthetic produces free and sincere inner states for the subject. It does not open to an aesthetics of the sublime, nor does it acknowledge the cognitive claims of the symbol.

Habermas's occasional comments on the "disclosure" character of the work of art and its central category of "possibility" suggest, however, that Habermas could remove this confusion in his account of aesthetic discourse if he would rethink his position by retrieving his own earlier hermeneutical interests. More exactly, any claim to truth in the work of art is a claim to a manifestation (and concealment) of possibility, including utopian possibilities for individual human happiness and the communal good life. As Heidegger, Gadamer, and Ricoeur have argued, this claim (and not the claim to expressive sincerity) is the central validity claim of all true art.

As I have argued elsewhere, the notion of the public character of all symbols (warranted by both a theory of symbol and the hermeneutical notion of truth as manifestation of possibility) renders the classic works of art and religion available to the public realm for dialogue and argument and not merely for the private states of the religious or aesthetic subject. The technicization of the public realm, so well analyzed by Habermas under the rubric of the colonization of the lifeworld, is linked in modernity to the marginalization of art and the privatization of religion. To ignore the claims of religion and to narrow the claims of art to claims of personal sincerity can only, I fear, increase the colonization of the lifeworld that Habermas so forcefully wants to overcome. The vestiges of reason in our lifeworld include the vestiges of possibility for individual happiness and communal good in the great classics of art and religion.

Without such rethinking of the claims to disclosure possibility in the aesthetic and religious symbols, our resources for public dialogue on the good life will be seriously impoverished. Two examples of those resources must here suffice.

(a) The utopian impulse found in the eschatological symbols as analyzed by Ernst Bloch and Walter Benjamin and as directly employed by modern political, liberation, feminist. and womanist theologians implies a notion of the cognitive status of symbols and a disclosive (not merely expressive) understanding of both the aesthetic and the religious. A rethinking, therefore, of the validity claims of aesthetic discourse would help Habermas retrieve, on non-Romantic grounds, the earlier analysis of the public character of utopian symbols by Bloch and Benjamin. The prophetic and eschatological symbols and the symbols descriptive of the dangerous memories of the suffering of the oppressed serve as disclosures of a genuine utopian possibility for a better life for all in our society. On this model, aesthetic and religious symbols should not be confined to the realm of inner sincerity but be allowed their properly public function. These resources for the good should, of course, be subject to further argument to see if they cohere with the demands of justice and the right. But before these further arguments can occur we must rethink the character of the aesthetic realm. Gadamer's dialogical model of understanding and Ricoeur's communication model of understanding and explanation have revised Heidegger's original insight on the claim to truth in the work of art in a more explicitly communicative direction that Habermas, in principle, could accept. My suggestion is that the same kind of hermeneutical, dialogical revision of the insights of Bloch and Benjamin could allow for a more substantive recovery of their utopian proposals. This understanding of both aesthetic and religious symbols could also illuminate how, in the American context, Reinhold Niebuhr was able to use the Christian understanding of the dialectic of grace and sin so effectively for discussion in the public realm and how Martin Luther King, Jr., could appeal so tellingly to both classical biblical resources and classic American political symbols to change the terms of the discussion on justice and the good life in the American civil rights movement.

(b) A hermeneutical reformulation of the validity claims of aesthetic and religious symbols as disclosive of possibility could also help to illuminate contemporary debates (often under the rubric of postmodernity) on the role of avant-garde art. One need not accept the over-claims of, for example, Jean-François Lyotard (or for that matter Theodor Adorno) to understand the legitimate claims in contemporary postmodern praise for avant-garde art. In fact, the French postmodern reading of the role of the avant-garde (starting with the surrealists) is misunderstood if it is interpreted as only trying to provide some inner space for private sincerity, authenticity, and happiness in the bleak modern situation. Rather, at their best (aside from polemical exaggerations) the intellectual program of the French postmoderns includes a crucial insistence that Habermas's interpretation of aesthetic discourse does not. That insistence is the need to find better ways to allow for difference and otherness as other than particular exemplifications of general rational principles. If "difference" is simply a synonym for particularity, it is difficult to see how avant-garde art (with its heightening of the role of difference, again starting with the surrealists) and postmodern philosophies of difference and otherness could perform any public function.

But, as Adorno and even Habermas (with his praise of avant-garde art) argue, new *forms* of art can be interpreted as disclosing realities of otherness and difference that both subvert the colonization of the modern lifeworld and bear new and needed possibilities for that public realm. To be sure, these possibilities include alternatives for rethinking both subjectivity and sincerity. But avant-garde art (at least hermeneutically construed) also includes new possibilities of difference and otherness for the public realm. As Julia Kristeva's and Michel de Certeau's recovery of the marginalized claims of the classic mystics show and as Kristeva's post-Derridian and post-Lacanian reflections on the category of a "subject-in-process" suggest, we need not be left, in our discussion of resources for the public realm, with merely formal notions of rationality or merely exaggerated postmodern notions of the "death of the self."

In sum, if Habermas would rethink his notion of the aesthetic realm in the hermeneutical terms he could, in principle, use, he could still argue persuasively against the over-claims of the postmoderns in the same way he argued against the over-claims of Weber's "iron cage" metaphor and Adorno and Horkheimer's "Dialectic of Enlightenment." As he was able to learn from Bloch, Benjamin, and Adorno on the import of the "avant-garde" for the modern lifeworld despite his other serious differences from them, so too Habermas could learn in principle far more from the postmoderns than he characteristically does without abandoning persuasive arguments against their problematic readings of modernity. He could learn, in short, that a defense of modernity need not confine aesthetic discourse to validity claims of sincerity. Rather we can read the postmodern thinkers (sometimes, to be sure, against their own intent) as providing new and often utopian resources for possibilities of difference and otherness. As such, they also provide resources for the dialogue in the public realm.

This same kind of rethinking could free Habermas's theory to learn far more from other cultures. More exactly, we all need to find better ways to learn from the classics of other cultures and thus remove the vestigial ethnocentrism of our Western theories of communicative action. Such, at least, is my final suggestion — a suggestion that, as I argued in a recent book, means that dialogue rather than argument is the more encompassing category needed.[2] Dialogue, as Plato knew, allows for all the necessary arguments that either an Aristotle or a Habermas could desire. Dialogue demands, moreover, the same general criteria for communicative competence as argument proper. But dialogue, as Plato eventually saw in the middle and later dialogues, also opens beyond dialectical argument to the equally rational realm of these disclosure possibilities for the true, the good, and the beautiful implicit in all the classic myths and symbols. Dialogue demands both an ethical responsibility to the other and an aesthetic and religious sense of disclosure possibility. Dialogue, furthermore, not merely allows for, but demands a testing of every disclosure possibility as a genuinely rational one by a willingness to argue its coherence or incoherence with what we otherwise know or, more likely, believe to be true (in science) and right (in formal communicative ethics). But dialogue also frees the aesthetic realm from its narrow confines in subjective sincerity and helps to release the further questions — the limit questions — which the religions, at their best, enunciate as reasonable questions for any reflective modern person. Plato's model of dialogue also helps one see how every morality of rights also implies some vision of the good and how scientific thought need not objectify and dominate nature. Dialogue may call the attention of the too vigorously separated cognitive realms of modernity (science, ethics, and aesthetics) to the limit-questions of religion and theology implied by all three spheres and by their necessary interactions. The model of dialogue, too, one can now see — thanks to Habermas's critical social theory — must, in our modern period, take on a further task that Plato's need not have: an understanding of the intrinsic link of any dialogical theory of communicative reason in our day to a testable sociological theory of modernity.

In the meantime, all who understand the complexity and urgency of our modern dilemma as partly a dilemma about finding forms of communication that respect both differences and commonalities need to find better ways to assure both dialogue and solidarity-in-action. For what dialogue and argument are to the life of the mind, solidarity must be to the life of action. In spite of my criticisms, therefore, of certain aspects of Habermas's social theory, I find myself not merely in critical dialogue and argument with Habermas but in solidarity with him in his defense of communicative reason and the basic project of modernity.

Any contemporary Christian theology that would employ classic prophetic and mystical symbols in its critical correlative task will also willingly join Habermas in his utopian hope for a better society and his resistance to the colonization of the lifeworld and the technicization of the public realm. The recovery of the prophetic and eschatological symbols by critical theorists like Bloch and Benjamin and theologians like Metz, Gutiérrez, Ruether, and Cone, as well as the recent French postmoderns' rethinking of the marginalized mystical traditions as disclosure of difference and otherness provide some theological ground for both hope and resistance. Such acts of dialogue, argument, and solidarity can give all conversation partners hope that both theologians and critical social theorists may find their conversation not only fruitful but necessary. Such, at least, are some of the reasons for the hope that lies in me.

NOTES

1. Clifford Geertz, *Local Knowledge: Further Essays in Interpretive Anthropology* (New York: Basic Books, 1983), 234.
2. David Tracy, *Plurality and Ambiguity: Hermeneutics, Religion, Hope* (San Francisco: Harper & Row, 1987).

BIBLIOGRAPHY

The principal resources used in this essay may be found in the following:

In Habermas, see especially Jürgen Habermas, *The Theory of Communicative Action*, vols. 1 and 2. Boston: Beacon Press, 1984, 1986. Also *Der philosophische Diskurs der Moderne. Zwölf Vorlesungen* (Frankfurt am Main: Suhrkamp, 1985) [ET: *The Philosophical Discourse of Modernity: Twelve Lectures*, trans. Frederick G. Lawrence (Cambridge: MIT Press, 1987)].

On Habermas, see especially the following:

For early work (and bibliographies) see Thomas McCarthy, *The Critical Theory of Jürgen Habermas*. Cambridge, Mass.: MIT Press, 1978.

For later work (especially recommended and frequently used for the descriptive sections of this essay), see (with bibliographies) Stephen K. White, *The Recent Works of Jürgen Habermas: Reason, Justice and Modernity*. Cambridge: Cambridge University Press, 1988.

For other references, see the citations in the following:

David Tracy. *The Analogical Imagination: Christian Theology and the Culture of Pluralism*. New York: Crossroad, 1981.

————. *Plurality and Ambiguity: Hermeneutics, Religion, Hope*. San Francisco: Harper & Row, 1987.

————. *Dialogue with the Other: The Inter-Religious Dialogue*. Louvain: Peeters Press, 1990, and Grand Rapids: Wm. B. Eerdmans Publishing Co., 1991.

John B. Thompson and David Held, eds. *Habermas: Critical Debates*. Cambridge, Mass.: MIT Press, 1982.

Seyla Benhabib. *Critique, Norm, and Utopia: A Study of the Foundations of Critical Theory*. New York: Columbia University Press, 1986.

2

Enlightenment and Theology as Unfinished Projects

Helmut Peukert

The relationship between critical theory and theology can be correctly determined only when we take into account the challenge that confronts both of them in our historical situation. It is a situation in which it has become more and more apparent that certain trends within our social-cultural formation threaten us. It is a situation in which — to put it a bit dramatically — humanity as a whole has become the *object* of our political decisions and of our economic activity, yet in which it is not yet the *subject* of its activity: that we would have available regular forms of public decision making or even have the necessary insights at our disposal that would be adequate to the size of the problems. This may meanwhile appear as something banal. But it is still our situation, and nothing is more resistant to analysis than a banality or something that has been declared a banality.

Granted this situation, what is the significance of projects like that of critical theory or of theology? And what relationship do they have to each other?

Ever since its beginnings, the critical theory of the Frankfurt School has considered itself as standing in the tradition of the Enlightenment. Indeed, the authors of the *Dialectic of Enlightenment* specifically understand Enlightenment as the project of human culture in general. This project is founded on the ability of human persons to step out of their blind, prereflective bond with nature and to become more and more aware of the conditions of their own existence, and with the help of their distancing-reflective reason, to lead a life in which they themselves give it its direction on the basis of mutually shared, free insight.

Some might hesitate to also call theology a "project." It is true that at the core of religion there is something at stake that is simply not in our power, that therefore cannot simply be the result of our efforts. But Kierkegaard, who knew this quite well, did not hesitate to speak of the project of thinking that is assigned to us with the exacting demands of becoming a Christian.[1] The dimensions of this project are first clear when one admits that since the rise of the great world religions, theology, as a methodically controlled reflective form of religion, has been concerned with the basic problems of advanced civilizations that developed simultaneously with it. The thesis seems plausible to me that the unsolved fundamental problem of advanced civilizations is that of mastering the tendency toward power accumulation.[2]

The concept of power is multi-layered. Power denotes first of all the ability through an action to bring about certain effects. Power increases through the expansion of possibilities of action within the framework of the general cultural development. But its character is first revealed, according to Max Weber, when power appears as the ability in situations of social conflict to push through a will even against resistance, when along with this, the expanded possibilities of action are systemically organized, and when such systems of power engage in competition with one another and place themselves under the pressure through this competition to surpass each other by increasing their own power. The structure of power then manifests itself in the self-driven competition of systems accumulating power in the political-military, in the economic, and in the — media-determined — cultural realms. The fundamental problem of our historical situation then appears to be that these mechanisms of accumulation are barely controllable and threaten to lead toward self-destruction. In my opinion, religion, and in its reflected form, theology, at least since the beginning of the world religions, cannot be understood simply as the attempt to endorse these mechanisms. Rather, religion must be understood as the attempt to put them into question and to develop *alternative* ways of dealing with reality from a grounding in another kind of experience.

Both projects, that of the Enlightenment and that of theology, remain unfulfilled. This is true not only because both share in the fallibility of human knowledge, and therefore as projects are limitless and unfinishable. It is true also in a more radical sense: in an increasingly precarious social-cultural situation both theology and the Enlightenment find themselves placed under the suspicion of having contributed to the rise of this situation in their previous expressions and activity. If they are to be continued, it can only be after they undergo fundamental corrections.

This has been true of theology for a long time. Ever since modernity's critique of religion, theology is suspected of having covered up and also legitimizing the mechanisms of accumulation and of the unjust sharing of power. And, in general, theology is accused of obscuring the true recognition of the human condition by producing an illusory consciousness. The most extreme perversion of religion, then, consists in the exploitation once again of the angst of existence and the desperation of human beings by a religious system interested in exerting its power. The fundamentalistic regressions, which presently can be observed even inside the major churches, sufficiently illustrate the danger of this perversion. Theology, then, must first always prove itself anew as a critical endeavor. The attempts of a new "political theology," of a "theology of liberation," or of a "theology of the public realm" must be counted as attempts in the great tradition of theology to develop and bring to bear the critical potential of religion even within theology itself.[3]

But this same suspicion also applies to the Enlightenment, and, indeed, has been sharpened in the radical critique of reason within our century.[4] The critique of reason by reason belongs itself to the tradition of the Enlightenment. What is new, however, is the assumption that our enlightened rationality does not measure up to the consequences of its actions, so that, in the end, the repercussions of the expanding, competing and accelerating systems of action on a finite world cannot be comprehended, much less controlled. The critical theory of the Frankfurt School, whose own origin and development bears the imprint of the self-destructive effects of social-cultural processes, can be counted as one of the most important attempts to continue the project of Enlightenment — exactly because it itself underwent a radical self-criticism. This is true both of its original form and of its reconstruction by Jürgen Habermas with his theory of communicative action.

Both projects, theology as well as Enlightenment, need to enter into public conversation with each other to continue. This is clear for the project of theology insofar as it makes a claim to speak in a way that is understandable and reasonable to all. And, to my mind, this claim constitutively belongs to theology which then, however, must become engaged in the argumentative discourse. But my thesis is that the Enlightenment also handicaps itself if it does not face the challenge of the religious traditions of humanity and their reflective formulations in theologies in which the basic human condition has been reflected upon in a radical way.

I would like to expound these theses in the following steps. First,

I present the basic approach of the first generation of critical theory and its relationship to theology. Second, I try to explain Jürgen Habermas's criticism of this approach and his reconstruction of critical theory in his theory of communicative action. This reconstruction is carried out in a double way: on the one hand, as a systematic analysis of the structure of human communication and its ethical implications, and, on the other hand, as a reconstruction of the genesis of the modern process of rationalization in which religion is replaced by a communicative ethics. In the third section, with respect to this claim I ask how a theology can be devised that can do justice both to its historical tradition and to the questions of critical theory. Finally, I consider what conclusions relevant for the public realm can be drawn from the discourse between critical theory and theology.

THE FIRST GENERATION OF CRITICAL THEORY AND THEOLOGY

The beginnings of critical theory date back more than two generations. The historians and interpreters of critical theory have shown that it is not possible to give a single theory or a homogeneous system that would have united so diversely creative thinkers from their different disciplines. Yet there were experiences from the first decades of the century that all of them found disturbing. To them belonged the rise of authoritarian movements and eventually of fascist systems in Southern and Central Europe. There was also the splitting up of the labor movement into social-democratic and communist factions. On the one side, this made workers susceptible to authoritarian movements in Western countries; on the other side, it led to the degeneration of the Russian Revolution into Stalinism. Further, there was the development of a new mass culture with new media that clearly tended to neutralize the potential of art for generating fundamental change. This then contributed to the stilling of protest and to the numbing of consciousness. For an explanation of these developments, obviously neither the theories of Marx on the development of capitalistic societies nor Max Weber's interpretation of the rise of modern societies from processes of rationalization and the expansion of administrative-bureaucratic power would be sufficient. The basic focus of their inquiry was to investigate how authoritarian structures of society were transformed into intrapsychic mechanisms in such a way that even the suffering borne under these structures could contribute to their stabilization. If one wants to speak of a hard core of the research program of critical theory in its first phase, this was found in a social-psychological approach that linked Marx's theory of society to Freud's psychoanalysis. This was expected to explain precisely this interdependence of psychic and social foundational structures. When Horkheimer took over the direction of the Institute of Social Research in 1931, he declared its goal to be the exploration of "the interconnection between the economical life of society, the psychic development of the individual and transformations in the realm of culture."[5]

The methodology of this program of research that linked analytical psychology, a critical theory of society, and dialectical philosophy was indeed the same "hermeneutics of suspicion" of which Paul Ricoeur later spoke. For these thinkers, consciousness itself is no longer an absolute. Instead now the Cartesian doubt is carried "to the very heart of the Cartesian stronghold."[6] But with this methodology, through a "hermeneutics of retrieval," a more encompassing concept of reason and the conception of a transformative praxis were supposed to be gained. This transformative praxis would make possible an overcoming of these social and psychic mechanisms and the realization of this broader idea of reason.[7]

It has always been considered to be the most frustrating moment in the development of critical theory when at least Adorno and Horkheimer gave up the hope of reaching a broader concept of reason through a research project that brought together empirical sciences and dialectical philosophy. In the preface to their *Dialectic of Enlightenment* they wrote: "However, the fragments united in this volume show that we were forced to abandon this conviction."[8] In the meantime, the Second World War and the Holocaust had begun. In 1944, near the end of the war, at the highest point of the industrialized extermination of human beings on the battle fields and in the concentration camps, they characterized their project in the following way: "It turned out, in fact, that we had set before ourselves nothing less than the discovery of why humanity, instead of entering into a truly human condition, is sinking into a new kind of barbarism."[9] The suspicion had become more radical; it was now directed against the concepts of Enlightenment and of reason themselves.

The *Dialectic of Enlightenment*, which Habermas describes as the "blackest book" of critical theory,[10] actually remained a fragment. Horkheimer and Adorno attempted to reconstruct the history of human culture as a history of Enlightenment and thereby as a history of reason. For them, reason signifies the ability to free oneself from a prereflective bond with nature and to be differentiated from it. This capacity of distancing, however, contains within it at the same time the possibility of transforming nature into an object of domination; things become "the substrate of domination." The motive for this domination is the "will of self-assertion" and, ultimately, the fear of being dominated oneself.[11] That is why the will of self-assertion as a will of domination over nature also becomes a will of domination over fellow-human beings. "For those in positions of power, however, human beings become raw material just like the whole of nature is for society."[12] This can only succeed when those who seek to dominate others, also have dominion over themselves. Human beings dominate themselves, in order to be able to dominate others as well as nature, in order not to be dominated themselves. Reason thus degenerates into an instrument of domination.

For Horkheimer and Adorno, the inner contradiction in the concept of reason can be traced through history:

reason comprises the idea of a free, human social life in which men organize themselves as the universal subject and overcome the conflict between pure and empirical reason in the conscious solidarity of the whole. This represents the idea of true universality: utopia. At the same time, however, reason constitutes the court of judgment of calculation, which adjusts the world for the end of self-preservation and recognizes no function other than the preparation of the object from mere sensory material in order to make it the material of subjugation.[13]

For Adorno, this contradiction cannot be overcome. Twenty years later, in one of the gloomiest passages of the *Negative Dialectics*, he wrote:

Universal history must be construed and denied. After the catastrophes that have happened, and in the view of the catastrophes to come, it would be cynical to say that a plan for a better world is manifested in history and unites it. Not to be denied for that reason, however, is the unity that cements the discontinuous, chaotically splintered moments and phases of history — the unity of the control of nature, progressing to rule over men, and finally to that over man's inner nature. No universal history leads from savagery to humanitarianism, but there is one leading from the slingshot to the megaton bomb.[14]

This is the famous construction of a universal context of delusion in the face of which the question arises how it can be broken through at all. For Adorno, one possibility seems to appear in art. "That works of art do exist, indicates that non-being could come into existence."[15] I do not want here to go into Adorno's aesthetic theory, but it seems to me that at this point the theological motifs also show their relevance.

Theological elements of the Jewish tradition appear as undercurrents throughout the history of critical theory. Prime advocate for this tradition was Walter Benjamin. Inspired by his friend Gershom Scholem, Benjamin had intensively studied Jewish mysticism since the 1920s. In 1929 he had a number of conversations with Adorno on the relationship between avant-garde art, historical materialism, and theology. From then on the relationship of critical theory to theology became a central topic in the personal relations between Benjamin and Adorno, and later on, also between Benjamin and Horkheimer. After Adorno himself had met Scholem in 1938, he wrote to Benjamin that he liked Scholem most "where he makes himself the advocate of the theological motif in your, and perhaps I may also say in my philosophy, and it will not have escaped you that a number of his arguments concerning the task of the theological motif, above all, that it is in truth as little eliminated in your method as in mine, converge with my San Remo discussions. . . . "[16] Of course it was unthinkable for them to directly adopt the current theological language. For in their minds the Hebrew Bible's ban on images was linked very closely with a radical critique of any objectifying metaphysics. Here also the motif of historical materialism prevailed: that one must consider the historical process from the perspective of its victims. For them the point was to link theological and materialistic thinking to each other and thereby to conceive both more clearly in their interrelatedness: "A restoration of theology, or better, a radicalization of the dialectic into the very glowing core of theology, would at the same time have to mean an utmost intensification of the social-dialectical, indeed economic, motifs."[17] This "radicalization of the dialectic into the very glowing core of theology," however, would also transform theology and its expressions. Through his dealing with surrealism, Walter Benjamin had found the formula that "religious illumination" had to be transformed into "a profane illumination of materialist and anthropological inspiration."[18] Adorno called such profane illumination "inverse theology."[19]

Yet, this transformation of theology also had to signify a transformation of the profane and could therefore leave neither theology nor historical materialism unchanged. This is illustrated in Benjamin's concept of time. In his "Theses on the Philosophy of History"[20] he tried to show that truly revolutionary action, in which not only the conditions but also the subjects are changed, breaks through the linear time of the victor's history of progress and challenges the conclusiveness of the past. It thus puts into question the definitiveness of the fate of the victims of the historical process. The possibility of such a mode of action is not simply given, it must be prepared. Benjamin's concept of the "now-time" (*Jetztzeit*) thereby tries to join together both the apocalyptic-messianic discourse about the radical transformation in the moment of redemption with the conception transformed through negative dialectics of a revolutionary mode of action that breaks through the historical context of coercion and through delusive consciousness.[21]

It cannot be said that Benjamin or Adorno or any other repre-

sentative of critical theory was able to realize this transformation
of theology beyond outlining these approaches. In addition, it is a
question whether the conceptual tools with which especially Adorno
worked were not inadequate in themselves. This, anyway, is the criticism from Jürgen Habermas which stimulated him to reconstruct
critical theory. It remains open whether this reconstruction preserves
the cutting edges of the radical questions of the first generation of
critical theory, and whether it is able to show from the new foundation of a theory of communicative action what a transformation of
theological discourse might mean.

THE RECONSTRUCTION OF CRITICAL THEORY
BY JÜRGEN HABERMAS AND THEOLOGY

While Habermas's thinking essentially has to be understood as a
continuation of the work of the first generation of critical theory,
this continuation is equally an independent basic "reconstruction"
of the whole approach. In this reconstruction, Habermas proceeds
on the assumption that the statement of a universal context of delusion is not just an historical diagnosis, but has also been caused by
the theoretical means employed. For him, the older critical theory
could conceive modern rationality only as a technical-instrumental
rationality because it starts from a philosophy of consciousness within
which the subject was primarily taken as a subject that dominates. In
order to attain a concept of transformative praxis which would be
relevant for our historical and social situation, it also seemed crucial
to explicate another, equally important mode of human action. This
mode is anchored just as deeply in the natural history of the human
species and in the structure of human competences like instrumental
action. It does not, however, aim at objectification and domination,
but at the autonomous responsibility [Mündigkeit] of the individual
in an intersubjectivity of unconstrained agreement.

This ability, which is founded in the history of the species, is that
of interaction mediated through language. Language is the starting
point for the history of the species and for anthropology. It constitutes the connection of subjectivity and intersubjectivity and through
it a relationship towards reality as a whole. Habermas still finds the
sentences he formulated in 1965 fundamentally valid: "The human
interest in autonomy and responsibility is not mere fancy, for it can
be apprehended a priori. What raises us out of nature is the only
thing whose nature we can know: language. Through its structure autonomy and responsibility are posited for us. With the first sentence
the intention of a universal and unconstrained consensus is unmistak-

ably expressed."[22] With this interconnectedness of linguistic action, the autonomy of the individual and a general, unconstrained consensus, the basic idea of a theory of communicative action has been formulated.

I consider this approach as fundamentally correct in its central intuition — not only because it aims at a human praxis that breaks through the constraint of self-assertion accomplished through the accumulation of power, but also because theoretically this kind of approach seems to be the one most likely to solve the limit problems of a theory of the natural sciences and the human sciences.[23] Of course, the sentences quoted also call attention to the problems of the theoretical status of this approach: it asks for a new kind of association between philosophical reflection and the empirical sciences. It is in need (1) of a philosophical foundation that starts from the presuppositions which necessarily have to be made in communicative action. Yet, it also asks for an embodiment of these insights in an analysis of both (2) the architectonic and the ontogenesis of the competences of a subject capable of action, and (3) in an analysis of the rise of these competences in phylogenesis, in the history of the species. It should be clear that crucial problems in scientific theory are present in this connection.

In order to understand correctly the status of this approach, and thus its possible relationship to theology, one has to consider as well the philosophical-historical background from which Habermas argues. In 1954, Habermas in his dissertation *Das Absolute und die Geschichte. Von der Zwiespältigkeit in Schellings Denken* ("The Absolute and History. On the Conflict in Schelling's Thinking") had treated the basic problems of modernity's critique of metaphysics.[24] This critique in postwar Germany had been articulated on the one side by Heidegger and his pupils, and on the other side by thinkers within the Marxist tradition, above all, by representatives of critical theory. This philosophical critique, inasmuch as it joined the self-critique within classical philosophy, considered itself at the culmination of a dramatic development. It wanted to show that metaphysical thinking would inevitably be full of aporias, because it had always tried to grasp the whole of reality and, as its ground, an Absolute. Yet this Absolute, in becoming the object of thinking, was subjected to this thinking and could not be the Absolute anymore. It thus had to be distinguished again from the object of thought as something still more original, but only to appear thereby once again as a product of thinking.[25] This aporia within modern metaphysics that made everything into an object — an aporia which stimulated the subsequent philosophical development — had been most acutely analyzed by Schelling.[26] Starting from Schelling's analyses, Habermas tried to show that Feuerbach and Marx in their critique of metaphysics and theology had voiced a major suspicion: namely, that the construction of an absolute is the projection of a human being who is not yet free from illusion and able to find a place in a contradictory historical and social reality. Habermas's conclusion from this critique, taken in opposition to Heideggerian thought, is the turn to a "philosophy of history with a practical intent." Here, indeed, he saw himself in accord with radical Jewish mysticism. In 1971 Habermas characterized the relation of postmetaphysical thinking to theology in this way: "Post-metaphysical thought does not challenge any specific theological assertions; rather it asserts their meaninglessness. It wants to prove that, in the basic conceptual system in which the Judeo-Christian tradition is dogmatized (and hence rationalized), theologically meaningful statements cannot be asserted."[27] He adds: "This critique...strikes at the roots of religion."[28] This philosophical background must be considered if one wants to understand Habermas's approach to the theory of communicative action, as well as his position with respect to the history of religion and to theology.

At first, Habermas tries to demonstrate the structure and the normative implications of communicative action by examining the genesis of human competences for action. For this, he refers to the theories of developmental psychology that explain the acquisition of different capabilities: theories of the development of cognitive (Jean Piaget) and interactive abilities (George Herbert Mead; John H. Flavell; Robert Selman); of the abilities of moral judgment and action (Lawrence Kohlberg); and theories of the development of individual psychological drives, following Freud. Looking at a child's development it is possible to see each successive step towards greater autonomy and independence as being accompanied by a corresponding step towards greater mutual interaction in human relationships, reaching steadily outward. The entire development seems to progress according to an inherent tendency: an individual identity initially dependent on the simple physical attention of others, gradually, through a long, drawn-out, and painful process of transformation, becomes an identity which does not depend simply on certain inculcated rules, but is itself capable of assuming responsibility for shaping and formulating the rules of communal life. Similarly, the goal of the development of moral consciousness would then be the ability to build a communicative world in which human beings can find ways of living together which enable every individual to work out his or her own lifestyle based on the recognition and respect of others, and to do so ultimately in a universal perspective not confined to small groups or nations. Individual freedom and universal solidarity would then be harmonious rather than contradictory concepts.

This form of communicative action includes a normative core which defines the basis of ethics. The attempts to formulate this core concur, it seems to me, in the following basic thesis: If I enter into communication with another person at all, I accept that person in principle as someone who is able to speak and make herself or himself understood and to contradict me. I accept that person as an equal partner and am prepared in what I say to expose myself to that person's criticism and response and to attempt to reach agreement with her or him on the truth of statements or the correctness of norms. These fundamental and inescapable suppositions depend primarily on the recognition and acceptance of the other person, an acceptance which must prove itself in jointly worked out norms of behavior. This mutual acceptance, in principle, can exclude no one as a partner in communication. The moment I begin to speak I enter a universal dialogue.

It is at this point of the reconstruction of the human competences of action and the corresponding forms of social agreement on the scale of the history of the human race that religion finds its significant role. Large parts of Habermas's "Theory of Communicative Action" can thus also be read as a dialogue with religion.[29] The first volume is focused on a discussion of Max Weber's analysis of western rationalization and its religious presuppositions. The second volume treats the thesis that in social evolution religion, which according to Durkheim guaranteed the social integration of a society, is replaced by communicative ethics.

Max Weber's reconstruction of the history of religion and Western rationalization is directed by the intention of highlighting in its genesis the final result of this development, namely the loss of meaning and of freedom in modern society. This reconstruction contains a double critique: (1) of the direction of this rationalization, thus also of the Enlightenment; (2) of the development of religion and its rationalization by its transformation into an individualizing ethics in which people set out to prove themselves in a capitalistic society of competition and turn against an original ethics of brotherliness. Weber, therefore, is also interested in the critique of a state of society: precisely the meaningless and freedom-threatening rationalized world of economics, of politics and of science. Weber's demonstration of the shortcomings of religion can therefore be interpreted as a critique of society; he shows that social conditions only allow a certain way of realizing religion and dooms other ways of realization to failure or to mere particularity.[30]

In opposition to Weber, Habermas wants to put forward another

understanding of the social processes of modernization and rationalization. With the earlier critical theorists, he also accuses Weber of
only introducing a concept of rationality that is limited to purposive
reason (*Zweckrationalität*). In contrast, Habermas conceives the processes of modernization precisely as the release of communicative
rationality. He explains the pathologies of modern societies from
the functional constraints and the inner dynamics of the economical and political-administrative systems themselves. These "colonize"
areas that constitutively depend upon the priority of unconstrained
communicative action, for example, socialization, social integration
and cultural reproduction.[31] Pathological developments in the individual can then be explained as appropriations of the pathologies
of society.

At the same time Habermas tries to show in his treatment of
Durkheim that with the spreading of communicative ethics in society
the integrating function of religion becomes superfluous. Durkheim
had conceived religion as the social bond of a normative consensus
that receives the character of the sacred and is renewed in ritual.[32]
In this way, religion can camouflage and legitimize unjust conditions
of violence behind the veil of the holy. When in the course of the
development of social forms of agreement the normative consensus is joined to discursive agreement, the authority of the sacred
is dissolved. Religion loses not only its ability to protect structural
violence by curtailing communication, but to a large degree is itself dissolved.[33] As Habermas explains, "to the extent that language
becomes established as the principle of sociation, the conditions of
socialization converge with the conditions of communicatively produced intersubjectivity. At the same time, the authority of the sacred
is converted over to the binding force of normative validity claims
that can be redeemed only in discourse."[34]

Yet recently Habermas has stressed that communicative reason
cannot simply take over the role of religion. Above all, it cannot
console. This results in the ambivalent position of a tolerant standing
next to each other, a skeptical but peaceful coexistence:

Communicative reason does not enact itself in an aesthetic theory as the
colorless negative of consoling religions. Neither does it announce the dis-
consolateness of a god-forsaken world, nor itself pretend to console. It also
renounces exclusivity. As long as it does not find any better words in the
medium of reasoned speech for that what religion can say, it will, without
supporting it or combating it, abstinently co-exist with it.[35]

This is no longer simply the position that claims to have overcome
religion and theology in a meta-communicative way.[36] Nevertheless,
in public *argumentative* discourse neither of them has a real place. But

then are not religion and theology once again suspected of falling away from communicative reason?

THEOLOGY AND THE THEORY
OF COMMUNICATIVE ACTION

Theology, if it does not want to abandon itself, obviously cannot renounce making a claim to truth. Moreover, in a pluralist society it must attempt to formulate its subject matter in an intersubjectively understandable and communicative way. The first requirement for it is then that it does not evade the aporias and contradictions of the common historical situation.[37] Theology cannot break away from the extreme experiences of suffering and annihilation of our century into a beyond calmly speculated upon. In the "solidarity of all finite beings" (Horkheimer), the setting for theology's discourse remains wherever there can be individual and communal historical action in protest against extermination. It cannot suppress the question of theodicy through an amnesia that represses world history, nor, like conservative political theologies, leave the answer to innerworldly political or religious sovereigns. Theology, remembering this finiteness and death and in historical solidarity with humanity, must first of all hold the question of theodicy open. It also cannot use dialectic in theology to put itself in the position of the "totally Other"; by holding on to the historical negativity, rather, it must insist on that "radicalization of the dialectic into the very glowing core of theology."

For Habermas the claim to communicative reason is itself already a transcending power. "Again and again this claim is silenced; and yet in fantasies and deeds it develops a stubbornly transcending power, because it is renewed with each act of unconstrained understanding, with each moment of living together in solidarity, of successful individuation, and of saving emancipation."[38] Communicative reason then aims at both freedom and reconciliation at the same time: "The utopian perspective of reconciliation and freedom is ingrained in the conditions for the communicative sociation of individuals; it is built into the linguistic mechanism of the reproduction of the species."[39] The question then becomes whether theology can appropriate the talk of reconciliation, of saving emancipation and of the transcending power of communicative action in Habermas's sense; or, rather, having been freed itself from the mechanisms of self-assertion and competing accumulation of power, theology has to make itself understandable as the theory of a communicative action which in remembrance and anticipation lays claim to God in God's acting here and now as the prevenient absolute love for the other and for oneself.

Concretely, the dialogue between theology and the reconstructed critical theory will have to be carried on: (1) with respect to the interpretation of the history of religion against the background of a theory of development of modern societies; (2) as an attempt of an independent, systematic reconstruction of its approach as a critical, society-related theology that considers it possible to start from a theory of intersubjectivity.

Interpretation of the Role of Religion in a Theory of the Development of Modern Societies

The interpretation of history is by no means secondary for theology; it touches its very core. Theology will thus pay attention to the way in which historical development as a whole and, within this development, its own traditions are interpreted. These interpretations shape the fundamental understanding of religion and especially of the world religions. For Habermas their prime task is clear: "Whereas mythical narratives interpret and make comprehensible a ritual praxis of which they themselves are part, religious and metaphysical worldviews of prophetic origin have the form of doctrines that can be worked up intellectually, and that explain and justify an existing political order in terms of the world-order they explicate."[40]

The question, however, is whether, historically, the task of religion, and especially the world religions, has been adequately described. With good reasons one can support the thesis that the basic problem in the development of advanced civilizations since the Neolithic revolution — and until today — is the accelerating accumulation and systematic organization of power.[41] The world religions by no means have reacted to this development and to the social injustice of class-divided societies only by legitimizing them. Indeed, in their origin and in their core, they are often protest movements against the basic trend of a society's development and attempt to ground other ways for human beings to relate to one another and to reality as a whole. This could be shown, for example, in early Buddhist texts. Here, I just want to point out some results of research in the Jewish and Christian traditions.

Max Weber had already conceived the ancient Israelitic union of tribes as a "confederation" (*Eidgenossenschaft*). Research has shown that responding to the accumulation of power in the neighboring ancient Near Eastern empires was fundamental for the whole of Jewish tradition. In contrast, the Israelite confederation of tribes constituted itself as an egalitarian society.[42] The experiences from this conflict were a driving force in the development of the understanding of that reality which can be called "God" and in what way their confession of God includes a specific societal communicative practice. The original profession of faith of Judaism is that of liberation from the slavery of Egypt. This experience is intensified during the period of exile and finally in the fight against the Seleucid empire in the second century, B.C.E. The latter was a totalitarian system that not only practiced external repression, but also tried to control the consciences of individuals. The apocalyptic originates as an answer to this exterminating power of the state. In an ever more radical way, God is confessed as the one who, intervening eschatologically, robs this untamable power of its force. God deprives this eschatological animal, with its continually reappearing new heads, of its ability to exterminate human beings, and in a way that extends even beyond the grave: God is the saving power whose range of action does not end at the threshold of death. God can call even the dead to life and make up for past injustice.[43] The knowledge of God includes the knowledge that a communal existence is possible, an existence that is not dominated by the mechanisms of power accumulation.

Viewed historically, Jesus is the one who decisively changes this apocalyptical understanding of history. For him also, of course, God is the one who in an eschatological intervention ultimately transforms the world through its completion. But the evil nexus has already been broken. ("I watched Satan fall from the sky like lightning," Luke 10:18.) God has begun to reign in unconditioned goodness and to restore creation. It is now not only possible, but necessary, indeed a matter of course, that one should realize this prevenient goodness of God practically: in the unconditioned affirmation of the other, even the one who may be an enemy. For this person, too, has been affirmed unconditionally. The execution of Jesus becomes the starting point for the experience and the confession that this is also true for his own person: that precisely in his death, he is saved and that, from now on, an intersubjective mode of conduct has become possible for all, in which we progress toward God as the saving reality even in death. Intersubjectivity is qualified in a new way; God's dominion means the abandonment of the domination of human beings over each other.

The fundamental problem of the history of Christianity is that, once it achieved the possibility of sharing power, it did not follow in an unequivocal way this claim to which it owes its existence. Seen historically, the problem of the relationship between religion and power has not been solved in Christianity. But this does not mean that theology was not able to or was not called to continually formulate this claim across the history of religions again and again. On the contrary, theology acts against the ground of its existence when it becomes an ideology of oppression; "theology of liberation" does not have to be a self-contradicting term.

The Task of Reconstructing Theology from a Theory of Intersubjectivity

How can a theology then be developed which is equal both to the claims of its tradition and to its own historical situation, and which thus faces up to the Enlightenment critique and its own self-critique? The project of Christian theology is yet unfinished. I would like, however, to point out at least the dimensions of this task and some basic problems.[44]

(a) Theology must develop its expressions in discussions with the formal sciences, the natural sciences, with the human sciences in their genetic-reconstructive method, and with philosophy. Here the question of the foundation of ethics plays a decisive role. The classical transcendental foundation of ethics, as with Kant, obtains its evidence precisely from the circularity of its argumentation. Freedom only develops fully in the affirmation of another's freedom; by negating in principal another freedom, it destroys itself. Karl-Otto Apel's transformation of the Kantian ethics on the level of a theory of communication is also dependent upon such circular evidence when it falls back upon the procedure of argumentation: If I ask for reasons at all, I have always already acknowledged the other as a communication partner who is able to contradict me with reasons. Yet the starting point for this reasoning is the conception of the already fully developed autonomous subject. On the basis of its competences it interprets reality and acts in mastery over it. In this presupposition, however, lie the limits of this conception. For example, in situations of inequality and oppression, but also in therapeutic and pedagogical action, it is precisely the point that there must first be created for someone the possibility to agree with me or contradict me in freedom.

It, therefore, seems necessary to establish the ground of ethics on a deeper level. To intend the free recognition of the other in that person's freedom means to want the other person to *become* himself or herself by way of an intersubjectively reflected self-determination. Such action aims at the genesis of subjects; it wants to make life possible and recognizes itself as responsible for its preconditions. Such a radicalization of ethics aims at helping possible freedom realize itself as real freedom. This kind of ethics also changes the concept of intersubjective action. This can be illustrated in the understanding of language. From what we know from the foundations of logic, scientific theory, linguistics and philosophical pragmatics, to speak implies the creative projection of an interpretation of subjective, social and objective reality on to my conversation partner in a way that both opens up an understanding to that person and invites my partner to share her or his own creative interpretation with me. Thereby, we enter into a mutual process of *finding* a possible consensus which is not unequivocally preformed by conventions, but which preserves its character of being an innovative process for all participants. This way of provoking freedom through freedom is the condition of the possibility of an intersubjectively reflected commitment to agreements. In such a radicalized ethics, I also see the possibility of a discussion with "postmodern" theories of language.[45]

(b) The character of this ethics, however, only becomes fully apparent when one takes into account that communicative action is always situation-related, temporal action; as this action changes present situations, it remembers things past and projects the future. An ethics that proceeds from the implications of the conversations about validity claims is always in danger of losing sight of the temporality of human activity.[46] The practical recognition of the freedom of the other in communicative action, which means the willing of his or her genesis as a subject, aims, however, at the future realization of possibilities of freedom which, in part, can only first be disclosed in mutual activity. This recognition affirms in an unconditioned way a developing, yet still presumed integrity of the other which does not lie within the power of the one initiating the communication. This mode of communicative action that sets out from the freedom and the integrity of the other trusts in more than what it could achieve by itself.

(c) Such an ethics of intersubjective creativity, admittedly, makes the tragical and antinomical character of ethical activity even more obvious. A person who orients herself or himself toward the freedom of the other as an end in itself, exposes herself or himself. That person becomes all the more vulnerable the more she or he is oriented to the freedom of the other and abandons without limitation any strategic-manipulative action directed toward the preservation of her or his own existence or social system. Freedom reaches its fulfillment only in being freely recognized through the other; yet it is precisely this acknowledgement that is not at its own disposal. Innovative freedom thus exposes itself to the danger of being futile, indeed, of being extinguished. The paradox in the founding of practical reason consists in that freedom, by accepting an unconditional interest in the realization of freedom and reconciliation, takes on the risk of itself being destroyed.[47]

(d) This discussion about the destruction and annihilation of freedom is not merely metaphorical; it characterizes real historical experiences. The tradition of all great religions centers around the memory that men and women have perished in their attempts to act ethically in an unconditioned way. The remembrance of those just men and women who suffered and were destroyed, the *"memoria passionis et mortis"* belongs to the core of both the Jewish and the Christian traditions. For these traditions, the Holocaust, *the* experience of annihilation in our century, has proved an extreme challenge.[48] Its remembrance is not simply exhausted in the moral demand that this must never be repeated. For communicative action, which in the face of the annihilated victims still anticipates the communicative realization of possible freedom in a practical way and in this exposes itself to the risk of failure, the question of the salvation of the annihilated victims arises: the quest for an absolute freedom, saving even in death. The analytics and dialectics of communicative action point beyond themselves to the question of the foundation of theology.

(e) The question that emerges here is the question about that which in the Jewish and Christian traditions is called "God." The "concept" of God which is outlined in temporal, finite, self-transcending intersubjective action in the form of a question encouraged by hope is not the concept of an absolute that we could have demonstrated through the drives of our objectifying thought. It is the concept of an absolute freedom, a freedom before which we hope that in the mortally-finite surpassing of ourselves it shows its true self, namely, as absolutely liberating and saving love. Is such an analysis of intersubjective action and its structure illusionary?[49] It certainly would be, if it led us out of the concrete dialectic of our historical action. Yet, it does not lead us outside of our situation, but, rather, more radically into it.

(f) I realize that here all the classical questions of a philosophical doctrine of God and of the relationship between metaphysical thought and theology reappear. Yet, to refuse to give up at this point the task of reflection does not necessarily mean a relapse into an objectifying metaphysics.[50] A way of thinking which has untangled itself from the compulsion to objectify in grasping reality as a whole — a "postmetaphysical" thinking in this sense — does not also have to be a "posttheological" thinking. It can, however, draw attention to experiences which cannot simply be reduced to a mythical consciousness. Along these lines I understand Adorno's sentences in the *Negative Dialectics:* "What demythologization would not affect... is... the experience that if thought is not decapitated, it will flow into transcendence, down to the idea of a world that would not only abolish extant suffering but revoke the suffering that is irrevocably past."[51]

(g) I believe that a hermeneutics both of the interpretation of the praxis and preaching of the historical Jesus and of speech about resurrection (if this is not simply to be presented as something miraculous) can only be developed from a prior analysis of the dialectic of finite, temporal, and intersubjective action. For this speech, the common advance towards death is the hopeful advance towards God: a God who is that reality which in the midst of a death-bringing historical-social context reveals itself as liberating and as making conversion possible, and which proves itself as saving in death. In this discourse, it is clear that affirmation in solidarity as the assertion of the reality of God for the other person cannot be limited. It always already proceeds from the assertion of the salvation of the past, of the annihilated, from the "death of death." Then, however, a fundamental-theological hermeneutics of the reality of resurrection can make the resurrection of Jesus understandable as an event that is not completely isolated from us, but rather an event which first makes possible an existence in unconditional and unlimited solidarity and which is the ground of that ecstatic joy which belongs to the heart of Christianity.[52] This means, conversely, that this salvation in death has only been grasped if it holds good in the unconditioned acknowledgment of the other here and now. Then communicative action, in which human beings drawing from this experience expect from each other an existence in illimitable solidarity, is constitutive for Christian existence which works in a concrete society for its transformation.[53]

FINAL REMARKS

I have started from the thesis that in our historical situation both the projects of theology and that of Enlightenment (and within this, the project of critical theory) are proved to be unfinished. This situation is characterized by a heretofore unknown expansion of human possibilities of action and by the tendency to organize these possibilities into competing systems of power accumulation, whose repercussions again threaten us. Today we know more about the conditions of our common existence than all previous generations, but we seem a long way off from being able to conceive it as a whole, much less to fundamentally change it. In addition, the plurality of languages and the ambiguity of interpretations continue to grow.[54]

Religion and the Enlightenment represent attempts to grasp the *condition humaine* as a whole, whether it be in mythical images or, also in theology, in argumentative discourse. The Enlightenment tried to determine the kind of rationality that would make a universal discourse possible in which a consensus of *all* as a basis for transformative action could be achieved. To do this it had to determine the limits of rationality and to exclude certain modes of self-interpretation. The question remains, however, whether this must lead to the conclusion that the religious traditions of humanity and their theological argumentation must be altogether excluded from the universal discourse.

It could be that we grasp the dimensions of crucial themes in our common public discourse only when we include these traditions and forms of argumentation, that only then can we completely grasp what this involves: the integrity and inviolable dignity of human beings; human rights in the wider social context in addition to the codified basic rights and the rights to political participation; justice that is more than the equal treatment of unequals, but that seeks to make individual integrity really possible; forms of discourse that enable the voiceless to speak; innovative conciliatory action that opens up the possibility for peace; and a solidarity which also includes the dead and the generations to come.[55]

Translated by Peter P. Kenny

NOTES

1. Søren Kierkegaard, *Philosophical Fragments*, 2d ed., trans. David F. Swenson with revision by Howard V. Hong (Princeton, N.J.: Princeton University Press, 1962), 11ff.

2. Carl Friedrich von Weizsäcker, *Bewußtseinswandel* (Munich: Hanser, 1988), 179.

3. See Johann Baptist Metz, *Faith in History and Society* (New York: Seabury, 1980); Gustavo Gutiérrez, *A Theology of Liberation* (Maryknoll, N.Y.: Orbis, 1973); Clodovis Boff, *Theology and Praxis* (Maryknoll, N.Y: Orbis, 1987); David Tracy, *Plurality and Ambiguity: Hermeneutics, Religion, Hope* (San Francisco: Harper & Row, 1987).

4. See Helmut Peukert, *Bildung und Vernunft* (Frankfurt am Main: Suhrkamp, in press); Peukert, "Über die Zukunft von Bildung," in *Frankfurter Hefte*, FH-extra 6 (1984):129–37.

5. Max Horkheimer, "Die gegenwärtige Lage der Sozialphilosophie und die Aufgaben eines Instituts für Sozialforschung," in *Sozialphilosophische Studien* (Frankfurt am Main: Athenäum Fischer Verlag, 1972), 43; see Helmut Dubiel, *Wissenschaftsorganisation und politische Erfahrung. Studien zur frühen kritischen Theorie* (Frankfurt am Main, 1978); Martin Jay, *The Dialectical Imagination: A History of the Frankfurt School and the Institute of Social Research, 1923–1950* (Boston: Little Brown, 1973); see David Held, *Introduction to*

Critical Theory: Horkheimer to Habermas (Berkeley: University of California Press, 1980), 33.

6. Paul Ricoeur, *Freud and Philosophy: An Essay in Interpretation*, trans. Denis Savage (New Haven: Yale University Press, 1970), 33.

7. See Max Horkheimer, *Traditionelle und kritische Theorie. Vier Aufsätze* (Frankfurt am Main: Fischer Verlag, 1970); Herbert Marcuse, *Kultur und Gesellschaft*, vol. 1 (Frankfurt am Main: Suhrkamp, 1965), partially translated in *Negations: Essays in Critical Theory* (Boston: Beacon Press, 1968).

8. Max Horkheimer and Theodor W. Adorno, *Dialectic of Enlightenment*, trans. John Cumming (New York: Seabury Press, 1975), xi.

9. Ibid., translation slightly modified.

10. Jürgen Habermas, *The Philosophical Discourse of Modernity: Twelve Lectures*, trans. Frederick G. Lawrence (Cambridge: MIT Press, 1987), 106.

11. Horkheimer and Adorno, *Dialektik der Aufklärung* (Amsterdam: Querido, 1947), 79. This has been republished by Fischer Verlag (Frankfurt am Main, 1969).

12. Ibid.

13. Horkheimer and Adorno, *Dialectic of Enlightenment*, 83–84.

14. Theodor W. Adorno, *Negative Dialectics*, trans. E. B. Ashton (New York: Seabury Press, 1973), 320).

15. Theodor W. Adorno, *Ästhetische Theorie*, in *Gesammelte Schriften* (Frankfurt am Main: Suhrkamp, 1970), 17:200. [ET: *Aesthetic Theory* (London: Routledge Methuen, 1986).]

16. Letter, Adorno to Benjamin, May 4th, 1938, Adorno Estate; see Susan Buck-Morss, *The Origin of Negative Dialectics: Theodor W. Adorno, Walter Benjamin and the Frankfurt School* (Hassocks, Sussex: Harvester Press, 1977), 284 n. 49.

17. Letter, Adorno to Benjamin, August 2, 1935, in Theodor W. Adorno, *Über Walter Benjamin*, ed. Rolf Tiedemann (Frankfurt am Main: Suhrkamp, 1975), 117; translated in Buck-Morss, *Origin*, 144.

18. Walter Benjamin, "Der Sürrealismus. Die letzte Momentaufnahme der europäischen Intelligenz," in *Angelus Novus: Ausgewählte Schriften* (Frankfurt am Main: Suhrkamp, 1966), 213; translated in Buck-Morss, *Origin*, 125.

19. Letter, Adorno to Benjamin, November 6, 1934, Adorno Estate; see Buck-Morss, *Origin*, 282 n. 34.

20. Walter Benjamin, "Über den Begriff der Geschichte," in *Gesammelte Schriften*, ed. Rolf Tiedemann and H. Schweppenhäuser (Frankfurt am Main: Suhrkamp, 1980), 1:691–704.

21. See Richard Wolin, *Walter Benjamin: An Aesthetic of Redemption* (New York: Columbia University Press, 1982), 263.

22. See Jürgen Habermas, *Knowledge and Human Interests*, trans. Jeremy J. Shapiro (Boston: Beacon Press, 1971), appendix, 314.

23. See H. Peukert, *Science, Action and Fundamental Theology: Toward a Theology of Communicative Action*, trans. James Bohman (Cambridge, Mass.: MIT Press, 1984).

24. Dissertation, Bonn 1954; see J. Habermas, "Dialektischer Idealismus im Übergang zum Materialismus — Schellings Idee einer Contraction

Gottes," in *Theorie und Praxis. Sozialphilosophische Studien* (Frankfurt am Main: Suhrkamp, 1971), 172–227.

25. Walter Schulz, *Der Gott der neuzeitlichen Metaphysik*, 3rd ed. (Pfullingen: Neske, 1957).

26. Walter Schulz, *Die Vollendung des deutschen Idealismus in der Spätphilosophie Schellings* (Pfullingen: Neske, 1955).

27. Jürgen Habermas, "Wozu noch Philosophie?" in *Philosophisch-politische Profile*, enlarged edition (Frankfurt am Main: 1981) 29 [ET: *Philosophical-Political Profiles*, trans. Frederick Lawrence (Cambridge, Mass.: MIT Press, 1985); translation found in Peukert, *Science, Action and Fundamental Theology*, 162.

28. Ibid.

29. Jürgen Habermas, *The Theory of Communicative Action*, 2 vols., trans. Thomas McCarthy (Boston: Beacon Press, 1985, 1987).; see Rudolf J. Siebert, *The Critical Theory of Religion: The Frankfurt School* (New York: Mouton, 1985), 108–334); Klaus-Michael Kodalle, "Versprachlichung des Sakralen? Zur religionsphilosophischen Auseinandersetzung mit Jürgen Habermas' Theorie des kommunikativen Handelns," in *Allgemeine Zeitschrift für Philosophie* 12 (1987):39–66.

30. See Karl W. Dahm, Volker Drehsen, and Günter Kehrer, *Das Jenseits der Gesellschaft. Religion im Prozeßsozialwissenschaftlicher Kritik* (Munich: Claudius Verlag, 1975), 325.

31. See Habermas, *The Theory of Communicative Action*, 2:119ff.

32. Ibid., 43ff.

33. Ibid., 188ff.

34. Ibid., 93–94.

35. Jürgen Habermas, "Die Einheit der Vernunft in der Vielheit ihrer Stimmen," in *Nachmetaphysisches Denken* (Frankfurt am Main: Suhrkamp, 1988), 153–86, 185).

36. Peukert, *Science, Action and Fundamental Theology*, 160–62.

37. See Tracy, *Plurality and Ambiguity*.

38. Jürgen Habermas, "A Reply to my Critics," in John B. Thompson and David Held, eds., *Habermas: Critical Debates* (Cambridge, Mass.: MIT Press, 1982), 219–88, 221.

39. Habermas, *The Theory of Communicative Action*, 1:398.

40. Habermas, *The Theory of Communicative Action*, 2:188.

41. See Peukert, "Universale Solidarität — Verrat an Bedrohten und Wehrlosen?" in *Diakonia* 8 (1978) 3–12.

42. See Norman K. Gottwald, *The Tribes of Yahweh: A Sociology of the Religion of Liberative Israel 1250–1050 B.C.E.*, 3rd ed. (Maryknoll, N.Y.: Orbis 1985), esp. Part X: "The Religion of the New Egalitarian Society: Idealist, Structural-Functionalist, and Historical Cultural-Materialist Models," 591–663.

43. Klaus Müller, "Apokalyptik, Apokalypsen III. Die jüdische Apokalyptik," in *Theologische Realenzyklopädie III*, 202–51.

44. Peukert, *Science, Action and Fundamental Theology*, 143ff.; Helmut Peukert, "Fundamentaltheologie," in Peter Eicher, ed., *Neues Handbuch the-*

ologischer Grundbegriffe (Munich: Kösel, 1984), 2:16–25; see also Edmund Arens, ed., *Habermas und die Theologie* (Düsseldorf: Patmos, 1989); Rudolf Siebert, *From Critical Theory to Communicative Political Theology* (New York: Peter Lang, 1989).

45. See Helmut Peukert, "Intersubjektivität — Kommunikationsgemeinschaft — Religion. Bemerkungen zu einer höchsten Stufe der Entwicklung moralischen Bewußtseins durch K.-O. Apel," in *Intersoggetività — Socialità — Religione*, ed. Marco M. Olivetti (Padova: Cedam, 1986), 167–78.

46. See Habermas, *Vorstudien und Ergänzungen*, 553.

47. See Thomas Pröpper, *Erlösungsglaube und Freiheitsgeschichte*, 2d ed. (Munich: Kösel, 1988), 165–71.

48. See Johann Baptist Metz, "Im Angesicht der Juden. Christliche Theologie nach Auschwitz," in *Concilium* (Ger.) 20 (1984):382–89.

49. See Thomas McCarthy, "Philosophical Foundations of Political Theology: Kant, Peukert and the Frankfurt School," in *Civil Religion and Political Theology*, ed. Leroy S. Rouner (Notre Dame, Ind.: University of Notre Dame Press, 1986) 23–40.

50. See Klaus Schäfer, *Hermeneutische Ontologie in den Climacusschriften Sören Kierkegaards* (Munich: Kösel, 1968), esp. pp. 112ff. on the relation between Kierkegaard and Schelling. Precisely from Kierkegaard's critique of the "metaphysical" could the discussion about metaphysics begin again.

51. Adorno, *Negative Dialectics*, 403.

52. See Karl Rahner, "Grundlinien einer systematischen Christologie," in Karl Rahner and Wilhelm Thüsing, *Christologie — systematisch und exegetisch* (Freiburg: Herder, 1972), 17–78; Francis Schüssler Fiorenza, *Foundational Theology: Jesus and the Church* (New York: Crossroad, 1984), esp. 5–55).

53. See Matthew L. Lamb, *Solidarity with Victims: Toward a Theology of Social Transformation* (New York: Crossroad, 1982).

54. See Tracy, *Plurality and Ambiguity*.

55. Helmut Peukert, "Praxis universaler Solidarität. Grenzprobleme im Verhältnis von Erziehungswissenschaft und Theologie," in Edward Schillebeeckx, ed., *Mystik und Politik. Theologie im Ringen um Geschichte und Gesellschaft* (Mainz: Matthias-Grünewald Verlag, 1968), 172–85); Francis Schüssler Fiorenza, "Politische Theologie und liberale Gerechtigkeits-Konzeptionen," in ibid., 105–17.

3

The Church as a Community of Interpretation: Political Theology between Discourse Ethics and Hermeneutical Reconstruction

Francis Schüssler Fiorenza

Habermas's theory of communicative action contains a theory of society as well as an interpretation of modernity and a proposal for a discourse ethics. It develops categories for the understanding of society and modernity, and it seeks to reconceptualize ethics as a discourse ethics. This essay explores the significance and limits of Habermas's theory of communicative action and his discourse ethics for a political theology.[1]

Such an endeavor presupposes that political theology as a discourse for the public realm relates its analysis to the social and political order not in a direct and immediate way. Since political theology involves much more than a method of correlation, it cannot simply and immediately correlate its religious and moral tradition with social and political practice. Instead, it must take into account certain background theories about the nature of society, deal with issues of social and political ethics, and explore the retroductive claims and warrants arising from contemporary experience.[2]

I will, therefore, first examine the basic categories of Habermas's theory of communicative action and his conception of a discourse ethics. In his theory of communicative action, Habermas uses the distinction between lifeworld and system to interpret modern society, which provides a significant background theory of society over against one-sided idealistic or materialist interpretations. His discourse ethics challenges theological and political reflection insofar as it seeks to avoid the deficiencies of traditional moral discourse — be it neo-Aristotelian or Kantian.

Second, I will argue that Habermas's theory of communicative action is helpful, but it does not sufficiently take into account some characteristics of the modern development of religion and theology. These characteristics display significant transformations of theology and religion within modernity. Moreover, these characteristics show that the development of modern theology exhibits traits that fit the conception of modernity outlined by a theory of communicative action. Such characteristics also show that the development of modern religion and theology is a basic presupposition and precondition of political theology.

Finally, I will propose that religious communities have a constructive role to play within modern society. Such a role is not less but more necessary within modernity. Such an increased necessity results from the uncoupling of the lifeworld and system and from the pathologies of modernity. The role of religious communities, however, requires explication under the conditions of modernity. Its role, therefore, functions in the dialectic between a conception of justice elaborated within a discourse ethics, on the one hand, and the hermeneutical task of reconstructing the ideal potential of normative traditions, on the other. This dialectic pertains to the structure of moral understanding, the distinction between thin and thick conceptions of the good, the criterion of morality, and the relation between the belief in transcendence and the conception of the self. Consequently, the role of religious communities as communities of interpretation is to engage in a critical reconstructive interpretation of their normative religious and moral traditions in relation to social and political praxis. In doing so, they seek a broad reflective equilibrium between the reconstructions of the normative potential of the tradition and the attempts to achieve a discursive consensus in regard to the principles of justice.

CRITICAL THEORY AS A THEORY OF SOCIETY AND MODERNITY

The theory of communicative action is an attempt to avoid one-sided and reductionistic approaches to understanding society — the one-sidedness of externalist and internalist approaches. An externalist approach explains social phenomena in relation to the base of society, that is, to its material conditions, such as economic structure or social systems. An internalist approach explains society primarily through an interpretive understanding of the internal story and narratives of persons in society. Internalist and externalist approaches are often contrasted or played out against each other. Habermas's theory of communicative action, however, seeks to combine and to relate them to each other. It reformulates the relation between an internalist and externalist perspective in a comprehensive theory of society.

Lifeworld and System

In combining these two perspectives, the theory of communicative action reformulates major concepts of Marx and Weber, Durkheim and Mead, Parsons and Schutz.[3] The concepts lifeworld and system replace traditional concepts of substructure and superstructure. Lifeworld refers to the shared meanings that make ordinary interaction possible. It includes social institutions, practices, and norms. The lifeworld consists of the world of meanings into which we are born and in which we grow up. These meanings are elaborated and integrated through discussion and ordinary social interaction. Lifeworld also refers to the knowledge and norms that provide the background for the formation of the self and for the legitimation of society.

System refers to those administrative areas of modern society coordinated by money and power. Society is considered a self-regulating system. The media of this self-regulation are money and power. On the level of system, money and power — rather than consensus — coordinate and steer human action; they not only replace language as a medium of coordination, but they also coordinate human action in a way that differs considerably from that which takes place linguistically through communication. On this point, Habermas, although indebted to Parsons, disagrees with him, for he emphasizes that only money and power are steering-mechanisms on the level of systems, rather than influence and value-commitment.

The Rationalization of Modernity

The concepts of system and lifeworld serve to explain not only society but also modernity in relation to changes in the organization of societal systems, the formation of lifeworld, and the relation between system and lifeworld.[4] Three specific developments outlined in Habermas's theory of communicative competence are relevant for political theology.

First, modernity is a process of rationality in which areas of life and action, originally united, have become separated. This differentiation leads to the distinction between public and private spheres in which certain values and preferences are private and others are public. Second, the process of rationalization leads to the dissolution of traditional mythic worldviews. It thereby weakens the authority of world religions to contribute to public policy discourse based on rational arguments and public consensus rather than on mythic worldviews and religious convictions. Third, this process of rationalization has further transformed traditional conceptions of morality. It has dissolved conceptions of morality based upon a teleological worldview that presupposes some eternal order of the cosmos. Instead, it bases justice upon consensual agreement as to the right. These three transformations play an important role within Habermas's advocacy of a discourse ethics.

Modernity as a Separation of Spheres

Habermas describes modernity as a differentiation of the cognitive, normative, and aesthetic-expressive spheres of life. This differentiation is ambivalent; it makes possible an advance in rationality, but it also undercuts the ability of religion and metaphysics to provide the integration of society as traditional worldviews have done in the past.[5] In modernity, science, law, ethics, and aesthetics develop and grow with their own inner logic. Judgments and arguments are formed in accordance with the logic and reasoning appropriate to each.

This analysis of modern rationalization differs from Max Weber's conception in a significant way. Weber interpreted modern rationalization as the spread of *Zweckrationalität* (means-ends rationality). Habermas argues that the problem is not rationalization itself. Instead, it is the inability to balance the different aspects of rationalization — cognitive, moral, and aesthetic.[6] Cognitive-instrumental rationality refers to the rationality of science and technology; moral-practical rationality refers to the rationality expressed in law and morality; and aesthetic-practical rationality signifies the rationality expressed in eroticism and art.[7]

According to Habermas, the three cultural value spheres should be connected with corresponding action systems so that one secures the production and transmission of specialized knowledge with distinct validity claims. The cognitive potential of expert cultures should in turn be transferred to the communicative practice of everyday life and should be made fruitful for social action systems. The distinct spheres of cultural values should be institutionalized in such a balanced way "that the life-orders corresponding to them are sufficiently autonomous to avoid being subordinated to laws intrinsic to heterogeneous orders of life."[8]

A balanced model consists of several components: the institutionalization of the differentiated transmission of knowledge, the de-insulation of the knowledge of experts from that of citizens, and the balancing of the three spheres. The distinction between lifeworld and system underscores this point. In archaic societies, no differentiation exists between lifeworld and system. The customs of kinship groups and their religious rituals are intertwined with their political and economic activities. In modern society, however, an "uncoupling" takes place between system and lifeworld so that religious, social, political, and economic activities are differentiated.

The role of religion in such a framework is somewhat ambivalent. On the one hand, the normative core of religious beliefs and symbol systems is the root and background for the development of modern rationality. On the other hand, the increase of societal complexity leads to a decline of religion, insofar as societal differentiation increasingly separates cultural spheres from one another and the administrative system from the lifeworld. As a result, normative claims are differentiated. The more this differentiation of normative claims develops, the more moral authority becomes separated from its religious basis and sacral authority.

Modernity as the Dissolution of Mythic Worldviews
Religions have at their historical roots a normative consciousness. Habermas contends, however, that this core must give way to a communicative ethics. In his analysis of Durkheim's interpretation of the role of religion within society, Habermas underscores that the religious is "the archaic core of norm consciousness."[9] Yet he interprets the dissolution of this core as positive. He argues, "to the degree that the rationality potential ingrained in communicative action is released, the archaic core of the normative dissolves and gives way to the rationalization of worldviews, to the universalization of law and morality, and to an acceleration of processes of individuation."[10]

His interpretation suggests that the role of religion in archaic society is replaced and surpassed by a rational morality in modern society. In archaic societies, ritual practices originally functioned to integrate societies. In premodern societies, religions legitimate institutions. In modern societies, communicative action takes over these functions of legitimation and integration. The authority of an achieved consensus replaces the authority of the sacred.[11] The legitimizing function of religious views of the world is replaced by rationally motivated agreement.

Priority of the Right over the Good

The rationalization characterizing the transition to modernity entails more than the destruction of a mythic worldview and the breakdown of the ontological-teleological worldview. It also entails a transformation of ethics. Partly as a result of the first two transformations, moral theory is no longer based upon religious views of the world or upon a teleological metaphysical worldview. Instead, ethics becomes universalistic; insofar as it advocates a moral point of view, it does not simply explicate the intuitions of specific cultures or specific groups. A moral point of view should go beyond the prejudices of a specific race, gender, or class. Rather it should be open to universal consensus regarding its validity claims.

This transformation indicates the context in which modern liberal theories of justice have stressed the priority of the right over the good, from which two implications can be noted.[12] First, this priority provides a means of dealing with the pluralism of conceptions. It concedes that diverse conceptions of the good life can exist. Yet it insists that conceptions of justice can be defined independently of them. Theories of justice, therefore, seek to explicate conceptions of justice independent of comprehensive theories of the good. Such conceptions of the good, it is argued, belong to the private sphere, along with their related religious preferences. As a result, a liberal theory of justice understands itself not as a metaphysical but as a political conception.[13] The liberal theory of justice is then anchored, as John Rawls argues, not in a comprehensive view of the good but in an overlapping public consensus.[14]

Second, the priority of the right implies that conceptions of justice should be more fundamental than conceptions of the good, in the sense that conceptions of justice should limit what can be legitimately and justifiably claimed to be a conception of the good life. On this point, Habermas's discourse ethics gives justice a much more central and basic role than John Rawls does. Rawls distinguishes between justice as a basic political virtue of society and a full theory of the good within moral theory. For Habermas, the primacy of justice means that justice specifies, delineates, and determines one's conception of the good. His ethic brings together questions of the good life with those of justice and discusses them as questions of justice within a discourse about justice that takes into account interests and needs.[15]

The Pathology of Modern Rationalization

The modern differentiation of the cognitive, normative, and aesthetic-expressive has, therefore, made possible advances in rationality. It has led to the dissolution of mythic worldviews and it has given a priority to the right. Such differentiation has also led to corresponding negative consequences. These consequences are more than the reduction of rationality to an instrumental rationality, of a means-ends rationality. These consequences constitute the pathology of modernity. Habermas's project is to defend the advance in rationality made possible in modernity and, at the same time, to avoid the pathologies of modernity.

First, it becomes necessary to overcome the reduction of rationality to an instrumental and functional rationality. This attempt constitutes Habermas's conception of communicative rationality. Society should incorporate communicative rationality as the basis for its normative and practical discourses. This communicative rationality is the goal of discourse ethics.

The second pathology of modernity, the uncoupling of system and lifeworld, jeopardizes the communicative action of the lifeworld. This uncoupling of administrative systems from the lifeworld of values suggests that a new form of socialization may prevail in modern late capitalist societies so that the processes of communicative rationality will prevail over systems rationality. The uncoupling of system from lifeworld means that in economic and political spheres, the norms, values, and motivations of the lifeworld become increasingly irrelevant. The economic and political spheres become increasingly indifferent to values and their shared communication with the lifeworld. Economic and political organizations become increasing uncoupled from the goals, meanings, and motivations of their members.[16]

The colonization of the lifeworld is a third negative tendency that moves in the other direction. Not only is the administrative system uncoupled from the lifeworld, but the system erodes the lifeworld. Colonization of the lifeworld refers to the process of deformation of the normative and symbolic structures of the lifeworld. The institutionalization of money and power as media of social exchange within the system penetrates the lifeworld of communicative action. This feature of capitalistic modernization works against the advances that the increasing differentiation within modernity entail.

These three tendencies (the dominance of functional rationality, the independence of system from lifeworld of values, and the colonization of the lifeworld) are the negative characteristics of modernity. They stand in contrast to the advances in rationality. This diagnosis of modernity with its advance and pathology provides the context for Habermas's development of a discourse ethics.

Discourse Ethics within Modernity

Habermas develops a theory of discourse ethics to specify the validity of ethical norms without a naturalistic or emotivistic reduction. He seeks to avoid the realism of natural law theories, which confuse claims of moral validity with those of factual assertions and conflate normative judgments with correspondence judgments. He also seeks to avoid the arbitrariness of an emotive approach that reduces moral claims to statements of taste, or a conventional approach that reduces moral claims to conventional norms.[17]

The theory of a discourse ethics criticizes traditional attempts to base conceptions of justice upon religious conceptions or upon conceptions of the good life. It argues that moral norms should be established through the process of public and practical argumentation. A discourse ethics contrasts with three other types of ethics: with an ethics based upon religious conceptions, with ethics based upon conceptions of the good life (for example, a neo-Aristotelian ethics, such as MacIntyre in the United States or Ritter in Germany), and with similar liberal conceptions of justice (for example, John Rawls's *Theory of Justice*).

Habermas criticizes a religious foundation of ethics for several reasons. He equates religious beliefs with antiquated worldviews and sees these beliefs as based on traditional forms of authority. Religious beliefs, therefore, do not lend themselves to public discussion and critique. Moral convictions based on such religious beliefs are likewise not open to public discourse and discursive argumentation. In addition to their foundation on authority, Habermas argues that religious and metaphysical worldviews have lost their ability to convince. They have, therefore, become matters of subjective and individual choice and cannot provide principles that have the universality and collectivity required by the public realm.[18]

Habermas argues similarly against Alasdair MacIntyre's neo-Aristotelian position or Michael Sandel's communitarian position. He labels neo-Aristotelianism a "renewed traditionalism." It is inadequate because it establishes ethics on the basis of a lived ethos. Such attempts to base morality upon forms of life do not take into consideration a crucial question: How does one critically assess the morality of the form of life itself and its ethos.[19] In addition, Habermas argues that all neo-Aristotelian approaches "must demonstrate how an objective moral order can be grounded without recourse to metaphysical premises."[20]

Finally, Habermas contrasts his discourse ethics with John Rawls's attempt to develop the basic conception of justice from a hypothetical starting-point. Such an approach is individualistic in that individuals themselves, behind a veil of ignorance, select the principles of justice.[21] In contrast, a discourse ethics does not start from either a concrete tradition or from an abstract original position behind a veil of ignorance. Instead, it emphasizes communicative interaction with regard to validity claims and includes the interpretation of needs. Habermas's discourse ethics seeks to transform Kant's categorical imperative from a monological to a dialogical imperative. The Kantian imperative is categorical if one can universalize a maxim, that is, if one can will it to universal law. In a discourse ethics, however, one submits the maxim to others in order to test its claim to universality discursively.

Habermas's discourse ethics, with its focus upon justice as the social virtue par excellence, correlates conceptions of justice and conceptions of the self in its relation to others. The development of judgments of justice corresponds to the development of the self's relation to others. A correlation exists between the formation of self-identity and the formation of moral judgments about justice. This correspondence between justice and self-identity relates to an understanding of identity in which a correspondence exists between personal identity and community identity.[22] Personal identity develops intersubjectively. A reciprocity exists between one's identification with other subjects and one's self-identity. Likewise, a reciprocity exists between the structures of the group and the identity of the ego. An interdependence, therefore, exists between the system of norms and the structures of self-identity.

RELIGION AND THEOLOGY IN MODERNITY

The theory of communicative action overlooks the transformations of religion and theology.[23] Several elements comprise this transformation. Religious beliefs (1) have become increasingly independent of cosmological worldviews, (2) are based upon personal conviction rather than upon authority, and (3) have explicated their anthropological and ethical content. These transformations bring the critical principles of the Enlightenment into religion itself and into theological reflection.[24] They are important if one is to understand how the churches as communities of interpretation enter into public discourse in modern pluralistic society.

Transformations of Religion and Theology

Modernity is not simply that which stands over against traditional religion. The modern Enlightenment is not adequately described as the "Rise of Modern Paganism."[25] Instead, in the modern post-Enlightenment period, forms of religious faith and reflection emerge that incorporate the critical principles of the Enlightenment. These principles are so incorporated as to constitute the very integrity of religious belief and reflection. Although Habermas's theory of communicative action analyzes religion and the sacred, his interpretation of modernity, unfortunately, does not adequately take these transformations into account. His analysis of the process of rationalization with regard to the development of modern religion should have highlighted significant changes in theology as the reflective activity of religion.

The first transformation is the increasing uncoupling of theology from mythological and cosmological worldviews. This disassociation of theology from specific cosmological worldviews is widespread within modern theology. In the nineteenth century, the most influential example is Schleiermacher. He defined religion as distinct from metaphysics and from ethics. He proposed that the third form of dogmatic statements (those relating religious propositions to the constitution of world and cosmos) are the most readily dispensable propositions — a proposal on which the structure of the *Glaubenslehre* (*The Christian Faith*) is based.[26] Likewise, at the end of the century, Albrecht Ritschl and his school elaborated a notion of theology that contrasts religious faith with both metaphysics and worldviews. In our century, Rudolf Bultmann's program of demythologizing continues this disentanglement of religious affirmations from cosmic statements.[27] Likewise, H. R. Niebuhr's affirmation of radical monotheism serves to affirm the radical distinction between the conception of God and the conception of the world.[28]

In all these instances, modern theology has undergone a radical transformation. The cosmological underpinnings of much of traditional religious beliefs have become sundered. Theological ethics also has developed ethics increasingly independent of a cosmic order. Even major exceptions — process theology and neo-Thomism — display this transformation. Process theology synthesizes religious beliefs with scientific images of the world in such a way that the cosmos does not serve as an eternal order grounding ethical norms. Instead, process theology interprets the cosmos as a process of becoming that exhibits the lure of emerging norms. Neo-Aristotelians or neo-Thomists traditionally understand natural law less biologically and naturalistically than previously.

The second transformation involves the move of theology away from its traditional reliance on definite and specific authorities and toward the human subject, with an emphasis on the formal structures and universal anthropological characteristics of religion. This

transformation of theology away from the reliance on principles of
authority has been so decisive that it has been described as the collapse of the house of authority.[29] This collapse has led to attempts
to overcome the subject-object dichotomy in theology and has affected the understanding of theology as transcendental and its task
as constructive.[30]

The transformation of religion within modernity involves a for-
malization and universalization of religious beliefs, exhibited within
the evolution of religion from archaic or traditional religions to
premodern world religions. Local gods of the tribe or geographi-
cal area become increasingly understood as universal. Their ethical
demands are likewise universalized. The radical monotheism and
ethical universalism of the prophets are Western examples of this
tendency.

Another type of universality emerges in the double awareness in
modernity of both the universality of religion and the particularity of
one's own tradition of beliefs. Other religions are no longer simply
interpreted as the "other," as nonbelief, or as false belief. Instead,
their beliefs relate to their own cultural traditions just as ours do.
The specificity of concrete historical religions is seen as historically
conditioned expressions of universal attempts to deal with ultimacy,
limit experiences, meaning, or even human religiousness.[31]

A third transformation, resulting in part from the first two, is
the ethical dimension of religious beliefs. Ethical criteria within religious symbol systems become increasingly retrospective criteria by
which the symbol systems are assessed. At the same time, an increased
awareness exists that these criteria are in turn dependent upon specific historical and cultural contexts.[32] Religious symbol systems are
more and more explicitly related to their ethical ground and practice. Nevertheless, this ethical grounding is not an a priori abstract
foundation. Instead, it exists itself within historical interpretations of
the ideal potential of the religious tradition and is in part determined
by them.[33]

The role of the increasingly ethical grounding of religious traditions is illustrated by eschatology. Previously one interpreted apocalyptic cosmic mythology primarily in terms of reward and punish-
ment or in terms of a perfectionist vision of the good life. Modern
theology, however, interprets this mythologic imagery primarily as
an ethical vision or as metaphorical language that expresses visions
of social justice and political peace. Contemporary political and liberation theologies explicate the utopian language and images of
traditional eschatology to exercise a critical function in relation to
injustice, oppression, and discrimination. These theologies explicate
eschatology in terms of justice. As a result eschatology is both shaped

and normed by conceptions of justice as it is an ideal representation of this eschatology. For example, feudal versions of eschatology interpreted eschatological images as ideal images of a hierarchical feudal order. Modern versions, in contrast, present images of radical equality, justice, and peace.

Eschatology is just one example illustrating how modern theological notions of justice have influenced religious conceptions. The normative potential of the belief is its ideal vision of justice and peace (rather than one of hierarchical inequality and oppression) that serves as a counterfactual, transcendent, and critical image to the injustices, oppressions, and discriminations of society. The religious belief itself is not simply an image of the ideal good life; it is an image radically constituted by principles of justice and equality. Similar examples of such transformations in relation to principles of justice and equality are evident.

Creation is another example. Previously, the belief in creation was a belief underpinning the hierarchical order of society. In modernity, the belief in creation has become transformed. The religious belief that all are created by God has become a belief in the ultimate equality and dignity of all persons. The belief in creation now entails the conviction that all persons be accorded equal rights and justice. Another example is the transformation of religious and theological evaluations of concrete practices such as work.[34]

The Public-Private Distinction

These three transformations of modern religion and theology express what Habermas's theory of communicative action has not sufficiently analyzed. This neglect affects his interpretation of the distinction between the public and private sphere and his relegation of religion to the private sphere within modern society. This distinction underlies, in part, his assessment of the function of religion in modernity. This distinction, however, has been sharply criticized.

In contemporary political philosophy, feminist theorists have brought significant criticisms against interpretations of modern society that underscore the separation between the public and the private realm. Although somewhat sympathetic to Habermas's theory of communicative action, several feminist philosophers (Seyla Benhabib, Nancy Fraser, and Iris Marion Young),[35] have criticized the interpretation of the distinction between the public and private. They point to its ambiguity, and they highlight its neglect of important elements of rationality. Their criticisms are significant, not only for feminist thought and political theory, but also for theology.

They emphasize that the public/private distinction exhibits not just a certain ambiguity, but also overlooks significant aspects of rationality. The ambiguity consists in a twofold use of the public/private distinction. On the one hand, the public/private distinction separates the economic, political, juridical, and administrative system of modern societies from the private domain of the family. Public refers to what is open to all, whereas private refers to the particular and special ties among individual persons.

In this sense, the distinction between public and private is not parallel to the distinction between system and lifeworld. The formation of public opinion belongs to the public domain, yet it belongs to the lifeworld. On the other hand, the public/private distinction contrasts general interests with private interests. In this respect, the economic area in which private welfare and profit is pursued is private, whereas the state and its administrative system should represent the general common interest.

The interrelationship of these two senses of the public/private distinction raises the question of rationality and values. If rationality is simply identified with the public sphere, open to all, and if the common good and private good are contrasted, then the result is a false dichotomy between an impartial public rationality and a private familial rationality. Feminist scholars have explored the gender subtext of this distinction. They have shown how such claims to an impartial universal rationality are false. The rationality displayed is, in fact, partial, for it excludes dimensions of rationality.[36]

The feminist critique of the public/private distinction is important. Both Jürgen Habermas and John Rawls relegate religion as well as conceptions of the good life to the private sphere. Insofar as religious beliefs and conceptions of the good life are brought together, they are related to the private sphere.

REFLECTIVE AND INTERPRETATIVE APPROACHES TO JUSTICE

Communities of Interpretation and Lifeworld

Habermas's analysis of modernity develops two basic insights. On the one hand, the uncoupling of the lifeworld and the system leads to advances in rationality.[37] On the other hand, this uncoupling also leads to a system increasingly devoid of the values of the lifeworld, and to the lifeworld colonialized through the media of money and power. Habermas interprets modernity not as the neutrality of the public sphere as classic liberalism does. Instead, modernity is, in part, the impoverishment of the system and lifeworld as a result of this so-called uncoupling and colonization. Therefore, his interpretation of modernity raises the question of the locus of public discourse about issues of justice, right, and good in view of the increasing colonization of the public sphere of the lifeworld.

The question is, where in the lifeworld are there concrete communities of discourse about issues of ethics and justice? In my opinion, Habermas has, in severing his discourse ethics from any religious foundations and institutions, failed to provide an institutional locus, both social and cultural, for the discussion of moral-practical issues. He has not developed an adequate institutional base for discourse ethics.

My proposal is that churches as communities of the interpretation of the substantial normative potential of their religious traditions can provide one such institutional locus. The churches constantly endeavor to interpret the normative potential of their traditions. Their endeavor includes not only full conceptions of the good, but also ethical issues of justice. The question is: what is the significance of this interpretation for moral practical discourse in modern society? In this respect, political theologies explicate the relevance of what Habermas acknowledges in his recent writings, but does not develop, namely, the transcending dimension of the unity of the lifeworld toward which moral discourse is aimed.[38] Yet this task of interpretation needs to take place under the conditions of fallibilism as well as the conditions of modernity within which the churches themselves are located. It needs to take into account the transformations of religion and theology that take place as part of the process of rationalization. It also needs to consider those issues raised by contemporary debates on justice and the public sphere.

Two Contrasting Approaches: Universalist and Historicist

Contemporary discussions on the nature of justice contain two fundamentally diverse approaches: a universalist and a historicist position. The universalist position (represented by John Rawls, Ronald Dworkin, and Alan Gewirth) stresses that the notion of justice should raise claims of validity capable of universalization.[39] The notion of justice should provide standards that can assess and judge a particular society and its practices; it enables one to judge the forms of human life of particular societies.

The historicist approach (represented by Michael Walzer, Michael Sandel, Charles Taylor, and Alasdair MacIntyre) takes a contrasting position.[40] It argues that notions of justice are relative to particular cultures and societies, with their concrete histories and traditions. All knowledge is historically and socially conditioned, including moral knowledge. Therefore, it does not seem possible to arrive at an abstract standard independent of a concrete history and society.

These two approaches to justice are diametrically opposed. What the universalists consider to be essential to justice, namely, the ability to take a critical stance in the face of a particular society with its concrete norms and practices, the historicists deny as impossible. All knowledge, they claim, is historically conditioned. The historicists derive the good from the particular practices and insights of their cultural traditions. The universalists consider the historicists to have overlooked what is essential to justice — its ability to criticize de facto customs and practices. The moral point of view, the universalists argue, is that point of view transcending particular viewpoints and customs. Since the historicists underscore the degree to which all knowledge is conditioned, they consider the conception of justice advocated by the universalists to be false consciousness. Its claims to universality are, in reality, only the pretensions of a historical period. The liberal ideals advocated by the universalists are then simply expressions of the particular ideal of the Western modern Enlightenment.

A political theology situating itself within the context of modern society and the modern understanding of justice needs to take a position in relation to these debates. At first glance it might seem that a political theology would take the historicist position over against the universalist position. After all, political theology seeks to develop the insights of a particular religious and moral tradition and to relate these traditions to contemporary political and social issues. Political theologies explore the pragmatics of religious beliefs.[41] Therefore, political theology as the interpretation or hermeneutics of the political dimension of a religious tradition seems, at first, to take the historicist rather than the universalist position.

Such an approach, however, simplifies the problem in several ways. First, it too readily concedes that these two positions are mutually exclusive, so that one has to choose between the two. It does not seek to place in tension the particularity of all knowledge and the need for moral judgments to go beyond and to critique the particular.

Second, it fails to consider that a religious tradition, though particular, exists within a pluralistic society. It needs to articulate the potential of its particular tradition in a way that enables it to engage in public discourse within the public realm. Therefore, political theology within a pluralistic society needs to engage in a discourse that takes into account the dimension of pluralism and the requirements of publicly accessible discourse and claims.

Third, such an approach fails to explore possibilities for developing a position that transcends the weakness of each position. Such a position should acknowledge the historicity of all moral knowledge and should, at the same time, attempt to provide moral knowledge, though revisable, and articulate principles that can critically assess both the customs of society and the standards of its tradition.

Justice and Reconstructive Interpretation

An approach that seeks to overcome the one-sidedness of each of these positions needs to develop a dialectic between the critical principle of Enlightenment rationality and the hermeneutical insight into the historical conditioning of reason and experience. This dialectic affects the structure of moral understanding, thin and thick conceptions of the good, and the criterion of morality. This dialectic entails a broad reflective equilibrium between hermeneutic reconstructions of normative traditions and the discursive attempt to obtain reasoned agreements in regard to justice.[42]

Structure of Moral Understanding

The hermeneutical insight — that moral understanding explicates implicit knowledge and that practical knowledge and experience are essential to the application of morality — is the central insight that the historicists bring to the current discussions of justice.[43] But moral understanding is more than making explicit the implicit practical judgments of moral cultural traditions. Moral judgments also criticize cultural traditions, and moral theory has to take into account epistemological crises within cultural traditions. New experiences bring to the fore conflicts within the tradition. Such conflicts arising from new experiences and from new background theories require revision and reconstruction of the tradition. Such revisions lead to a new understanding of what in the tradition should be considered as paradigmatic and essential.[44]

At the same time, the formalistic and universalist position sharply separates the foundation of moral norms, not only from their motivation, but also from their application. This separation of justification and application is central to the Kantian tradition of moral theory. Such a distinction, however, does not adequately deal with complex moral situations or with concrete conflicts of moral values. In cases of basic principles (for example, one should not lie or one should not murder), the justification of the moral principle is clearly distinct from its application. But in complex and conflicting moral cases, the issue of justification is inseparable from the issue of application. The issue is: What in this situation or case is the moral norm or the overriding moral principle? Such complex and conflicting cases require practical judgment, prudence, and wisdom as emphasized by those underscoring the hermeneutical nature of experience, including moral experience.[45]

Such considerations, however, do not support either the universalist or the historicist position. What the historicist correctly grasps is that application cannot simply be separated from justification as the universalist imagines. But the historicist overlooks that criteria transcending the situation, culture, and tradition may have to be formulated as counterfactual standards. Hence what is called for is a dialectic in which the issues of justification, discovery, and application are interrelated but not identical. Therefore, it is necessary to examine this dialectic in relation to the criterion of morality.

Thin and Thick Conceptions of the Good

The distinction between "thin" and "thick" conceptions of the good is central to John Rawls's political conception of justice. In a pluralistic society, it is not feasible to obtain agreement about a common comprehensive conception of the good, especially if such a conception includes religious convictions and should be subject to revision. Nevertheless, it is possible that some overlapping conception of the good, less full and comprehensive, is shared within a society. Such a shared conception relates to a society's understanding of right and justice.

Such a conception is called by Rawls a "thin" conception of the good. He defines it so:

In contrast with teleological theories, something is good only if it fits into ways of life consistent with the principles of right already on hand, but to establish these principles it is necessary to rely on some notion of goodness, for we need assumptions about parties' motives in the original position. Since these assumptions must not jeopardize the prior place of the concept of right, the theory of the good used in arguing for the principles of justice is restricted to the bare essentials. This account of the good I call the thin theory: its purpose is to secure the premises about primary goods required to arrive at the principles of justice. Once this theory is worked out and the primary goods accounted for, we are free to use the principles of justice in the further development of what I shall call the full theory of the good.[46]

A basic question emerges: What is the relation between the "thin" and the "thick" or "full" conceptions of the good? Is the former independent of the latter or is it somehow related to the latter? How does one distinguish between what is "thin" and what is "thick"? The pluralism of modern society may demand a minimalist conception of the good in contrast to a fuller and more comprehensive conception, but the distinction between "thin" and "thick" rests on a slippery slope.

The distinction is such that it is embedded in what I shall call a dialectical relation between "thin" and "thick" — a relation that points somewhat away from Rawls's conception. The dialectical relation is that in any society there will be a mutual reciprocity between the "thin" and "thick" conceptions. If the "thin" conception is what is essential to justice and the premises of primary goods, then fuller conceptions of the good should be consistent or should cohere with these essentials and premises. Likewise, the fuller conceptions will necessarily influence what is considered essential to the "thin" conception of the good. The distinction is important insofar as societies do, in fact, have an integrating and an overlapping consensus on significant moral issues. Nevertheless, concretely and historically, one has to explore the dialectical relation between the "thin" and the "thick." This relation raises the issue between the reconstructive interpretation of normative traditions within society and their relation to "thin" conceptions. It also raises the question: Where does public discourse take place about this interrelation between fuller or more substantial conceptions of the good and the "thin" conceptions about which there is overlapping consensus?

The interpretation of modernity within a communicative theory of action argues that the uncoupling of lifeworld and system has led to an impoverishment of political discourse. The recent U.S. presidential campaigns have illustrated this impoverishment. The candidates have not so much engaged in substantive ethical or political discourse, as they have appealed to popular fears and prejudices. They reduced complex policy statements to thirty-second TV "sound-bites." The public realm of society in political campaigns and debates becomes increasingly devoid of substantive discussion of issues concerning the right as well as the good, concerning "thin" as well as "thick" conceptions of the good.

In contrast, the churches as communities of interpretation of normative traditions have contributed to public policy in recent years. They have issued public statements on such controversial issues as nuclear warfare, the economy, and the death penalty. They have condemned racism and militarism with a moral language that the administrative political domain does not use. They have dealt with issues concerning the nature and priority of diverse social goods.[47]

Criterion of Morality

Moral theory is primarily concerned with the justification of moral principles and concrete moral judgments. The interest in justification stems from a search for foundations of moral knowledge that are not merely conventional but are accessible to others. Since individuals acquire their moral views through socialization into specific historical cultural traditions, one must reflect on the ethical question: How does one distinguish valid moral principles from inherited prejudices, and how does one distinguish correct moral decisions from parochial mores? Coherence, consistency, and universality are usually given as criteria enabling us to distinguish principles from prejudices and mores.

Such an approach can become ideological, if, in stressing the justification of moral principles through rational reflection, it also asserts that moral knowledge is acquired through rational reflection and can be justified only through a rational reflection independent of historical traditions and background theories. For example, in the nineteenth century, a moral injunction barring women from higher education was widespread. This injunction was based on unquestioned social assumptions about women's unequal social status and medical assumptions about women's intellectual ability and biology. This sexism and discrimination could not simply be eliminated by reflective reasoning. It was only through women's historical protests stemming from their experience that society came to question the social, anthropological, and moral assumptions.

Habermas's theory of discourse ethics represents his move away from an emphasis on the "ideal speech" situation to an argument from the general presupposition of discourse. The requirement of universalization is formal, and the idea of formal-pragmatic presuppositions of every communication is abstract unless it is embedded within the awareness of a solidarity among all. The formal universalization is the other side of the coin that all humans (despite race, gender, political system, and creed) are brothers and sisters. The normative kernel of the universality of the principles of justice for all is not only the universality of brotherhood and sisterhood under one God, as it developed in the central religions. It is not simply a historical conviction. It is also the present power and life-embodiment of rational discourse. Solidarity is the one side; justice is the other side.[48] These are not two coins, one past and one present, but one coin. The formal, procedural, and universal exists in tandem with the historical, substantial, and even religious beliefs.

Political Theology and Discourse Ethics

Habermas's discourse ethics has two aspects. On the one hand, there are formal structures and categories. On the other hand, there is the importance of the consensual agreement of all participants. Criticisms of his work often overlook this double aspect.[49] Through his notion of a discourse ethics, he seeks to follow Hegel and to steer a middle ground between two positions: the abstract universalism of the Kantian conception of justice and the concrete particularism of the Aristotelian and Thomistic emphasis upon the common good. He accepts Hegel's critique of both positions. Yet he wants to overcome the one-sidedness of each position with Kantian means. Through the procedural approach of a discourse ethics, he hopes to take into account the substantive as well as formal claims in justifying justice.

In distinction, I am proposing that political theology use a broad reflective equilibrium that includes a reflective equilibrium between what is normative in a tradition (narrow equilibrium) with what is publicly normative through principles of justice, where mutual and reciprocal criticism takes place. This proposal aims to overcome the one-sidedness of both positions. It suggests a broad reflective equilibrium of both a normative tradition and universal conceptions of justice. Such a procedure seeks to take into account the intent of a discourse ethics. At the same time, it seeks to overcome the one-sidedness of a discourse ethics that does not sufficiently take into account that normative traditions should also be open to discussion and subject to revision along with conceptions of justice and right.

Such a political theology would not as sharply distinguish foundation and application as Habermas does within discourse ethics. Insofar as a political theology seeks to relate its tradition with its conceptions of justice and the good life to contemporary society with its diverse interests, needs, and ideals, it encounters complex moral situations and moral conflicts. The discourse engendered within communities should be reflective about what is morally right in relation to the concrete context. What is brought to discussion as the contribution of a specific tradition of ethical reflection is at the same time open to the validity claims of a discourse ethics. In this way, discourses engendered by attempts to reconstruct ethical and moral traditions have the reciprocity and symmetry essential to Habermas's conception of a discourse ethics. The notion of a broad reflective equilibrium points to the importance of constantly criticizing conceptions of the good life and normative traditions in relation to discursive consensus in regard to justice, and vice versa.

Community, Self, and Ultimacy

In addition to the dialectic of the interpretation of normative traditions and justice, issues of the formation of self-identity and of personal empowerment also are essential to political theology. These issues are often excluded from accounts of justice developed exclusively as a formal and universalistic account. The churches as religious communities have a function within an impoverished and colonized lifeworld not just as communities of interpretation of substantial normative tradition. As communities they are also significant for the formation of personal identity and for the institutional empowerment of personal agency within society.

These two issues (self-identity and transcendence, community and personal empowerment) are central to political theology. They need to be explored both in relation to a theory of communicative competency and to a fully developed political theology. Likewise, the significance of universal solidarity as developed by Helmut Peukert and Karl Bauer would need to be explored,[50] as well as the ideas of James Fowler and Sharon Parks on religious convictions and ego development.[51] Likewise, one would need to discuss issues of the relation between motivation and justification of moral belief, and between an Aristotelian emphasis on character and virtue and the Kantian challenge to these emphases. Any consideration of these issues should take into account not only the transformation of modern religion, but also the mutual criticisms within a broad reflective equilibrium. Such topics, although essential and relevant to my analysis, would excessively expand the scope of this essay.

CONCLUSION

In this essay, I have argued that churches within modern society function as communities of interpretation in which issues of justice and conceptions of goodness are publicly discussed. Moreover, I have argued that a broad reflective equilibrium is necessary to bring out the dialectic between universalizable principles of justice and the reconstructive hermeneutic of normative tradition. Habermas's interpretation of modern society, religion, and ethics does not propose such a role for churches and the interpretation of their normative traditions. In fact, he seems to exclude it because religious and moral traditions are relegated to authoritarian forms of belief and are bound to teleological worldviews. "Even religious or classic-philosophical ethics that explicate the moral life-relation neither understand nor justify what is moral from itself, but from the horizon of a salvation-historical or cosmological viewpoint of totality."[52]

Nevertheless, his theory of society and modernity underscores two significant theses: The thesis of the uncoupling of the political and administrative system from the values and norms of the lifeworld as well as the thesis of the colonization of the lifeworld by the media of money and power underscores an impoverishment of the lifeworld and the system of modernity. This theory of society seems sadly confirmed by the recent presidential debates in the United States devoid of substantive ethical and political issues. Moreover, the pluralism of modern liberal societies places a priority on the procedural over the substantial, emphasizes the priority of the right over the good, and acknowledges at the most a "thin conception of the good" as an "overlapping consensus."

In such a modern situation, the need exists for a public discussion of substantive issues of justice and administrative policy. Such a discussion cannot be limited to expert cultures of philosophy departments but should have a broader base. My proposal suggests that the churches are increasingly taking on this function. They do so the more they become communities of public discourse about such issues of justice. This argument is of course primarily an institutional argument insofar as it locates ethical discourse within religious communities. This does not of course deny that there should be or are in fact other communities of ethical discourse within societies. I would hope that the academy is also another one of these communities.

Yet the churches have a special role insofar as religious communities have at their core religious traditions. These religious traditions are such that they bring to the fore normative traditions not only of the good life, but also of justice. As religious institutions and communities, they also provide a locus for the discussion of the affective and expressive spheres of human life. In this regard the church keeps alive the utopian dimension that has been central to critical theory.[53]

NOTES

1. For a history of the concept of political theology, see Francis Fiorenza, "Religion und Politik," in *Christlicher Glaube in Moderner Gesellschaft*, vol. 27 (Freiburg: Herder, 1982).

2. Francis Schüssler Fiorenza, "Politische Theologie und liberale Gerechtigkeits-Konzeptionen," in Edward Schillebeeckx, ed., *Mystik und Politik Theologie im Ringen um Geschichte und Gesellschaft* (Mainz: Matthias-Grünewald Verlag, 1988), 95–104.

3. See David Ingram, *Habermas and the Dialectic of Reason* (New Haven: Yale University Press, 1987).

4. Jürgen Habermas, *The Philosophical Discourse of Modernity: Twelve Lectures* (Cambridge, Mass.: MIT Press, 1987).

5. Jürgen Habermas, *Theory of Communicative Action* (Boston: Beacon Press, 1984), 1:83–164.

6. Jürgen Habermas, *Communication and the Evolution of Society* (Boston: Beacon, 1979); translation of *Zur Rekonstruktion des Historischen Materialismus* (Frankfurt am Main: Suhrkamp, 1976).

7. For an analysis of Habermas's conception of rationalization, see Thomas McCarthy, "Reflections on Rationalization," in *The Theory of Commu-*

nicative Action, ed. Richard Bernstein (Cambridge, Mass.: MIT Press, 1985), 176–91.

8. *Theory of Communicative Action*, 1:240. See the commentary by Stephen K. White, *The Recent Work of Jürgen Habermas: Reason, Justice, and Modernity* (Cambridge: University of Cambridge, 1988), 134–36.

9. Jürgen Habermas, *Theory of Communicative Action*, 2:46.

10. Ibid., 2:46.

11. Ibid., 2:77.

12. John Rawls, *A Theory of Justice* (Cambridge, Mass.: Harvard University Press, 1971), and from a utilitarian point of view, Richard B. Brand, *The Good and the Right* (Oxford: Oxford University Press, 1979).

13. John Rawls, "Justice as Fairness: Political not Metaphysical," *Philosophy and Public Affairs* 14 (1985): 223–51.

14. John Rawls, "The Idea of an Overlapping Consensus," *Oxford Journal of Legal Studies* 7 (1987): 1–25, and "Social Unity and Primary Goods," in Amartya K. Sen and Bernard Williams, eds., *Utilitarianism and Beyond* (Cambridge: Cambridge University Press, 1982), 159–85.

15. Jürgen Habermas, "Moralität und Sittlichkeit. Treffen Hegels Einwände gegen Kant auch auf die Diskursethik zu?" *Moralität und Sittlichkeit*, ed. Wolfgang Kuhlmann (Frankfurt am Main: Suhrkamp, 1986), 16–37; now translated in Jürgen Habermas, *Moral Consciousness and Communicative Action* (Cambridge, Mass.: MIT Press, 1990), 195–215; "Über Moralität — Was macht eine Lebensform rational?" in *Rationalität*, ed. Herbert Schnädelbach (Frankfurt am Main: Suhrkamp, 1984), 218–35. "A Reply to My Critics," in John B. Thompson and David Held, eds., *Habermas: Critical Debates* (Cambridge, Mass.: MIT Press, 1982), 219–94.

16. For a critical analysis of Habermas's interpretation of the relation between system and lifeworld see Hugh Baxter, "System and Lifeworld in Habermas's *Theory of Communicative Action*," *Theory and Society* 16 (1987): 39–86.

17. Jürgen Habermas, "Zwei Bemerkungen zum praktischen Diskurs," *Konstruktionen versus Positionen*, ed. Kuno Lorenz (Berlin: Walter de Gruyter, 1979).

18. Jürgen Habermas, *Moralbewußtsein und kommunikatives Handeln* (Frankfurt am Main: Suhrkamp, 1983), 85.

19. "Über Moralität — Was macht eine Lebensform rational?" 218–35.

20. Habermas, *Moral Consciousness*, 213–14.

21. For a comparison of Rawls and Habermas, see Seyla Benhabib, "The Methodological Illusions of Modern Political Theory: The Case of Rawls and Habermas," *Neue Hefte für Philosophie* 21 (1982): 47–74.

22. This is clearly emphasized by Edmund Arens, in his excursus, "Habermas' Identitätskonzept," *Kommunikative Handlungen. Die paradigmatische Bedeutung der Gleichnisse Jesu für eine Handlungstheorie* (Düsseldorf: Patmos, 1982), 304–5.

23. On the one hand, Jürgen Habermas and his students, e.g., Rainer Döbert and Klaus Eder, trace the social evolution and historical development of religion. On the other hand, Habermas's conceptual and systematic

evaluations of religion treat religion as if religion could not contribute to contemporary political discourse because it belonged to some previous stage of social evolution. See Rainer Döbert, *Systemtheorie und die Entwicklung religiöser Deutungsysteme* (Frankfurt am Main: Suhrkamp, 1973), and Klaus Eder, *Seminar. Die Entstehung von Klassengesellschaften* (Frankfurt am Main: Suhrkamp, 1973).

24. Edward Farley, *The Fragility of Knowledge* (Philadelphia: Fortress Press, 1988).

25. The subtitle of Peter Gay's influential book, *The Enlightenment — An Interpretation: The Rise of Modern Paganism* (New York: Random House, 1966).

26. *The Christian Faith* (New York: Harper and Row, 1963), no. 30

27. Rudolf Bultmann, *Jesus Christ and Mythology* (New York: Scribner's Sons, 1958).

28. *Radical Monotheism and Western Culture* (New York: Harper & Row, 1943; 1960 revised edition).

29. Edward Farley, *Ecclesial Reflection: An Anatomy of Theological Method* (Philadelphia: Fortress Press, 1982).

30. For a contemporary and consistent development of the notion of theology as constructive that underscores the ethical dimension of the constructive task, see Gordon D. Kaufman, *An Essay on Theological Method*, 2d ed. (Atlanta: Scholars Press, 1979) and *Theology for a Nuclear Age* (Philadelphia: Westminster, 1985).

31. See for example Wilfrid Cantwell Smith, *Towards a World Theology* (Philadelphia: Westminster Press, 1981).

32. See Ernst Troeltsch, *Christian Thought: Its History and Applications* (London: University of London Press, 1979), especially the essay "The Place of Christianity among the World-Religions."

33. See Francis Schüssler Fiorenza, *Foundational Theology: Jesus and the Church* (New York: Crossroad, 1984).

34. See Francis Schüssler Fiorenza, "Work and Critical Theology" in *A Matter of Dignity: Inquiries in the Humanization of Work*, eds. William Heiser and John Houck (Notre Dame, Ind.: University of Notre Dame Press, 1977), 23–44, and "Religious Beliefs and Praxis: Reflections on Theological Views of Work," in *Concilium* 131 (1980): 92–102.

35. Seyla Benhabib, *Critique, Norm, and Utopia: A Study of the Foundations of Critical Theory* (New York: Columbia University Press, 1986). See also Nancy Fraser, "What's Critical about Critical Theory?"; Iris Young, "Impartiality and the Civic Public: Some Implications of Feminist Critique of Moral and Political Theory"; and Seyla Benhabib, "The Generalized and the Concrete Other: The Kohlberg-Gilligan Controversy and Feminist Theory," in *Feminism as Critique: On the Politics of Gender*, eds. Seyla Benhabib and Drucilla Cornell (Minneapolis: University of Minnesota, 1987), 31–56 and 57–76.

36. See Susan Moller Okin, "Justice and Gender," *Philosophy and Public Affairs* 16 (1987): 42–72.

37. Hugh Baxter, "System and Lifeworld in Habermas's Theory of Communicative Action," *Theory and Society* 16 (1987): 39–86. Baxter claims

that Habermas's account of the interchange between lifeworld and system is inadequate, that it misconceives the economic and political system and equivocates in his use of the concept of the lifeworld.

38. Jürgen Habermas, *Nachmetaphysisches Denken. Philosophische Aufsätze* (Frankfurt am Main: Suhrkamp, 1988).

39. Ronald Dworkin, *Taking Rights Seriously* (Cambridge, Mass.: Harvard University, 1977); *A Matter of Principle* (Cambridge, Mass.: Harvard University Press, 1985); *Law's Empire* (Cambridge, Mass.: Harvard University Press, 1986); Alan Gewirth, *Reason and Morality* (Chicago: University of Chicago Press, 1978).

40. Michael Walzer, *Exodus and Revolution* (New York: Harper & Row, 1984), *Spheres of Justice* (New York: Basic Books, 1983), and *Interpretation and Social Criticism* (Cambridge, Mass.: Harvard University Press, 1987); Charles Taylor, *Philosophy and the Human Sciences*, Philosophical Papers 2 (Cambridge: Cambridge University Press, 1985); Michael J. Sandel, *Liberalism and the Limits of Justice* (New York: Cambridge, 1982); "The Procedural Republic and the Unencumbered Self," *Political Theory* 12 (1984): 81–96; Alasdair MacIntyre, *After Virtue* (Notre Dame, Ind.: University of Notre Dame Press, 1981; 2d ed. 1984), and *Whose Justice? Which Rationality?* (Notre Dame, Ind.: University of Notre Dame Press, 1988).

41. See Francis Schüssler Fiorenza, "Political Theology as Foundational Theology," *Proceedings of the Catholic Theological Society of America* 32 (1972): 79–107.

42. For the notion of broad reflective equilibrium that has been developed in the discussions following Rawls's work, see Fiorenza, *Foundational Theology*, 301–21.

43. For an attempt to define neo-Aristotelianism, see Herbert Schnädelbach, "Was ist Neoaristotelismus?" *Moralität und Sittlichkeit*, 38–63.

44. Francis Schüssler Fiorenza, *Foundational Theology*, 301–21. See also "Theory and Practice: Theological Education as a Reconstructive, Hermeneutical, and Practical Task," *Theological Education* 22 (1987, supplement): 113–41.

45. Fiorenza, *Foundational Theology*, 285–301.

46. John Rawls, *A Theory of Justice*, 396. See also "Social Unity and Primary Goods," in Amartya K. Sen and Bernard Williams, eds., *Utilitarianism and Beyond* (Cambridge: University Press, 1982), 159–85.

47. For a discussion of social goods, see Nanette Funk, "Habermas and Social Goods," *Social Text* 6, no. 3 (1987): 19–37. Philip Petit, "Habermas on Truth and Justice," in *Marx and Marxisms*, ed. G. H. R. Parkinson (New York: Cambridge, 1982), 207–28, raises the issue of the relation between Habermas's consensus theory of truth and his conception of justice.

48. For Habermas's own reflections on solidarity, see Jürgen Habermas, "Gerechtigkeit und Solidarität. Eine Stellungnahme zur Diskussion über 'Stufe 6.'" *Zur Bestimmung der Moral*, ed. Wolfgang Edelstein and Gertrud Nunner-Winkler (Frankfurt am Main: Suhrkamp, 1987), 291–318.

49. See Arens, *Kommunikativen Handlungen*, 380–82.

50. Helmut Peukert, *Wissenschaftstheorie — Handlungstheorie — Fundamen-*

taltheologie (Düsseldorf: Patmos, 1976); Karl Bauer, *Der Denkweg von Jürgen Habermas zur Theorie des kommunikativen Handelns. Grundlagen einer neuen Fundamentaltheologie?* (Regensburg: S. Roderer Verlag, 1987).

51. James W. Fowler, *Stages of Faith: The Psychology of Human Development and the Quest for Meaning* (San Francisco: Harper & Row, 1981), and Sharon Parks, *The Critical Years* (New York: Harper & Row, 1986).

52. Habermas, *Moralbewußtsein und kommunikatives Handeln*, 178.

53. Seyla Benhabib has argued that Habermas's exclusion of issues of the good life from the discourse-ethic undercuts the utopian dimension of critical theory. See "The Utopian Dimension in Communicative Ethics," *New German Critique* 35 (1985): 83–96.

4

Communicative Praxis and Theology: Beyond Modern Nihilism and Dogmatism

Matthew Lamb

Die große Scholastik, vorab die Summen des Thomas, hatten ihre Kraft und Würde daran, daß sie, ohne den Begriff der Vernunft zu verabsolutieren, nirgends ihn verfemten: dazu ging die Theologie erst im Zeitalter des Nominalismus, zumal bei Luther, über.
— Theodor W. Adorno, *Vernunft und Offenbarung* (1957)

The great works of scholasticism, especially the *Summa*s of Thomas, had their power and dignity in that, without absolutizing the concept of reason, they nowhere ostracized it: theology first went that way in the age of nominalism, especially with Luther.

A discussion of the relevance of the critical theory for a theology of the public realm is, perhaps, a suitable occasion to peer beneath the surfaces of critical theory, rummage under the stage of its splendid (if often frustrating) conceptuality, and encounter the deformed dwarf of theology, described by Walter Benjamin as an underground agent in philosophical discourse. In his own way, Benjamin applied to dialectical philosophers what Nietzsche said of German philosophers: "What are they then, if not furtive theologians?"[1]

Has not the jargon of authenticity given way to a jargon of publicity? Is not sophism alive and well in the great communication networks of our age? Are not all forms of communication in danger of being reduced to utilitarian and pragmatic "communicative techniques"? Could it be that modernity provides the best communication networks in world history, but has nothing substantive to communicate? Is not informed political participation waning precisely in those cultures with omnipresent television? Are not individuals in those cultures less able to engage in understanding their own narratives and more empowered to adopt the packaged narratives of talk shows and soap operas? Are we really communicating in this age of instantaneous communication?

Immanuel Kant defined the Enlightenment as emerging out of immaturity by having the courage to use publicly one's own understanding. We now, as Johann Baptist Metz recently wrote, have a crisis of a second-order immaturity in which the public forum of "enlightened" societies fails to support vigorous and reasoned public debate and consequently political participation declines. Politics and communication have been so instrumentalized that serious judgments are rarely made and even more rarely communicated.[2]

Philosophers of communication and culture in the age of communications are not unlike theologians in the age of faith. Dialectical discernment is imperative. The traditions of critical theory teach important lessons in dialectical discernment in how they criticize the instrumentalism and functionalism and yet avoid romanticism and historicism.

I will argue in this chapter that theology can contribute creatively and transformatively to an understanding of communicative praxis that avoids the nihilism and dogmatism threatening modernist and postmodernist discourses. First, I will sketch a few of the lines that link modern dogmatism and nihilism, suggesting that the dogmatic self-assertion of modernity evokes its shadow, nihilism. Then I will argue that what is normative in modernity is communicative praxis understood as a process of raising ever further relevant questions. Finally, I will suggest three areas in which communicative praxis and theology help to realize reason in history and to remove those distortions that cast religion in utilitarian or fanatical roles.

MODERN NIHILISM AND DOGMATISM

Modernity Is Now History

Modernity is no longer modern.[3] Modernity now has to be defended in the name of continuity, moderation, even tradition.[4] It may be that the postmodernists are no more than ultramodernists, but they hardly exemplify modern rational self-assurance. The defenders of the modern project, the *via moderna*, now adopt an orientation that the defenders of the *viae antiquae* (ancient, medieval, and renaissance) used before them. The modern way is not only self-critical, we are told, but its central orientation is toward mutual understanding rather than coercive domination. Reading Jürgen Habermas's brilliant and incisive *The Philosophical Discourse of Modernity*, I was reminded of Friedrich Schleiermacher's *On Religion: Speeches to Its Cultured Despisers*. What modernity once did to religion, in the name of a supposedly pure reason, is now done to modern reason — its purity long tarnished if not extinguished.[5]

"Self-critical," "mutual understanding," and "reciprocal recognition" are hardly hallmarks of modern history, any more than the moral and intellectual virtues were hallmarks of ancient Greece or Rome, the theological virtues of faith, hope, and love were hallmarks of medieval history; or absolute faith in Christ's Gospel was a hallmark of the Reformation. Modernity now has a history and discrete repentance should be the order of the day. The name of discretion is ambiguity. Analogously to the orientation David Tracy takes to religion in *Plurality and Ambiguity*, Habermas calls attention to the ambiguity intrinsic to modern processes of rationalization.[6]

Hans Blumenberg's arguments for the legitimacy of modernity cut both ways. The autonomy of modernity means that it is intrinsically responsible for its own horrors. The easy ascription of these horrors to mythic or premodern residues illustrates, in my judgment, reason's degenerating into rationalizations.[7] The defenders of modernity keep insisting on what they think are its undeniable achievements. The cultured despisers of modernity concentrate on its palpable distortions. Today belief in automatic progress through science and technology is intellectually and morally indefensible, and modernity needs self-reassurance (*Selbstvergewisserung*) that escapes the cycle of dogmatic self-assertion countering nihilistic condemnation.

Those who critically defend modernity must recognize that dogmatic self-assertion resides at the heart of the modern age. Hans-Georg Gadamer's critique of the Enlightenment's *Vorurteil gegen Vorurteile* ("prejudice against prejudice"), Wayne Booth's critique of the modern dogmas of scientism and motivism, and Alasdair MacIntyre's critiques of emotive individualism and liberalism do more than suggest that enlightened modernity is reaping the harsh value-judgments it has sown against other periods and cultures.[8] How enlightened and true were the judgments forcing previous generations into prehistories of modern developments?

Third and Fourth World critics who want to do to modernity what modernity did to the Middle Ages and Renaissance are more strident: they use modernity's tools (science and technology) but negate its culture.[9] These harsher critiques haunt First and Second World debates as the limits to industrial growth and mounting global pollution pose the question: Are massive poverty and misery in the Third and Fourth Worlds remnants of modernity's past that progress will eventually eradicate, or intimations of our fated future? Are we left with the choice but to join either the optimists who envisage progress as a myth with a moral, or nihilists for whom it is a myth without a moral?[10]

This is not a purely academic question. The destructive powers that science and technology provide to the military systems could decide it by annihilating the questioners. What is done to the poor, to native peoples, and to endangered species throughout the world could be done to all humankind. Modern dogmatic self-assertion is profoundly nihilistic, just as modern nihilism is irresponsibly dogmatic. Apocalypse has been instrumentally rationalized. If you think I exaggerate, recall the Holocaust, and visit Iron Mountain, your nearest Strategic Air Command, or a Trident Submarine Base. Modern dogmatism is nihilistic.

Max Weber and Democratic Dogmatism

For Weber the distinction between value and fact is very much in line with a neo-Kantian separation by which counterfactual values are robbed of cognitive validity. Weber did this by first setting up instrumental rationality as normative for the rationalization process of modernity. He then stated how from the viewpoint of instrumental reason "the greater the value the greater its irrationality."[11] Weber is much closer to a Nietzschean void than the North American students of his sociology (especially Talcott Parsons) have admitted.[12]

Weber explicitly distinguished the empirical sciences of action, such as sociology and history, from what he terms the "dogmatic disciplines... such as jurisprudence, logic, ethics, and esthetics, which seek to ascertain the 'true' and 'valid' meanings associated with the objects of their investigations."[13] Sociology and history are empirical and factual. Jurisprudence, ethics, aesthetics, and even logic are dogmatic. Within such a context, counterfactual moral values (that is, moral values that are grounded in the capacities of humans to transcend all factual injustices and immoralities), along with claims to truth and validity, are treated in dogmatic disciplines since they are dogmatic assertions. The methodological foundations of his social theory led Weber to an extrinsicist instrumentalism in social analysis. Social relations and institutions are primarily understood as structures of command and obedience, what Weber terms *Herrschaft*, or domination. For Weber domination is intrinsic to social organization; the only relevant question is whether the domination is legitimate.

Modernity is constituted by the shift from traditional to rational forms of domination, from the established beliefs of ancient traditions to a "*belief* in the legality of enacted rules and the right of those elevated to authority under such rules to issue commands."[14] Weber believed we moderns have moved from a dogmatism of traditions to a dogmatism of conventionally established rules. Like traditional dogmatism, the dogmatism of conventionally established rules may be established by "consensus."[15]

The difference is that the "consensus" now is not mediated through hereditary or hierophanic agents, but by elected agents. We get to elect our *Herrschaften*, our controllers and commanders, and we call that freedom. The democratic character of the mediation, however, does not make the rules any less dogmatic. Their validity or truth are empirical only through the decisions establishing or grounding them. Truth or validity (*Geltung*) become decisionistic. Freedom in this context either means negating natural determinism in favor of conventional rules, or moving from one type of consensus to another, from one conventional set of rules to another, from one dogmatism to another. If such is the case, it is difficult to avoid Nietzsche's farewell to the dialectic of Enlightenment and his move to a radically nihilistic self-assertion of the will to power.

We are concerned just as little with these questions of the religious as with the questions of the philosophical dogmatists, whether they be idealists or materialists or realists. Their object, one and all, is to compel us to a decision in domains where neither faith nor knowledge is needed.[16]

Were the classic members of the Frankfurt School, with their Jewish memories, troubled by terrible insights into the concrete nihilism of modern dogmatism? Granted, as Habermas remarks, the "dark" writers of the bourgeoisie appealed to Max Horkheimer. Granted Horkheimer and Adorno's *Dialectic of Enlightenment* is an "odd book."[17] But in the name of reason and enlightenment, how were two German Jewish intellectuals to "make sense" of the terror of Holocaust casting very deep dark shadows over Europe? Do the abstractions and formalism of communicative logic — as Fred Dallmayr claims[18] — conjure up "a specter of solipsism"? Does this specter block a rather fateful insight of Horkheimer and Adorno, namely, that the horrors of Nazi Germany were not aberrations outside the pale of an enlightened modernity, but an apocalyptic fulfillment of its latent tendencies?

Only a thoroughly modern industrialized bureaucracy could have killed so many millions with such sterile efficiency. How are contemporary critics of modernity to make sense out of the terrors so scientifically stored in nuclear weapons? How are they to deal with the fact that modern industrialization, urbanization, and automation are responsible for massive environmental pollution?

Could it be that "the palpable distortions" in modernity are not irrational deviations from its Enlightenment project? Could the "palpable distortions" be intrinsic to its "undeniable achievements"? These questions are implicit in Walter Benjamin's thesis that there is no document of civilization that is not also a document of barbarism, as well as his image of the angel of history with the terrible wreckage created by the storm we moderns call progress.[19]

COMMUNICATIVE PRAXIS AS NORMATIVE

If we are troubled by these insights and questions we shall not misread Jürgen Habermas's reconstruction of critical theory in communicative action as a sophisticated variation of solipsism or whistling in the dark. In my judgment Habermas seeks to shift away from modern dogmatism while also avoiding its nihilism. I will first sketch just how he does this by showing how human questioning grounds his communicative action. Then I will indicate how a philosopher and theologian, Bernard Lonergan, developed a normative notion of human questioning as basic to all communicative praxis.

Jürgen Habermas's Performative Dialectics

How is reason practiced in such a way that reasonable judgments are not dogmatic in Weber's sense? I refer to communicative praxis rather than communicative action in order to indicate that the normative "action" is never totally objectified or expressed. Indeed, what is normative for human intelligence and reason is the praxis of raising ever further relevant questions. The root of dogmatism and nihilism in modernity, as in other epochs, is the fallacy of misplaced normativeness. It is the process of making the products of intelligence and reason as normative rather than the questioning praxis of intelligence and reason. We create something that is intelligent and marvelously rational; then we project onto it the powers of our own creative intelligence and reason. Religious, who recognize intelligence and reason as divine in origin, call this idolatry; secularists term it reification.

Communicative praxis within modernity must admit that praxis or performance can never be totally identified with its expressions in theory or narrative, and that institutionalizing enlightenment is always a communicative praxis in which reason is defined by the praxis of raising ever further relevant questions. Jürgen Habermas illustrates this in criticizing postmodern, totalizing critiques of modernity. *The Philosophical Discourse of Modernity* argues, in the words of Thomas McCarthy, that "the defects of the Enlightenment can only be made good by further enlightenment." There are "performative contradictions" involved in using reason to negate reason:

It is precisely the ambiguity of rationalization processes that has to be captured, the undeniable achievements as well as the palpable distortions; and this calls for a reconstructed dialectic of enlightenment rather than a totalized critique of it.[20]

How does Habermas "capture" the ambiguity of rationalization processes? He makes at least two major moves. First, he deconstructs the notion of totality realizing itself in the modern age; then he develops a dialectical notion of communicative reason that can concretely and empirically transcend efforts to stifle or negate it.

History Is Human, Not Automatic

Habermas, as Martin Jay and others have indicated, has broken with his own earlier commitment and that of others in the Frankfurt School to the concept of totality in Hegelian Marxism.[21] There is a "dogmatic version of the concept of a history of the human species," which presumes a *"unilinear, necessary, uninterrupted, and progressive development of a macrosubject."*[22] Habermas wants to develop "a weaker version" of the unity of history and the human species. In general he sees "society" as "a species undergoing social evolution." This is empirically accessible and can be developed without the intuitive or conceptual totality of rigid idealism and mechanical materialism.[23]

There are two significant features of this weaker version. First, adapting notions from Durkheim and Mead, Habermas holds for a growing "linguistification of the sacred" by which the "authoritarian and enforced" consensus of archaic norms dissolves, giving way to "the rationalization of worldviews, the universalization of law and morality, and accelerated processes of individuation."[24] The questions and concerns expressed in world religious traditions must be socially mediated and philosophically transformed in each generation, if the "semantic potential" of many values is not to be lost.[25] The "linguistification of the sacred," as Thomas McCarthy indicates, is reconstructed "as a learning process" in which communicative interaction leads to ever more active appropriations by the participants in mutual understandings, judgments, values.[26]

Second, Habermas does not leave the learning process in vague generalities but shows how it has been socially and culturally differentiated in the modern age. Modifying some categories from Weber, Habermas claims that the specific contribution of modern cultures to the human learning process can be seen in the "decentration" of worldviews, that is, in the shift to a recognized pluralism of world-views. Such decentration, however, does not lead to social or cultural anarchy or nihilism. For it is accompanied by a decentering of con-sciousness that enables persons to adopt different basic attitudes or orientations: (1) cognitive-scientific-instrumental, (2) moral-practical, and (3) aesthetic-practical-expressive. These basic attitudes are iso-morphic (or heuristically relate) to different domains of reality: (1) the objective domain of facts, (2) a normatively regulated inter-subjective realm, and (3) a subjective domain of the self's inner experiences.[27]

But what happens when "rationalization of worldviews" becomes a functionalist ideology? When "universalization of law and morality" enforces particular laws or customs on others? When "individualiza-tion" ends, not in an empowered intersubjectivity but in monadic competition?

Communicative Reason Goes beyond Failures and Achievements

What enables Habermas to recover orientations, including self-critical orientations, that have not been realized? His interest in the modern classics in philosophy and social theory is not primarily her-meneutical or historical but dialectical. He has an acute sense of the further relevant question capable of exposing performative contra-dictions between an author's positions and the concerns informing the communication. Reason and rationality are not only tools of dom-ination, of more or less violent struggle, of forced control. Within rationalization processes are *noncoercive communicative orientations that call into question whatever jeopardizes the learning processes constituted by persons raising further relevant questions.*

In the pluralistic, decentered worldviews of modernity there is a center within humankind open to transcending or going beyond past and present failures and achievements. Habermas once stated this transcending empowerment in a reply to his critics:

Marx wanted to capture the embodiments of unreason. In the same sense, we are also concerned today with the analysis of power constellations that suppress an *intention intrinsic to the rationality* of purposive action and lin-guistic understanding — the claim to reason announced in the teleological and intersubjective structures of social reproduction themselves — and that allow it to take effect only in a distorted manner. Again and again this claim [to communicative reason] is silenced; and yet in fantasies and deeds it de-velops a *stubbornly transcending power*, because it is renewed with each act of unconstrained understanding, with each moment of living together in solidarity, of successful individuation, or of saving emancipation.[28]

The desire for intelligence and reason, the troubled and struggling intention toward uncoerced and genuine communication is as close to the center of Habermas's dialectics as anything he has yet, to my knowledge, articulated.

The emancipatory interest in communicative praxis is anything but dogmatic self-assertion. It is one with "the stubbornly transcending power" of communicative reason. It can be traced in intersubjective self-correcting processes of learning, and some of these traces are institutionalized within modernity, and so can subvert the totalizing identification of power and reason. Dogmatism and nihilism confuse the normativeness of "universalistischen *Fragestellungen*" with the long since abandoned validity ascribed to particular answers, theories, and systems.[29]

The totalizing critiques of modernity depend upon fictitious "normative intuitions" (*normativen Intuitionen*) that become trapped, if I understand Habermas's argument correctly, in "performative contradictions" (1) by projecting pictures or figures of undamaged intersubjectivity or necessary macrosubjects, or progressive competitive system expansions; and yet (2) are unable to recognize the stubbornly transcending power of communicative reason to emancipate us from instrumental totalitarian objectifications and totalizing, inclusive ideologies by means of uncoerced insights, judgments, and communicative actions.[30]

Fred Dallmayr, among others, thinks Habermas passes too quickly over the philosophy of the subject into communicative action theory. Had Habermas deconstructed the Cartesian subject, with its self-asserting replacement of both the conscious immediacy of questioning and discursive knowing with *thinking*, he may have been able to pursue more thoroughly his criticisms of the dogmatism in Kant, Hegel, and Marx. Communicative reason, raising ever further relevant questions, articulates the heuristic dynamics of Habermas's formal-pragmatic relations with their basic attitudes and objective, social, and subjective worlds in a way that avoids the pitfalls of reifying language, thereby emphasizing Habermas's own concrete references to speech acts and intentions.[31]

Working out the dialectical transitions from the philosophy of the subject to communicative action would also exploit the heuristic praxis orientations in such sources as Piaget and Kohlberg. As Piaget analyzes the growth process in a series of adaptations and mediations, so the social intersubjective sets of self-correcting processes of learning (cognitive, moral, aesthetic, religious) continually differentiate into sets of adaptations and mediations that are world disclosive and world transformative. Working through the dialectical transitions from modern philosophies of the subject to communicative praxis would also indicate more adequately how individual freedom and universal solidarity are not contradictory (as they tend to be cast in liberal capitalism and socialist collectivism) but profoundly harmonious.[32]

Moreover, this would also highlight a central concern of Habermas. For he clearly affirms that there is no normative *content* to modernity, whether it be intuitions, concepts, systems, rules, axioms, or institutions, but rather that the effectively free exercise of intelligence and reason is normative in social and cultural interaction. Precisely this concern could be missed in his formulation of the formal pragmatic relations. He both corrects idealist tendencies to separate the expressive and imaginal from the rational and conceptual and the naturalist tendencies to collapse them. However, to date he only seems to recognize the nonobjectivated *environment* or *Umwelt* in terms of human moral-practical spontaneity (*Moral* as differentiated from *Recht*) and sensual spontaneity.[33]

As Thomas McCarthy and others indicate, this concedes too much to Weber's *Zweckrationalität*, and tends to hand over the natural sciences to empiricist and instrumentalist philosophies. How does that differ from the "strategic retreats" that the human sciences have been making vis-à-vis empiricism? Are not the instances now multiplying where "the stubbornly transcending power" of communicative reason subverts the empiricist and instrumentalist misreadings of empirical science? Moreover, if cognitive spontaneity does not operate in all three spheres of human activity, what besides force can settle disputes in the cognitive-empirical sphere?[34]

What Habermas, in speaking of Benjamin and Peukert, calls "the communicative context of a universal historical solidarity" undercuts the facile misunderstanding of communicative praxis as a new and improved "paradigm" or "model," replacing older ones the way we replace television sets: the knowing subject (with theories of consciousness and presence) was replaced by the producing subject (with forces and relations of production), which is now replaced by a "new and improved" communicative action (with uncoercive consensus and universal pragmatics). Communicative praxis is not new. Like human subjecthood or agency, it is a set of human actions and relations that is not identified with the "theories" or "concepts" that we form about them. It is a praxis that occurs before we know about it; indeed, it is a praxis through which we come to know it.[35]

Bernard Lonergan's Dialectics of Reason

The philosopher of science Patrick Heelan shows how Bernard Lonergan's work in cognitional theory provides terms and relations needed for an understanding of quantum mechanics, and the structure of physical science generally, as communicative languages.[36] The interest in empirical science is not primarily control or instrumental domination, but rather questioning natural events, no longer as those events are mediated by unaided sense data, but through complex explanatory languages of instrumental measurement. While this certainly differentiates the learning process enormously, empirical sciences in the modern age are examples *par excellence* of research communities engaged in raising ever further relevant questions and correcting previous errors. Indeed, it is precisely the empiricist and positivist misunderstandings of the empirical sciences that alienate economic and political policies relative to scientific and technological projects.[37]

Bernard Lonergan's *Insight: A Study of Human Understanding* is unequaled in its articulation of the questioning dynamism of human intelligence. He relates intelligent spontaneity to the spontaneity of affective and moral desires. Ethics is related to intelligence. No one has to attend school to acquire questions, to experience the questioning that spontaneously desires to understand what one is sensing, perceiving, or imagining. There is a spontaneous intersubjectivity to illocutionary acts. Humans spontaneously question one another's, or their own, understandings of experience. We want not only to understand but to understand correctly. We are not satisfied with thinking — we want to know, to give reasons why our understanding is correct. Habermas expresses this desire for correct understanding:

Thus an interpreter cannot become clear about the semantic content of an expression independently of the action contexts in which participants react to the expression with a "yes" or a "no" or an abstention. And he does not understand this yes/no position if he cannot make clear to himself the implicit reasons that move the participants to take the positions they do . . . reasons of such a nature that they cannot be described in the attitude of a third person. . . . One can understand reasons only to the extent that one understands why they are or they are not sound."[38]

Unlike Lonergan, Habermas does not explore the spontaneously operative praxis of questions for understanding and questions for judgment.[39]

Judgment leads to the moral-practical spontaneity that questions whether something is worth doing, with the personal and interpersonal deliberations and evaluations that can give reasons for this or that course of action. No one needs a degree to wonder and to raise questions from experience for understanding, from understanding for validity and truth, from validity and truth for genuine values and goods. The communicative praxis of intelligence, reason, and responsibility is the performance of raising ever further relevant questions.[40]

The spontaneity of intelligence and reason precedes any distinction between one's self and others. That to which Lonergan calls our attention is anything but the objectified "subject" or "consciousness" or "presence" described in the modern theories of the same. Habermas perceives the shortcomings of all such theories, whether they be totalitarian objectifications or all-inclusive totalizing critiques. His concern for "performative contradiction" is articulated in Lonergan's analysis of how our spontaneous sensitivity, intelligence, reason, and evaluative activities are normed, not by extrinsic rules or axioms or principles, but by our spontaneous questioning that seeks to be attentive (sensitivity), intelligent (understanding), reasonable (truth), and responsible (value). In their disagreements, humans call attention to data overlooked, to alternate ways of understanding, to evidence or warrants not given, to values or goods not chosen. This self-correcting process of learning, as Lonergan indicates, is neither dominative nor dogmatically self-assertive.

Such intelligence and reason as questioning is anything but an absolute Geist intuiting absolute concepts. The related and recurrent operations of communicative praxis are the open and norming patterns of human freedom. While we all are inattentive, stupid, unreasonable, and irresponsible at times, we effectively expand our freedom when we attend to the questioning desires for attentiveness, intelligence, reasonableness, and responsibility.

Not only does this communicative praxis constitute lifeworlds, it also constitutes, in ever more differentiated manners, the sciences. Michael H. McCarthy has demonstrated that the totalizing orientations within modernity can be traced to a failure of philosophical reflection to understand how the emerging empirical sciences performatively broke with the Aristotelian ideal of certain knowledge of necessary causes. Descartes attributed necessity and certainty to thinking subjectivity. The positivistic misunderstanding of the empirical sciences is, as Habermas has remarked, related to traditional, classicist ontology.[41] For the pivotal role of judgment was collapsed into a curious type of Platonic dualism, now recast in terms of body versus mind, sensations versus ideas. Since no human ideas (even the "ego cogito") could survive Descartes's universal doubt, the empiricists simply transferred *necessity* and *certainty* to sensations or perceptions. This set the stage for the interminable modern debates between empiricists and idealists.[42]

The turn to communicative praxis is part of postempiricist philosophies of science that, in tune with critical theory, break with the absolutizing concentration on necessity and certainty. Unfortunately, modern philosophies of science, while fixated upon a basically classicist ideal of certain knowledge of necessary causes, tended to concur with the modern moral philosophies that rejected the Aristotelian theory of the virtues, with its development of practical judgments in contingently historical ways. The judgments of science, as postempiricist philosophies of science indicate, are more like the conditioned universality of moral judgments (*phronēsis*) than the deductivist universality of necessary and unconditioned axioms or principles.[43]

The postempiricist philosophies of science clearly reject the ideals of necessity and certainty informing the quest for a complete and coherent theoretical articulation of reason. This would make reason into a monistic absolute, as if reason could be completely expressed, as if all questions would be fully answered. These philosophies also reject the inference from the radical incompleteness of human rationality that reason must be totally criticized. Arational relativism or irrational anarchism, proposed by many postmoderns, is an inference premised on the mistaken assumption that if rationality exists, it must be capable of complete and coherent theoretic purity. Instead, postempiricist philosophies affirm the praxis of reason as the performance of raising ever further relevant questions within communities engaged in empirical, hermeneutical, and/or dialectical inquiry in order to articulate coherently, yet always incompletely, both the answers discovered by their questioning praxis, as well as the heuristic relations within these communities of inquiry and other forms of the questioning praxis of reason (e.g., the lifeworld of everyday commonsense living, aesthetic spheres, moral, religious).[44]

The universality of communicative praxis is not constituted by intuitions, concepts, theories, axioms, or principles. Nor is it mediated from "the top down." No theory or system can coherently *and* completely express rational praxis. It is a universality constituted by attentive, intelligent, rational, and responsible communicative praxis, and is mediated through the plurality of persons and communities communicating and questioning. Moreover, this universality is coherent but always incomplete, requiring openness to further relevant questions. Such openness is not the fiction of a Cartesian universal doubt, for questions are relevant to data and occur within multiple contexts of communication and belief.[45]

One need not read Descartes to experience one's own consciousness, Dilthey or Gadamer to experience one's desire to understand, Lonergan to desire to understand correctly, or Habermas to desire genuine communication. Communicative praxis is grounded in what Habermas terms "the stubbornly transcending power" and in what Lonergan describes as the desire raising ever further relevant questions in ongoing self-correcting processes of learning. This is what is normative. It is not dogmatically asserted. Lonergan explicitly invites his readers to verify in their own performance the activities and operations he derives from human questioning spontaneity. We read these philosophers to understand the genuine achievements of intelligence and the *performative contradictions* between human, intersubjective spontaneity and its distortions and derailments.

Like Habermas, Lonergan called for a second enlightenment to carry forward the advances of the first:

The Enlightenment — it becomes just the first Enlightenment if a second is recognized — was carried socially and culturally. Socially by the movement that would sweep away the remnants of feudalism and a lingering absolutism by proclaiming liberty, fraternity, equality. Culturally by the triumph of Newton, who did for mechanics what Euclid had done for geometry and who led philosophers to desert rationalism and swell the ranks of empiricists.

While the empiricism and positivism of the first Enlightenment may still dominate, Lonergan traces the emergence of what he terms the second enlightenment, which, from its cultural origin in the relativizing of Euclidean geometry, relativity theories, and quantum mechanics, has moved on to challenge empiricism and positivism in economics, politics, and the deductivist pretensions of both empiricism and idealism in philosophy.

Of itself this second enlightenment is culturally significant. But it may have as well a social mission. Just as the first enlightenment had its carrier in the transition from feudal to bourgeois society, so the second may find a role and task in offering hope and providing leadership to the masses alienated by large establishments under bureaucratic management.[46]

THEOLOGY AND PUBLIC REALMS

There are many implications in any dialogue between critical theory and theology for a theology of the public realm. I shall sketch three.

Communicative Praxis Is Never War

Helmut Peukert has shown that what is new in the twentieth century is not the use of reason to critique reason, which belongs to all traditions of enlightenment. What is new, and what Benjamin and other early critical theorists wrestled with, was an inverse insight:

enlightened reason cannot measure up to the consequences of its actions.[47]

For understandable reasons deriving partially from the European wars of religion, there are two fundamental presuppositions on which most Western modern philosophers agree, whether they are conservative, liberal, or radical. The first is that natural and historical realities are ultimately conflictive, as though reality is made up of contradictory forces contending for dominance. The second presupposition is that knowledge is power to control, a learning of secrets in order to enforce order and secure dominance. Little wonder, then, that Max Weber thought that social organization always involved domination (*Herrschaft*). Habermas also espouses this, at least in regard to the empirical-analytic sciences. They are supposedly informed by instrumentalist interests in technically dominating nature since "the human species secures its existence in systems of social labor and self-assertion through violence," while he differentiates communication and individuation from such dominative interest.[48]

It seems to me that neither Judaism nor Christianity can accept these two fundamental presuppositions. God's creative act is not an act of violence and domination — indeed, the Hebrew creation narratives repudiated the violent cosmogonies of the surrounding empires. The empires and superpowers of history have become what they are through force and violence, so it is hardly surprising that their visions of world birth would be violent. Quite different are the narratives of the victims of empires and superpowers. Creation is good, creation nourishes us and metaphors of gardening, not killing, are central. Indeed, Jewish and Christian revelations intensify intersubjective communication infinitely. God speaks and the universe comes into being. Humans emerge and are called to respond in faith and love, not in violence and force, which latter are the results of sin.

Insofar as religious faith is a knowledge born of love, it is important that the wisdom of such faith engage in communicative praxis with the sciences and technologies, which, unfortunately, seem urgently in need of a healing transformation away from the fears and aggressions engendering them.[49] But this "insofar as" has to be stressed. For just as there is needed a dialectic of enlightenment that differentiates the genuine exercise of reason from the abuse of reason to subject nature and persons as instruments to another, so there is needed a dialectic of religious experience that differentiates genuine religious praxis from the abuse of religion to dominate and control. As Helmut Peukert indicates, only such a mutually critical exercise of reason and religion can foster the collaboration between the sciences and religious or theological scholarship adequate to contemporary challenges.[50]

Christian Doctrine

Theology will not be able to aid a genuine dialectic of enlightenment if it continues to internalize the caricatures of itself that the
Enlightenment first portrayed. How often we hear, for example,
a dominative and "dogmatic" reconstruction of Christianity's own
dogmas. Is it not curious that whenever theologians uncritically as-
similate an imperial culture around them, they marvelously discover
how the origins of Christian doctrine in the Great Councils were
equally if not more imperial? Theologians still refer to the Imperial Church of the Constantinian epoch and completely identify the
Nicean confession of faith with that imperialism. Such theologians
accept with minor reservations the picture of the events provided
by the first of all self-important Christian court theologians, Eusebius of Caesarea. Eusebius was more interested in power than in
orthodoxy. In line with the first enlightenment's prejudices, modern
theologians, who accept Eusebius's distortions, negate orthodoxy as
intrinsically "dogmatic" in the pejorative sense, i.e., as a use of faith
to control and dominate.[51]

Such reconstructions illustrate the distorted communication with
the past, with the men and women who strove to live their faith in
Christ Jesus as intelligently and responsibly as they could. It weakens
those who strive to do so today, for they are not provided with the
social power that comes from a realization of our solidarity in the
Body of Christ. But just as the distorted pictures of the Enlightenment can be overcome by the self-correcting learning processes of
communicative reasoned praxis, so ongoing theological scholarship,
attuned to the dialectics of enlightenment and of religion, can begin
to indicate what a jejune and distorted reconstruction of orthodoxy
that is.

Athanasius was hardly a court theologian. Ejected many times
from his diocese and strong in his support for the thousands of
·devout Christian communities of study and prayer, he realized
that the God revealed in the life, death, and resurrection of Jesus
Christ is not the Imperial One, with Son and Spirit as imperial
emanations subordinate to Father. No, orthodoxy confessed the
God of Jesus Christ as a unity of Consubstantial Persons.[52] Indeed, it was within the orthopraxis of fervent local churches, out
of which the monastic communities of women and men emerged,
that Athanasius found the graced foundations of orthodoxy.[53]
The work of Bernard Lonergan demonstrates the need to recover the intellectual, moral, and religious orthopraxis that has
been the matrix out of which genuine orthodoxy lives down the
ages.[54]

Does Modern Secularism Project onto Faith Its Abuse of Reason?
Among the many tasks of a dialectic of enlightenment, or a second
enlightenment, is the recognition that religious faiths and practices
do not by definition lack intelligence and reason. A theology for the
public realm, especially here in the United States, will be effective
only if it overcomes the deep cultural tendency to treat religion as
utilitarian at best ("useful for the common weal") and at worst as a
type of occult or public fanaticism. The sociology of religion is hardly
helpful in this task, as long as it maintains the Weberian dichotomy
between fact and value, between cognitive and ethical orientations.
Charismatic and apocalyptic are often used in ways that blunt by being wrapped in fanatical connotations the serious questions they pose
to the culture. Like religion generally, charismatic is either benign
and so useful, or malignant and so fanatical.

This distortion masks, however, a deeper problem within the
Western Enlightenment. Bluntly stated, confronted with the tragic
wars of religion in Europe, Enlightenment intellectuals tended to
criticize religion rather than war. Just as religious truth was equated
with domination, so all truth remains linked with power and violence. A consequence remains the terribly violent orientation in all
national public realms.[55] Indeed, modern industrialized war-making
far overshadows all previous forms of organized violence. This is
the terribly apocalyptic significance of Holocaust, Hiroshima, and
the World Wars. The Middle Ages and Renaissance had a successor, the Modern Age. Will modernity have a successor? For the first
time in world history humankind's biological survival is questionable.
The intelligent and very reasonable insights into this shadow side of
modernity, the instrumentalization of apocalyptic evil, are misunderstood as negations of reason because the normativeness of reason is
wrongly identified with necessary, unilinear progress in a struggle
for survival.

The modern age did not invent communicative praxis. No one
culture has it copyrighted. There are achievements in wisdom,
in moral goodness, and in common sense that any enlightenment
would overlook at its own peril. The myth of necessary unilinear progress in the struggle for survival is not secularized Jewish
and Christian salvation history. Rather it stems from Euclidean
and Newtonian quantification of all reality in the empiricism of
seventeenth-century Europe, linked with the Hobbesian instrumentalization of intelligence as a tool in the supposed war of all against
all.[56]

It is still difficult for philosophers and theologians to understand
the genial insights of an Augustine and Aquinas regarding eternity and time, especially given the tendency to regard the former

as either a phenomenal or noumenal duration. Moderns wrongly stretch apocalyptic metaphors onto their own grids of duration and extension (as, for example, Newton's chronology of Daniel's apocalyptic prophecies). Indeed, there are many rather central theological doctrines in which contemporary theologians continue to misconstrue premodern classics.[57]

We are all moderns and, if we are to take the self-correcting processes of learning within scholarship seriously, we have much to learn from the men and women of past ages. Communicative praxis is not restricted to the present generation. Every age and culture has its mistakes, biases, and sins. Communicative praxis recognizes how cooperative consensus has to be universal if it is not going to self-destruct. One of the errors of modernity has been to misconstrue traditions and the past as no more than dominative and benighted authoritarian repression out of which modernity emerges. As Lonergan remarked, "any present is powerful in the measure that past achievement lives on in it."[58]

Modernity fails to discern the normative achievements of the past and to differentiate them from the errors, biases, and sins. For example, Habermas reads Durkheim and develops a notion of "the linguistification of the sacred" as a process of learning. By a very different route Lonergan discovered that what Augustine meant by *desiderium animi*, the desire of mind, and Thomas Aquinas meant by *lumen intellectus agentis*, the light of intelligence in act, was the human capacity to raise ever further relevant questions. That capacity was healed and intensified, not dogmatically broken or distorted, by religious faith. Aquinas structures the whole of theology as ongoing questions. Theodor Adorno glimpsed this, if we judge from the quotation at the beginning of this chapter.

Why did Augustine or Aquinas understand their faith in Jesus Christ as the incarnate son of God as a healing intensification of their intelligence and reason? For Augustine, it was the only way hate and domination in the imperial cities of man, which so tragically used intelligence and reason to destroy, could avoid extinguishing the quest for wisdom and intelligence. For Aquinas, the barbarity of evil in human history is adequately met only by the light of faith and agapic love. Humankind can excel in the intellectual and moral virtues only if these are strengthened and intensified by the theological virtues. We are back at the consequences of the use of reason to destroy reason. What else is the Holocaust? What else is the nuclear arms race? What else the enormous environmental pollution in modernity?

The Theodicy Question

Habermas seems to overlook in Benjamin just this struggle with the consequences of using reason to negate the reason of others. Is it not true that the theodicy problem *as it is posed in modernity* admits of no intelligent and rational answer?

There can be no intelligent and rational answer for several reasons. First, in modernity intelligence and rationality are distorted into conceptualistic instruments of all sorts. This distortion was then projected into infinity (as it was by Leibniz and others), as a divine intelligence and reason. The theodicy problematic put modern theologians in the dilemma of either denying the very real suffering of history or of claiming that the leap of faith is irrational. Only if they question the very presuppositions of the conception of intelligence and reason in modern theodicy are they able to avoid the dilemma.

Second, the truncation of modern reason (which has a prehistory: Lonergan on how Kant's critique is not of pure reason but of reason à la Scotus) led to a conflation of logic and conceptualist theories, which led to the conceptualist philosophies of the subject, consciousness, and unilinear progress, which we have already discussed. The appeal was for ever more comprehensive logical concepts or all-embracing theories. With the collapse of these pretensions, the postmodernists, whom Habermas criticizes, collapse reason too quickly into Nietzschean nihilism.

Third, Jewish and Christian prophetic and mystical traditions reveal an answer to the massively concrete histories of human suffering. But it is not a human conceptual answer. Any human and historical theory that made such claims should be denounced as idolatrous blasphemy in the presence of the dead and suffering. *No mere theory can console the suffering, no concept can raise the dead.* Peukert indicates how this is implied in Benjamin's very Jewish demand for an openness of the past (as well as the present and future) to messianic interruption. Messianic expectation is also present in Johann Baptist Metz's insistence on the eschatological proviso and the apocalyptic interruption of all modern myths of time entombing humankind in a closed and endless duration. The answer to the massively concrete histories of evil, oppression, and suffering — the only adequate answer — far exceeds all human hearts and minds.[59]

The *theological* affirmation that God's infinite understanding and love alone are the answer breaks the epistemic cynicism of modernity, a cynicism that claims that intelligence and love are merely more cunning weapons or tools in some great universal struggle for existence. Moreover, the theological affirmation that God alone is capable of transforming evil into good, death into life, sin into grace, is not cheap consolation or opium but a confession as well of the enormous evil and suffering from which we must be redeemed.

Political theology, as Metz understands it, unites the mystical and the prophetic. The mystical and mysterious assertion, "God is the Answer to massive evil and suffering," does not induce apathy, but informs strong and clear prophetic denunciations of evil and calls to decisive action with and for the oppressed. The prophetic and mystical traditions of Judaism and Christianity, and the concrete practices of discipleship down the ages, keep alive the faith, hope, and agapic love that inform a noninstrumental compassion and solidarity. These few reflections might at least suggest how we humans are not alone in struggling with these terrible questions.

Theologies for Public Realms

The public realm in the United States is in danger of becoming an abstract, conceptualized universality. In such a public realm the participants are led to believe that the plurality of their traditions, races, genders, and religions requires that they intellectually bracket those particularities, with their truth claims, for the sake of "civil" public discourse. The public realm is constituted, then, in two moves. First there are the efforts to develop abstract symbols, axioms, principles, or whatever minimum on which all could agree. Differences are abstracted out of the melting pot, for they are conflictual by definition. Second, there are ground rules for civil and legal negotiations of those differences that particular pressure groups are unwilling to bracket. Such an abstract universality, with its social, civil, and state formalism, is extrinsicist and dogmatic. The rules of the game, the procedures of the public realm, demand compromise and a relentless privatization of those cherished beliefs and values that disrupt a smooth functioning of the public realm.

It is misleading to imagine that there is only one public realm in the United States, and that we can develop "a" theology for it. That would be to approach the question with either deductive or inductive conceptualism. I find too much of that approach still operative, often without advertence, in works on world religions and in public discourse.[60] Communicative praxis would suggest that attention to all relevant questions within one's immediate contexts is a proper starting point. This means that the theologies of the public realms will indeed have a universal significance, but only as mediated in and through the many communities of religious discourse and ecclesial action operative in the many public realms constituting our society and culture. The universality of the many public realms is mediated in and through the particularities of the many communities. The discourse that would make this concretely possible has hardly begun, and must contend with the impoverishing abstractions fed by the communication media.

Religious truth claims cannot be bracketed, any more than faith should be cut off from intelligence in theological discourse. This requires that truth questions be clearly and consistently differentiated from domination, violence, and force. If such concrete truth claims are ignored in theology, then theology becomes as privatized as religion is in our culture.

No wonder, then, that there is a very strong tendency, especially in the United States, toward an individualism that is excessively monadic, if not egophanic, with an accompanying failure to understand the vast differences between *intentional* communities within institutionalized traditions, on the one hand, and voluntary associations of like-minded monads on the other. The public realms in the United States are particularly vulnerable to the misunderstandings that cast synagogues, churches, or mosques in the same lot as clubs and other voluntarily associated pressure groups. This privatizes religion drastically, since it is taken for granted that, in areas where religious traditions disagree with a modern or majority consensus, the intentional aspects of the disagreement can be ignored as the conflictive aspects are reduced to different groups contesting their relative powers in the legal and/or political realms.

Ironically, while this has been the fate generally of religious discourse in our culture for some time, a complaint is now heard that it has become the fate of our political discourse. Issues are not intelligently and rationally debated. They are settled by courts or elections. Without genuine communicative praxis, the decisions of either are only dogmatically decisionistic. Social power, not understood as having its source in ongoing cooperative communication, is alienated into power to impose one's will upon others by the judicious use of manipulative cunning, whether in legal or political forums.[61]

If, as is said, languages are dialects with armies and navies, then, when the source of social power shifts from cooperation to manipulation, communicative consensus would be opinions with bank accounts and pressure groups. Understanding and reasons are not discussed but simply presumed to be associated with forceful and authoritarian groups. The public realm, as it excludes the dead, the poor, and the marginalized, loses its human orientation and becomes a battlefield of warring opinions and decisions. Dogmatic competition replaces communicative praxis.

Christian theologians whose theology is rooted in communities of orthopraxis will realize that "the weak messianic power of the present"[62] is informed with a grace and Spirit that transforms our weakness into the gentle strength and Presence of God. In the Risen Christ we are united into a communion of communities that embraces and transforms humankind, not through dominative force but through quiet faith, undying hope, and a love that all the hate and indifference in the world cannot extinguish. Christian theologies for the public realms communicate a universality through the solidarity of the reign of God (*basileia tou theou*), which the whole Christ preaches and practices against the empires and superpowers down the ages.

NOTES

1. Walter Benjamin, *Zur Kritik der Gewalt und andere Aufsätze* (Frankfurt am Main: Suhrkamp, 1965), 78. Theodor Adorno's essay "Vernunft und Offenbarung" can be found in *Stichworte. Kritische Modelle 2* (Frankfurt am Main: Suhrkamp, 1969), 20–28.

2. Immanuel Kant, "Beantwortung der Frage. Was ist Aufklärung?" *Werke XI* (Frankfurt am Main: Suhrkamp, 1964), 53–61; Johann Baptist Metz, "Wider die zweite Unmündigkeit" in *Frankfurter Allgemeine Zeitung* December 15, 1987.

3. Jean-François Lyotard, *The Postmodern Condition: A Report on Knowledge*, trans. G. Bennington and B. Massumi (Minneapolis: University of Minnesota Press, 1984); and *Le Différend* (Paris: Editions de Minuit, 1983).

4. See David Kolb, *The Critique of Pure Modernity: Hegel, Heidegger and After* (Chicago: University of Chicago Press, 1986), 256ff.

5. See Jürgen Habermas, *The Philosophical Discourse of Modernity*, trans. Frederick Lawrence and introduction by Thomas McCarthy (Cambridge, Mass.: MIT Press, 1987). On parallels from the past, see Richard Jones, *Ancients and Moderns: A Study of the Rise of the Scientific Movement in Seventeenth-century England* (St. Louis: Washington University Press, 1961); Emile Poulat, *Modernistica: Horizons, Physionomies, Débats* (Paris: Nouvelles Editions Latines, 1982); Lucien Febvre, *The Problem of Unbelief in the Sixteenth Century: The Religion of Rabelais*, trans. B. Gottlieb (Cambridge, Mass.: Harvard University Press, 1982), 335–464.

6. Ibid., xv.

7. Hans Blumenberg, *The Legitimacy of Modernity*, trans. Robert Wallace (Cambridge, Mass.: MIT Press, 1984). For readings of modernity that expose the horror, see Zygmunt Bauman, *Modernity and the Holocaust* (Ithaca, N.Y.: Cornell University Press, 1989); Edith Wyschogrod, *Spirit in Ashes: Hegel, Heidegger, and Man-Made Mass Death* (New Haven: Yale University Press, 1985).

8. Hans-Georg Gadamer, *Wahrheit und Methode*, 5th rev. ed. (Tübingen: J. C. B. Mohr, 1986), 276ff.; Wayne Booth, *Modern Dogma and the Rhetoric of Assent* (Chicago: University of Chicago Press, 1974); Alasdair MacIntyre, *Whose Justice? Which Rationality?* (Notre Dame, Ind.: University of Notre Dame Press, 1988).

9. For example, see *Indigenous Peoples: A Global Quest for Justice* (London: Zed Books, 1987); L. S. Stavrianos, *Global Rift: The Third World Comes of Age* (New York: William Morrow, 1981); Ali Shari'ati, *Marxism and Other Western Fallacies: An Islamic Critique* (Berkeley: Mizan Press, 1980); and Gustavo Gutiérrez, *The Power of the Poor in History* (Maryknoll, N.Y.: Orbis Books, 1983), 169–233.

10. Franco Ferrarotti, *The Myth of Inevitable Progress* (Westport, Conn.: Greenwood Press, 1985).

11. Max Weber, *Economy and Society*, trans. Guenther Roth and Claus Wittich (Berkeley: University of California Press, 1978) 1:4–26, 85–86; 2:1116–17; on the rationalization process see Weber's *Gesammelte Aufsätze zur Wissenschaftslehre*, 2d rev. ed. (Tübingen: J. C. B. Mohr, 1951), 471ff.

12. See Leo Strauss, *Natural Right and History* (Chicago: University of Chicago Press, 1953), 35–80, esp. 65f.; also Allan Bloom, *The Closing of the American Mind* (New York: Simon & Schuster, 1987), 151, 194ff.

13. Weber, *Economy and Society*, 1:4.

14. Ibid., 1:212ff.

15. Ibid., 457–63.

16. Nietzsche, *Human, All Too Human*, trans. R. J. Hollingdale (Cambridge: Cambridge University Press, 1986), vol. 2, part 2, par. 16 (p. 308). Translation altered.

17. Jürgen Habermas, *The Philosophical Discourse of Modernity*, 106.

18. Fred Dallmayr, *Polis and Praxis* (Cambridge, Mass.: MIT Press, 1984), 250–53.

19. Walter Benjamin, *Illuminations*, trans. Harry Zohn (New York: Schocken Books, 1978), 257–58: "This is how one pictures the angel of history. His face is turned toward the past. Where we perceive a chain of events [extrinsicism], he sees one single catastrophe which keeps piling wreckage upon wreckage and hurls it in front of his feet. The angel would like to stay, awaken the dead, and make whole what has been smashed. But a storm is blowing from Paradise; it has got caught in his wings with such violence that the angel can no longer close them. This storm irresistibly propels him into the future to which his back is turned, while the pole of debris before him grows skyward. This storm is what we call progress."

20. Habermas, *The Philosophical Discourse of Modernity*, xiv–xvii.

21. Martin Jay, *Marxism and Totality: The Adventures of a Concept from Lukács to Habermas* (Berkeley: University of California Press, 1984), 462–509.

22. Jürgen Habermas, *Communication and the Evolution of Society*, trans. Thomas McCarthy (Boston: Beacon Press, 1979), 139.

23. Jürgen Habermas "Dogmatismus, Vernunft und Entscheidung — Zu Theorie und Praxis in der verwissenschaftlichen Zivilisation" in Jürgen Habermas, *Theorie und Praxis. Sozialphilosophische Studien* (Frankfurt am Main: Suhrkamp, 1971), 307–35 [ET: *Theory and Practice*, trans. John Viertel (Boston: Beacon Press, 1973)]; also his "Über das Subjekt der Geschichte. Diskussionsbemerkung zu falsch gestellten Alternativen" in his *Kultur und Kritik* (Frankfurt am Main: Suhrkamp, 1973), 389–98.

24. Habermas, *Theorie des kommunikativen Handelns* (Frankfurt am Main: Suhrkamp, 1988), 2:74ff.

25. Habermas, "Metaphysik nach Kant," in K. Cramer et al., eds., *Theorie der Subjektivität* (Frankfurt am Main: Suhrkamp, 1987), 431.

26. McCarthy, introduction to his translation of vol. 1 of Jürgen Habermas, *The Theory of Communicative Action* (Boston: Beacon Press, 1984), xxv.

27. Habermas, *The Philosophical Discourse of Modernity*, 110–13, 339–41; also his *The Theory of Communicative Action*, 1:234ff. It would take us too far afield to discuss how these differ from Habermas's earlier three quasi-transcendental interests in *Knowledge and Human Interests*. Have the psycho-analytic disciplines and emancipatory interests now been displaced by the aesthetic? How do they transform Karl Popper's three worlds? They do have general institutional correlatives in terms of (1) universities and scientific research institutes, (2) juridical and legal professions, and (3) autonomous centers of art production and criticism. The significance of Bernard Lonergan's work is that he shows how the related and recurrent operations of human interiority (the third domain in Habermas) relate to the first and second domains.

28. In John B. Thompson and David Held, eds., *Habermas: Critical Debates* (Cambridge, Mass.: MIT Press, 1982), 221; emphasis mine.

29. Habermas, *The Philosophical Discourse of Modernity*, 408, note 28. Regarding the claims of classical metaphysics, see below.

30. Habermas, *The Philosophical Discourse of Modernity*, 336ff. This argument expresses insights analogous to those of Anthony Giddens on the duality of structure, and distanciation from bureaucratic control, in *The Constitution of Society* (Berkeley: University of California Press, 1984), 5–40, 281–354.

31. Habermas, *The Theory of Communicative Action*, 1:279–337; on the questions raised, see Fred Dallmayr, *Polis and Praxis*, 224–53; also Dallmayr's "Critical Epistemology Criticized" in his *Beyond Dogma and Despair: Toward a Critical Phenomenology of Politics* (Notre Dame, Ind.: University of Notre Dame Press, 1981), 246–93; also the criticisms raised by Thomas McCarthy, Henning Ottmann, and John Thompson, along with Habermas's responses, in John B. Thompson and David Held, eds., *Habermas: Critical Debates*, 57–161, 219–83.

32. It seems to me in reading Habermas in terms of his performative questioning, it is toward such an articulation of rational praxis that he is heading. Making this more explicit would, for example, answer some of the questions posed by Anthony Giddens in his "Reason without Revolution?" in Richard J. Bernstein, ed., *Habermas and Modernity* (Cambridge, Mass.: MIT Press, 1985), 111ff. Working through the dialectical transitions from the modern philosophies of the subject to communicative reason would also strengthen Habermas's corrections to Kohlberg's stages. For relations between Lonergan's work and both Piaget and Kohlberg, see Walter Conn, *Conscience: Development and Self-transcendence* (Birmingham: Religious Education Press, 1981).

33. Habermas, *The Theory of Communicative Action*, 1: 236ff.

34. *Habermas: Critical Debates*, 57–115; *Habermas and Modernity*, 177–91.

35. Habermas, *The Philosophical Discourse of Modernity*, 14ff.

36. Patrick Heelan, *Quantum Mechanics and Objectivity: A Study of the Physical Philosophy of Werner Heisenberg* (The Hague: Martinus Nijhoff, 1965). This has been further elaborated by a student of Heelan, Patrick Byrne, in "Lonergan on the Foundations of the Theories of Relativity," in Matthew Lamb, ed., *Creativity and Method: Essays in Honor of Bernard Lonergan* (Milwaukee: Marquette University Press, 1982), 477–94.

37. David F. Noble, *Forces of Production: A Social History of Industrial Automation* (New York: Alfred Knopf, 1984); Seymour Melman, *Profits without Production* (New York: Alfred Knopf, 1983); Joshua S. Goldstein, *Long Cycles: Prosperity and War in the Modern Age* (New Haven: Yale University Press, 1988).

38. Habermas, *The Theory of Communicative Action*, 1:115–16.

39. If Habermas were to explore the implications of judgment, as Lonergan has, he would be able to break more decisively with his Kantian presuppositions; see Giovanni Sala, "The Apriori in Human Knowledge: Kant's Critique of Pure Reason and Lonergan's Insight," in *The Thomist* 40, no. 2, 179–221. The exploration of judgment is also central in understanding the question of God; see Giovanni Sala, *Kant und die Frage nach Gott* (Berlin: Walter de Gruyter, 1990).

40. Bernard Lonergan, *Insight: A Study of Human Understanding* (New York: Philosophical Library, 1957), 207–17, 289–98, 607ff. Also his "Cognitional Structure," in the *Collected Works of Bernard Lonergan* (Toronto: University of Toronto Press, 1988), 4:205–22.

41. Habermas, *Knowledge and Human Interest*, 302–3.

42. Michael H. McCarthy, *The Crisis of Philosophy* (Albany: State University of New York Press, 1990).

43. See among others Richard Bernstein, *Beyond Objectivism and Relativism: Science, Hermeneutics, and Praxis* (Philadelphia: University of Pennsylvania Press, 1983); Alasdair MacIntyre, *After Virtue: A Study in Moral Theory* (Notre Dame, Ind.: University of Notre Dame Press, 1981); *Whose Justice? Which Rationality?* (Notre Dame, Ind.: University of Notre Dame Press, 1988); David Tracy, *Plurality and Ambiguity* (San Francisco: Harper & Row, 1987).

44. See Matthew Lamb, "The Dialectic of Theory and Praxis within Paradigm Analysis," in Hans Küng and David Tracy, eds., *Paradigm Change in Theology* (New York: Crossroad, 1989), 63–109.

45. Lonergan, *Insight*, 703–18.

46. Bernard Lonergan, "The Second Enlightenment," in his *A Third Collection* (New York: Paulist Press, 1985), 63–65. The non-Euclidean geometries indicate how the quest for necessary and deductively certain principles was mistaken: "from being regarded as the unique deduction of necessary truth from self-evident principles (e.g., in Kant) it became just one of many possible geometric systems deduced from freely chosen postulates."

47. Helmut Peukert, "Praxis Universaler Solidarität" in Edward Schillebeeckx, ed., *Mystik und Politik. Theologie im Ringen um Geschichte und Gesell-*

schaft (Mainz: Matthias-Grünewald, 1988), 172–85. On inverse insights, see Lonergan, *Insight*, 19–26, 387, 687–89.

48. Habermas, *Knowledge and Human Interests*, 313; also Thomas McCarthy, *The Critical Theory of Jürgen Habermas* (Cambridge, Mass.: MIT Press, 1978), 53ff.

49. Matthew Lamb, "Christianity with the Political Dialectics of Community and Empire," in N. Biggar, J. Scott, W. Schweiker, eds., *Cities of Gods: Faith, Politics and Pluralism in Judaism, Christianity and Islam* (New York: Greenwood, 1986), 73–100. On the relevance of this to Habermas's work, see Steven Lukes, "Of Gods and Demons: Habermas and Practical Reasons" in John B. Thompson and David Held, eds., *Habermas: Critical Debates* (Cambridge, Mass.: MIT Press, 1982), 134–48, 254ff.

50. Helmut Peukert, "Über die Zukunft von Bildung," in *Frankfurter Hefte* 6 (1984), 129–37. Also Matthew Lamb, "The Dialectic of Theory and Praxis within Paradigm Analysis," 86ff.

51. Variations on this theme are widespread. For a recent version, see Elaine Pagels, *Adam, Eve, and the Serpent* (New York: Random House, 1988). Pagels turns Augustine into an "imperial church" theologian, a claim she can make only by ignoring the dialectics Augustine elaborated between empire and church in *The City of God*. Augustine, like Athanasius, realized that overcoming imperialism was the task of all humankind graced by God's Incarnation carried on in the communion of the church. Pelagius, like Eusebius, simply underestimated the power of imperialism. Pagels seems to do so as well.

52. Aloys Grillmeier, *Christ in the Christian Tradition*, trans. John Bowden (Atlanta: John Knox Press, 1975), 250–71, 308ff. for a differentiation of the imperial church from the Nicean faith.

53. See Athanasius's *Life of Anthony*, which had a profound impact on both Orthodox and Catholic Christianity. Also Armand Veilleux, *The Pachomian Koinonia*, 3 vols. (Kalamazoo: Cistercian Publications, 1980), for important writings from the Egyptian monasteries in which Athanasius sought refuge when he was persecuted by the imperial forces. Note that the communities of monks and nuns did not understand themselves as fleeing from a corrupt church that had compromised with empire (*pace* von Harnack et al.), rather they understood themselves as in communion with the local churches genuinely following Christ. Armand Veilleux, "The Monastery as a School of Orthopraxis," not yet published. W. H. C. Frend, *The Rise of Christianity* (Philadelphia: Fortress Press, 1984), 423, 477–88, illustrates an uncritical assimilation of Eusebius of Caesarea and a failure to understand the issues at stake both in monasticism and in the Trinitarian controversies.

54. Bernard Lonergan, *De Deo Trino* (Rome: Gregorian University Press, 1964), and *De Verbo Incarnato* (Rome: Gregorian University Press, 1965). These Latin works, along with English translations, will be included within the twenty-two volume edition of the *Collected Works of Bernard Lonergan*, which the University of Toronto Press has begun publishing.

55. Anthony Giddens, *The National State and Violence* (Berkeley: University of California Press, 1985); also his *The Consequences of Modernity* (Stanford:

Stanford University Press, 1990). There is also the extensive work of Michel Foucault on the modern equation of knowledge and dominative power.

56. Amos Funkenstein, *Theology and the Scientific Imagination from the Middle Ages to the Seventeenth Century* (Princeton: Princeton University Press, 1986). The author's scholarship on Aquinas is inadequate. See Michael Buckley, *At the Origins of Modern Atheism* (New Haven: Yale University Press, 1987).

57. Sir Isaac Newton, *Opera quae exstant Omnia* (Stuttgart-Bad Cannstatt: F. Frommann Verlag, 1964); also his *Theological Manuscripts*, selected and edited with intro. H. McLachlan (Liverpool: University Press, 1950). In a forthcoming study I shall attempt to show the inadequate interpretations of St. Augustine by such scholars as Peter Brown, Jaroslav Pelikan, and Paul Ricoeur.

58. Bernard Lonergan, "Dialectic of Authority," in his *A Third Collection*, 5. Lonergan's entire way of posing the dialectic of authority is fundamental, in my judgment, for a proper understanding of communicative praxis.

59. Johann Baptist Metz, "Productive Noncontemporaneity," in Jürgen Habermas, ed., *Observations on the Spiritual Situation of the Age* (Cambridge, Mass.: MIT Press, 1984), 169–77. For another perspective, see Terrence Tilly, *The Evils of Theodicy* (Washington, D.C.: Georgetown University Press, 1990).

60. For example, Paul Knitter, *No Other Name* (Maryknoll, N.Y.: Orbis Books, 1985). Knitter seeks to find an orientation agreeable to all religions. This, it seems to me, is an inductively impoverishing abstraction. Ecclesiocentrism is immediately abandoned, yet it is only in and through religious institutions that the long-term dialogue of world religions occurs.

61. Bernard Lonergan, "Dialectic of Authority" in *A Third Collection*, 5–12. Also Matthew Lamb, "The Notion of the Transcultural in Bernard Lonergan's Theology," *Method: A Journal of Lonergan Studies* 8, no. 1 (1990): 48–73.

62. Habermas, *The Philosophical Discourse of Modernity*, 14–15: "It is no longer only future generations, but past generations as well, that have a claim on the weak messianic power of the present. The anamnestic redemption of an injustice, which cannot of course be undone but can at least be virtually reconciled through remembering, ties up the present with the communicative context of a universal historical solidarity. This anamnesis constitutes the decentering counterpoise to the dangerous concentration of responsibility that modern time-consciousness, oriented exclusively toward the future, has laid on the shoulders of a problematic present that has, as it were, been tied in knots."

5

Critical Theory and Reconciliation

Fred Dallmayr

Turris fortissima nomen....

As I understand it, the term "practical theology" signals a complex interlacing of theology, or thought of the divine, and human praxis or practical engagement. Bypassing segregation and coincidence, such interlacing means that theology is not divorced from the world of practical and political concerns, just as human praxis does not shun its linkage with the divine (or the transcendent). Taken in this sense, the term itself points to the theme I have chosen: reconciliation, and more particularly the relation between critical theory and reconciliation. On the one hand, reconciliation plays a central role in Christian theology — and perhaps in all religious thought tracing its roots to the Scriptures. On the other hand, reconciliation is a prominent topic in some forms of Western philosophy and social-political thought. Not being a theologian, I shall limit myself to brief remarks in that field.

In the New Testament, reconciliation has chiefly two meanings — which, however, are closely connected: reconciliation between human beings and God (initiated through a divine act of redemption) and reconciliation between human beings and fellow human beings (on the basis of the same redemptive act). In both cases the assumption is that of an initial breach or enmity, which then requires a process of healing or mediation leading to restored friendship. As Paul writes in 2 Corinthians 5:19 regarding the humankind-God relationship: "In Christ God was reconciling the

119

world to himself, not counting their trespasses against them, and entrusting to us the message of reconciliation." To this he adds in the letter to the Romans (5:10): "If, while we were enemies, we were reconciled to God by the death of his Son, much more now that we are reconciled, shall we be saved by his life." Divine redemption at the same time furnishes the ground for a new fellowship among people formerly divided by enmity. Thus, Paul says in Ephesians 2:11: "Remember that at one time you Gentiles in the flesh ... were separated from Christ, alienated from the commonwealth of Israel.... But now you who once were far off have been brought near in the blood of Christ. For he is our peace, who has made us both one, and has broken down the dividing wall of hostility."[1]

In Western philosophy, reconciliation is not an uncommon theme, even outside the range of medieval philosophical theology. Traces of it can be found in Plato's notion of *eros*, in Aristotle's conception of *dynamis*, and in socialist utopias from Thomas More to Marx. In the modern context, however, the foremost philosophical advocate of the theme is Hegel with his focus on dialectical "mediations" and their consummation in the "absolute spirit." In an eloquent and captivating passage, Gadamer once portrayed Hegel as the philosopher of reconciliation par excellence — a description that meshes not accidentally with his status as "Christian" thinker. According to Gadamer, the basic experience triggering the entire labor of Hegel's system was the experience of division or enmity (*Entzweiung*). "As the starting point of Hegel's thought," he writes, "division entails as its corollary the reconciliation of division or, in his own terms, the 'reconciliation of corruption.' Thus, the task which Hegel pursues as a thinker is the reconciliation of all forms of divisiveness, accomplished in the medium of philosophical reflection." Gadamer illustrates his comments primarily by reference to the "phenomenology" of everyday experience — to the twists and turns of interpersonal relationships — reaching the basic conclusion that reconciliation is "the secret of Hegelian dialectics." Yet, he also recognizes that this dialectics is predicated on the premise of divine intervention or the redemptive power of the absolute. To this extent, he notes, Hegel's philosophy also seeks to embrace the "truth of Christianity" and thus to achieve a reconciliation of faith and reason.

The latter point has been corroborated by another leading Hegel scholar of our time, Michael Theunissen, particularly in his study entitled *Hegel's Doctrine of the Absolute Spirit as Theological-Political Treatise*. According to Theunissen, "mediation" is a vernacular term for reconciliation just as "absolute spirit" is a translation of the divine redemptive spirit made manifest in Christ's ministry. As he states: "God's concrete incarnation reveals the truth of the spirit, especially by highlighting the incommensurability of divine glory and human servitude." Operating in the same medium of the spirit, the goal of philosophy (for Hegel) was hence to represent conceptually "nothing else but the actual reconciliation effected by Christ in objective reality."[2]

My own focus here is not directly or centrally on Hegel's philosophy; but his impulses are bound to reverberate in the following discussion. Hegel's system has cast a long shadow, or rather a long light, on subsequent developments — an influence by no means exhausted. Immediately after his death, Hegel's legacy was appropriated by left- and right-Hegelian factions, and through the former it was bequeathed to Marx and his heirs. In this somewhat circuitous way, the legacy finally left its imprint on the Frankfurt School, and particularly on its founders, Horkheimer and Adorno. To be sure, in the course of its travels or peregrinations, Hegel's opus underwent changes or shifts of accent; foremost among these was the eclipse of the notion of a final synthesis accomplished on the level of absolute spirit — an eclipse inaugurated by the left-Hegelians and later seconded and intensified by most existentialist and neo-Marxist writers. Notwithstanding this change the Hegelian notion of reconciliation continued to play a powerful role in the work of the early Frankfurt School; only more recently has the notion come to share the apocryphal status of the absolute spirit. My presentation is going to proceed in three steps. First I want to show the centrality of reconciliation in "early" critical theory, by concentrating on selected writings of Horkheimer and Adorno (from *Eclipse of Reason* to *Negative Dialectics*). Next I want to turn to Habermas's reformulation of critical theory and to his progressively sharpened critique of his predecessors, a critique which in large part centers on their notion of reconciliation. Finally, I shall assess the successive phases of critical theorizing and conclude by vindicating an unorthodox (linguistically transformed) Hegelian conception of absoluteness and redemptive reconciliation.

RECONCILIATION IN EARLY CRITICAL THEORY

As a distinctive outlook or perspective, critical theory was first developed by Frankfurt theorists after the demise of the Weimar Republic during the initial years of their exile. As formulated by the school's founders the perspective was designed as an antidote to the dominant bourgeois mentality or social-theoretical paradigm of the time, which they designated as "traditional theory" — a synonym for positivism or positivist empiricism. From the vantage of positivism, reality (including nature and society) was an array of neutral facts or external data amenable to "objective" analysis by the scientist or human observer. Given the underlying subject-object dichotomy, reality could be transformed — and in fact was progressively transformed in modernity — into a target of technical control serving the supposed survival needs of subjects or the human species. Paralleling this transformation, reason as reflective insight was increasingly streamlined into a calculating or instrumental capacity geared toward enhanced mastery or power over nature. Anticipated in Bacon's equation of knowledge and power, the project of technical control reached its culmination in twentieth-century positivism and scientism — and finally revealed its dark or sinister side in fascism. Opposing the instrumentalism of positivist science, critical theory narrowed the subject-object gulf by marshalling some of the resources of dialectics — a dialectics construed largely along left-Hegelian lines with the accent on emancipatory social praxis.[3] Yet, almost from its inception, critical theorizing found itself challenged or contested by a steadily darkening global horizon. The outbreak of World War II and the intensification of technological imperatives cast doubt on the prospect of even modest dialectical mediations — without succeeding, to be sure, in canceling the founders' critical-oppositional stance. Both the gloom of the war years and the founders' desperately maintained hope found eloquent expression in a study written by Horkheimer in 1944 and subsequently published under the title *Eclipse of Reason.*

In line with early impulses of critical theory, Horkheimer's study focused again on the rise of modern scientism, and particularly on the triumphant reign of positivism or logical empiricism with its celebration of purely abstract-formal rationality (in contrast to substantive reasoning). This scientific ascendancy, in his view, was paralleled in the social domain by the structure of capitalist or market economy as a network of causal, quasi-objective relationships juxtaposed to the individual producer and consumer. On both levels, the consequence of modern developments was the radical split between subject and object, inside and outside, human beings and nature. "As the end result of the process," Horkheimer wrote, "we have on the one hand the Self, the abstract ego emptied of all substance except its attempt to transform everything in heaven and on earth into means for its preservation, and on the other hand an empty nature degraded to mere material, mere stuff to be dominated, without any other purpose than that of this very domination." Under the impact of these developments, reason itself has increasingly both formalized and instrumentalized — formalized through the expulsion of all substantive ends, and instrumentalized through the equation of purpose with mastery and control. Although seemingly holding the promise of greater latitude and emancipation, these changes actually were the harbingers of a new closure — by stunting the human capacity to appreciate the dimension of the noninstrumental (or nonpurposive). "The story of the boy," Horkheimer added, "who looked up at the sky and asked, 'Daddy, what is the moon supposed to advertise?' is an allegory of what has happened to the relation between man and nature in the era of formalized reason. On the one hand, nature has been stripped of all intrinsic value or meaning. On the other, man has been stripped of all aims except self-preservation; he tries to transform everything within reach into a means to that end."[4]

According to the study, modern (instrumental) rationality unleashed not a benign, but a destructive dialectic — domination of nature rebounded or boomeranged on the human subject or agent of control. "In the process of emancipation," we read, "the human being shares the fate of the rest of his world: domination of nature involves domination of man. Each subject not only has to take part in the subjugation of external nature (human and nonhuman), but in order to do so must subjugate nature in himself: thus domination becomes 'internalized' for domination's sake." Internalization of control is closely tied to the ascendancy of the abstract-rational ego or *cogito* with its tendency to repress internal instincts and the imaginative potential of the unconscious. Following the dictates of survival or self-preservation, the ego serves simultaneously the function of inner-psychic self-management and effective adaptation to external constraints in an increasingly rationalized and instrumentalized world. Apart from the effects of internal repression, ego-centered instrumentalism further rebounds on social relations by forcing them into a rigid structure of super- and subordination. In Horkheimer's words: "The history of man's efforts to subjugate nature is also the history of man's subjugation by man. The development of the concept of the ego reflects this twofold history." In its endeavor to triumph over external nature, over internal impulses, and over fellow-beings in society, the ego generally is perceived to embody the functions of "domination, command, and organization"; its characteristic gesture is the "out-stretched arm of the ruler, directing his men to march or dooming the culprit to execution." Social domination, in turn, is frequently camouflaged through internalization or sublimation — and sometimes through a combination of mastery and the (partial) release of instinctual frustrations (as in fascism).[5]

Regarding the prospect of healing or mediating modern divisions, *Eclipse of Reason* was circumspect and subdued. As Horkheimer insisted, subject-object or human-nature splits could by no means be overcome by collapsing the tension into one of the constitutive poles.

"The later development of rationalism and of subjective idealism," he noted, "tended increasingly to mediate the dualism by attempting to dissolve the concept of nature — and ultimately all the content of experience — into the ego, conceived as transcendental" — which was a solution by fiat rather than reflection. Under liberal-pragmatic auspices, the ego's role was expanded into a collective or anthropocentric enterprise geared toward the "ideas of progress, success or happiness" — without greatly improving matters. The reverse strategy consists in the suppression of reason in favor of a simplistic "return to nature" or else the revival of "old doctrines" and the creation of "new myths" — which is a recipe for primitivism if not barbarism. Just as modern dilemmas could not be resolved through one-sided contractions, they could not be dispelled in unitary visions or instant syntheses by-passing the labor of mediation. "The dualism of nature and spirit," Horkheimer stated, "can no more be denied in favor of their alleged original unity than the real historical trends reflected in this dualism can be reversed. To assert the unity of nature and spirit is to attempt to break out of the present situation by an impotent *coup de force*, instead of transcending it intellectually in conformity with the potentialities and tendencies inherent in it." In Horkheimer's view, the dilemmas brought about by modernity could not simply be undone, set aside, or magically wished away — because (as he said) "we are, for better or worse, the heirs of the Enlightenment and technological progress." To ignore the latter or to cancel them through recourse to crude formulas or to regress to more primitive stages was bound to aggravate rather than alleviate the "permanent crisis" of our age. Instead, without truncating one side nor "committing the fallacy of equating nature and reason," humankind was challenged "to reconcile the two" — which could only happen through radical reflection attentive to nature as its "seeming opposite."[6]

Reconciliation through genuine mediation thus was the proper remedy of modern divisions. According to the study, subject-object or humankind-nature rifts had as a corollary the conflict between "subjective" and "objective" modes of rationality — one tending to spontaneity and romanticism and the other to alienation and reification. "The task of philosophy," we read, "is not to play the one stubbornly against the other, but to foster a mutual critique and thus, if possible, to prepare in the intellectual realm the reconciliation of the two in reality." Hegel's philosophical system owed its "incomparable force" to his critical awareness of the pitfalls of one-sided perspectives. In Horkheimer's presentation, the rifts between subject and object, and spirit and nature, were both a "mere" appearance and a "necessary" appearance created by a dialectical momentum. To move beyond the level of appearances it was imperative to grasp both the "separateness" and the "interrelatedness" of the polar opposites, that is, to penetrate to their tensional correlation. Subjugation of nature, he stated, was bound to imply human subjugation and vice versa "so long as man does not understand his own reason and the basic process by which he has created and is maintaining the antagonism that is about to destroy him." Reason or spirit could be "more than nature" only by concretely realizing "its own 'naturalness,'" that is, its own "trend to domination, the same trend that paradoxically alienates it from nature." In this manner, reason could become "an instrument of reconciliation," and indeed "more than an instrument." The latter prospect was advanced if, instead of exerting control, reason allowed nature to mirror itself peacefully in reflective thought and language — differently phrased: if it recaptured some of the playful-mimetic (that is, nonpurposive or noninstrumental) impulses of childhood and precognitive existence. If, through reflective and linguistic sublimation, Horkheimer wrote, nature becomes able to "mirror itself in the realm of spirit," it thereby gains "a certain tranquillity by contemplating its own image" — a process which is "at the heart of all culture." In sum, channeling mimetic impulses into the "general medium of language" rather than regressive behavior means "that potentially destructive energies work for reconciliation."[7]

A similar perspective, sketched in even bolder, more dramatic strokes, emerges in a book composed roughly at the same time and published likewise in 1947: Horkheimer and Adorno's *Dialectic of Enlightenment*. Like Horkheimer's study, *Dialectic of Enlightenment* concentrates on modern conflicts and divisions, particularly on the growing gulf between subject and object, human beings and nature. Again, the rift is ascribed to an inner momentum of reason that cannot simply be reversed or canceled but that urgently demands mediation and reorientation. According to the authors, the advancement of knowledge and social progress inevitably involves a retreat or exodus from unreflective naturalism, that is, from primitive-natural forces and mythical constraints; however, precisely by exiting from and superimposing itself on nature, reason becomes an instrument of domination — thus entangling itself in reification and turning into a "second nature." Basically, the program of rational enlightenment — they write — was always "the disenchantment of the world, the dissolution of myths, and the substitution of knowledge for fancy." Yet, by equating itself with power and with the sway of causal-natural laws (fixed by science), reason was in a sense remythologized and redogmatized. Thus, enlightenment revealed its own darkness or dark underside, and progress its nexus with regress.

In the authors' words: "We are wholly convinced — and therein lies our *petitio principii* — that social freedom is inseparable from enlightened thought. Nevertheless, we believe just as clearly to have recognized that this very way of thinking — no less than the actual historical forms (the social institutions) with which it is interwoven — already contains the seed of the reversal universally apparent today. If enlightenment does not accommodate reflection on this regressive element, it seals its own fate."[8]

In terms of the study, the regressive counterpoint of enlightenment — its dialectical underside — results from the equation of knowledge and power, an equation that in turn reflects the growing division between human beings and nature. Ever since the time of Bacon, Horkheimer and Adorno note, the linkage of reason and science has shown a "patriarchal" face: by conquering superstition, mind or reason is meant to "hold sway over a disenchanted nature." In the course of modernity or modernization, this patriarchal legacy has led to a progressive widening of the Cartesian rift between *res cogitans* and *res extensa* — which coincides with the gulf between inside and outside, between logical form and substantive content. Increasingly, they write, "being divides into the *logos* (which with the advance of philosophy contracts to the monad, to an abstract point of reference), and into the mass of all things and creatures without. This single distinction between inner existence and external reality engulfs all others." On the subjective side, the *cogito* in modernity is stylized into a sovereign selfhood, a self-contained identity that ejects from itself as modes of reification, all forms of otherness; in large measure, modern emancipation has this connotation of self-recovery or self-possession. It is only through retreat into inwardness, we read, that human beings obtain "self-identity," a selfhood that cannot be "dissipated through identification with others" but "takes possession of itself once and for all as an impenetrable mask." Under the impact of this self-enclosure, disenchanted or disqualified nature turns into the "chaotic matter of abstract classification," while the sovereign self becomes addicted to "mere having or possession, to abstract identity." The upshot of this bifurcation is the radical subordination of matter to mind, that is, the domination of the rationally emancipated human being over nature. "Systematizing spirit or reason and the creator-God resemble each other as rulers of nature," the study observes. "Man's likeness to God consists in the sovereignty over the world, in the countenance of mastery, and in the ability to command." Modern science, in particular, considers objects only to the extent that they are "makeable," producible, and controllable: "In this metamorphosis the nature of things reveals itself as always the same: as target of domination."[9]

Reason or rationality in modernity shares the fate of the *cogito:* it is truncated into a self-contained logical formula through which means-ends relations can be deductively or inductively pinpointed. This tendency was first evident in the sequence of modern philosophical "systems"; later it became virulent in functional-sociological models seeking to grasp the totality of social life. In the authors' words: "From the start, enlightenment recognizes as being and occurrence only what can be apprehended in unity; its ideal is the system from which all and everything follows." The primary means for accomplishing unification — a means extolled especially by positivism and the "unified science" movement — is number, that is, the reduction of all qualitative differences to quantitative measurement. "Number," Horkheimer and Adorno note, "became the canon of enlightenment: the same equations govern bourgeois justice and commodity exchange." In exorcising qualitative differences, formal-quantitative reasoning also prepared the ground for the streamlining and homogenization of social life and thus for the establishment of various social controls and disciplines. While wedded to universal categories, formal rationality also promoted a hierarchy by defining "truth" as the rule of (universal) form over (particular) content, of rational knowledge over nonrational experience. This schema exacted a price: namely, the alienation of reason from the goal of genuine cognition. In exorcising "mimetic magic," we read, the rational ego also "tabooed the kind of knowledge which really reaches its object; its hatred extended to the image of the vanquished prehistory and its imaginary bliss." This tabooing (of the nonrational) was intensified in the same measure that the ego was internalized and transcendentalized: sensuality was exiled from the realm of reason. According to the judgment of enlightenment (as well as Protestantism), regress into "prehistory" is the lot of all who abandon themselves to life "without rational reference to self-preservation." From the vantage of reason, instinct is "as mythical as superstition," serving a God not postulated by the self "as irrational as drunkenness." For both prayer and submergence in naturalness, progress has prepared the same fate: "by anathematizing the self-oblivion of reason as well as that of pleasure."[10]

As in Horkheimer's work, exposing the "dialectic of enlightenment" is not meant here as a plea for primitivism. Some help in avoiding the twin pitfalls of regression and rational triumphalism can be found in Hegel's dialectics, and particularly in his notion of "determinate negation." With that notion, Horkheimer and Adorno assert, Hegel "revealed an element that separates the Enlightenment from the positivist decay with which he lumps it together." Yet, this endorsement is qualified. They add that, by ultimately "absolutizing" the outcome of negation (his system and historical totality), Hegel himself "contravened the prohibition (of images) and lapsed into mythology." As a result, the authors recommend a more subdued, post-Hegelian dialectics — but one clearly geared toward the healing of modern divisions. Again, hope cannot and must not be pinned on instant solutions or magical reunions of opposites. "All mystical unification is deception, the impotent-inward trace of a missed radical renewal." Only through relentless reflection — mindful of its complicity with power — can thought break the spell of reification. Precisely by forestalling any "hypostatization of utopia" and by unfailingly exposing domination as division, the rupture between subject and object — which thought does not allow to be obscured — becomes simultaneously "the index of its own untruth and of the truth." At this point, enlightenment is more than enlightenment: namely, "nature which becomes perceptible in its alienation" (or otherness). In the self-cognition of reason as predicated on division, nature begins to be reconciled with spirit and with itself. By curtailing itself and acknowledging its natural premises, reason "abandons the claim to dominion that precisely subjects it to nature." Thus, healing of divisions is at least initiated (if not completed) through radical "self-reflection of thought" pushing beyond instrumentalism; phrased differently, through a "recollection of nature in the rational subject" — a remembrance that holds the hidden key to the "truth of all culture." As the authors conclude, enlightenment fulfills and "sublates" itself when the means-ends nexus is suspended — at the point where the "nearest practical ends" reveal themselves as the "most distant goal" and where repressed nature is remembered as the "land of origin" as well as the portent of hope.[11]

Qualified endorsement of Hegelian dialectics is the hallmark also of Adorno's later writings, particularly his postwar essays on Hegel and his *Negative Dialectics*. "Qualified" here means acceptance of healing mediations *minus* resort to the "absolute" or to any comprehensive synthesis (especially synthesis presumed to be operative in reality). This ambivalence is clearly evident in the essay on Hegel's notion of "experience" or "experiential content" (of 1958). Adorno observes there: "Hegel's thought — more than that of any previous philosopher — suffered from the alienation between subject and object, between consciousness and reality." Yet, instead of regressing backward or retreating into immediacy, Hegel trusted in the healing power of mediations: in the ability of rationality to reflect upon itself and to discover the "wounds of unreason" in its own dominion. The chief means of mediation — the inner "nerve of the dialectic" — is again located in "determinate negation," in the sustained engagement and labor of thought with concrete conditions. However, while applauding these and related aspects of Hegelian dialectics, Adorno distances himself from its "idealism," from its tendency to soar into a realm of absoluteness where real conflicts or divisions are already synthesized or reconciled (though only in thought). Opposing this escapism, Adorno underscores the conflictual, torn, and fragmented character of real-life experience. "The history of this unreconciled age," he writes, "cannot be one of harmonious development: the latter is only the figment of an ideology which ignores historical antagonisms. Conflicts and contradictions — its only true ontology — are the governing law of history which only proceeds antagonistically and through untold suffering" — as Hegel himself recognized when he called history a "slaughter bench." Once this grim reality is bypassed, idealism turns into an ideological legitimation of prevailing conditions; even determinate negation at this point is placed into "the service of an apologetic function, the justification of existing reality."[12]

Adorno's chief reservation in the essay concerns the presumed "rationality of the real" (as asserted in the Preface to Hegel's *Phenomenology*). "Such a philosophy," Adorno complains, "marches with the stronger battalions," treading under its heels alternative possibilities and utopian hopes. At this point the truth of Hegelian dialectics turns into its "untruth" — an untruth rightly denounced by left-Hegelian critics. By postulating a merely abstract-theoretical reconciliation, Hegel is said to have shortchanged real-life opportunities and political tasks. A philosophy, we read, which dissolves everything "into spirit" and celebrates "the identity of subject and object on a grand scale," is bound to become quietistic and to serve as alibi for prevalent modes of domination. Particularly in the higher reaches of Hegel's system, the difference between "contingency and absoluteness" is cancelled (through subsumption of the former under the latter) — in a manner violating real-life experience. Adorno's essay provides a strict counterpoint. Reality, he affirms, is definitely "not rationality or the rational" but its reverse. Above all, the "division between subject and object" cannot be overcome through mere theory — as long as the conflict persists in reality. In effect, he claims, the grand synthesis Hegel envisaged is nothing but a replica of the existing social totality with its built-in domination and coerced conformism: "The subject-object identity to which his philosophy ascends is not a system of reconciled absolute spirit but a synonym for the real world experienced as system. Absolute spirit is the name for the relentless unification of all parts and particular moments of bourgeois society into a totality under the auspices of the exchange principle." Countering Hegel's conception of absolute truth, Adorno's essay culminates in the thesis that "totality or the whole is untruth." Hegel absolutizes domination. Only with a view toward the future can the truth of the whole be recovered — but as redemptive task: "The ray of light revealing the whole in all its parts as untrue is none other than the ray of utopia — the utopia of a whole truth still to be accomplished."[13]

On a broader scale and with more subtlety, a similar perspective is outlined in the *magnum opus* of Adorno's later life: his *Negative Dialectics* (1966). Its "negative" character here means that dialectics confines itself to the (determinate) negation of existing ills and divisions while foregoing the imagination and portrayal of a completely reconciled condition. As before, the thrust of this outlook — while accepting the task of mediation — is directed against Hegel's "absolutism," against his presumed identification of subject and object on an abstract-speculative level. Adorno observes that although Hegel recognized nonconceptual otherness, his system "pre-thinks" or conceptually prearranges every concrete particularity; thus, objects and phenomena are streamlined and integrated into a grand synthesis or harmonious order — which is the order of pure thought. Despite protestations to the contrary, phenomena ultimately congeal into "exemplars of concepts"; notwithstanding the proclaimed need of objectification, thought remains contained in its own domain, endlessly rehearsing its own categories. In Adorno's view, the only way to rupture this self-enclosure is through thought's attentiveness to nonthought or reason's turn toward the "nonidentical" — which precludes a premature synthesis. In his words: "If thought really yielded to its object, if it focused on the thing rather than its categories, then things themselves would turn articulate under its lingering glance." In this manner, thinking would regain (in Hegel's own terms) its "freedom to the object" — a freedom lost under the spell of the subject's "meaning-giving autonomy." Basically, philosophy's genuine concern in our time, he adds, is with those matters in which Hegel, at one with the tradition, expressed his disinterest: namely, "nonconceptuality, singularity, and particularity" — things which ever since Plato have been dismissed as "transitory and insignificant." Philosophy's theme thus consists of "those qualities it downgrades as contingent, as a *qualité negligeable*."[14]

According to Adorno, the corrective to Hegel's speculation is the rigorous and persistent reliance on the notion of (determinate) negation. Only negation is able to break through the enclosure of thought and the reification of objects. This fact lends preeminence to "negative" dialectics over its idealistic variant. "To change the direction of conceptuality, to turn it toward non-identity," we read, "is the hinge of negative dialectics. Insight into the constitutive character of the nonconceptual in the concept would end the compulsive identification which the concept entails unless halted by such reflection." Confined within the domain of thought, traditional idealism offered a truncated dialectics ultimately unable to overcome modern divisions. In its idealist version, dialectics was tied to the "sovereign subject" as source of conceptualizations. However, this primacy of the subject is now "historically obsolete," even in its Hegelian guise; none of the reconciliations proffered by absolute idealism were "tenable" or stood the test of time. Only a negative dialectics holds out promise under present circumstances; by being attentive to the otherness (or other side) of thought it undermines ingrained divisions — without granting access to instant conceptual synthesis. In Adorno's words: Being mindful of the "breach between subject and object" and its traces or furrows in all experience, such dialectics "in the end turns its face toward reconciliation — one which would release the non-identical, ridding it even of mental coercion, and thus would open the road to the multiplicity of differences." In this sense, reconciliation would be "recollection of the manifold seen as no longer hostile — something which is anathema to subjective reason." Dialectics, properly understood, is "in the service of such reconciliation."[15]

In ridding itself of its idealist legacy, dialectics also extricates itself more thoroughly from the nexus of domination, in regard to both nature and society. In terms of the study, idealism, by privileging subjectivity, merely "spiritualized" the Darwinian struggle for survival, thus reinstating a repressive naturalism. By proclaiming itself the Baconian master and even idealist creator of all things, the epistemological-metaphysical subject participates and entangles itself in this nexus: "In exerting mastery it becomes part of what it believes to master, succumbing like the lord" (in Hegel's master-slave relationship). In relinquishing subjectivity and identifying rationality, negative dialectics softens and heals the enmity between thought and reality, human beings and nature. Dialectical thinking, Adorno writes, "respects that which is to be thought — the object or subject matter — even where the latter does not heed the rules of logic." Instead of being narrowly confined by its own rules, thinking is able "to think against itself without self-cancellation. If dialectics allowed definition, this would be one worth suggesting." Thus, in making reality its target, thinking does not solely obey a modified Darwinism; although doing violence to things through its synthetic constructs, reason also is able to "heed a potential slumbering in things," thereby "making amends" to them for its own acts. Differently phrased: "irreconcilable reasoning is matched by the hope for reconciliation" — a hope predicated on the fact that the resistance of thought to mere thingness intends in objects even that which eludes reification. This elusive element is the domain of otherness or difference — a domain captured in Eichendorff's phrase of "beautiful strangeness" (*schöne Fremde*). As Adorno states: "The reconciled condition would not annex the alien through an act of philosophical imperialism; instead, its happiness would consist in allowing it to remain distant and different even in proximate surroundings, beyond the pale of heterogeneity and sameness."[16]

HABERMAS'S CRITIQUE AND REFORMULATION

The preceding discussion, I believe, revealed new and captivating vistas — but probably also some dilemmas besetting "early" critical theory. While correcting speculative hyperbole, the turn to negation undoubtedly exacted a price. For if the "whole" is entirely untrue and beyond the pale of redemption, how can even parts be reconciled or redeemed — without resort to a *creatio ex nihilo* (which further aggravates instrumentalism or the plight of willful fabrication)? How, in other words, can thought recover the potential slumbering in nature if the latter is hopelessly corrupt? Moreover, who could serve as agent of transformative healing — given the general nexus of perversion? These and other *aporias* — to which I shall return later — do not detract, in my view, from the authors' basic effort: their undaunted plea for an emphatic type of reconciliation, construed in unorthodox Hegelian terms. By comparison, Habermas's work has always been more circumspect and subdued, more intent on mapping out knowable terrain than on exploring *terra incognita*. Regarding Hegel's legacy, Habermas shares with Horkheimer and Adorno — and with left-Hegelians in general — aversion to absolutes (especially the "absolute spirit") and sympathy with the pervasive shift from speculation to human praxis or pragmatics. Going beyond his predecessors, however, he also casts doubt on the prospect of comprehensive "reconciliation" (in Hegel's sense) — preferring to reduce it to more limited or manageable proportions, chiefly under the heading of intersubjective "communication." The latter change is accompanied by dramatically upgrading the function of reason or rationality, that is, by deemphasizing the "*dialectic* of enlightenment" in favor of a restored (though linguistically reformulated) Enlightenment rationalism. Habermas's opus as a whole is a precarious blend of praxis orientation and quasi-Kantian rationalism — with the latter ingredient tending to ascend and prevail over the former (without cancelling a broadly pragmatic framework). A few examples must suffice to illustrate this point.

One of Habermas's earliest writings that attracted wide attention was a critique of Marxist "philosophy," that is, of dialectical theorizing, from the vantage of a left-Hegelian praxis focus. Remnants of this outlook were still present — though mixed with rationalist features — in his first major work, published shortly before Adorno's death, *Knowledge and Human Interests* (1968). While the linkage of knowledge and interests postulated in this work was an attack on positivist and other modes of detached theorizing, the concern with epistemology or knowledge theory concurred uneasily (if at all) with left-Hegelian or pragmatic premises. In fact, Kant was singled out in the study as the last great practitioner of modern epistemology — a form of cognitive reflection that fell on bad days already with Hegel's turn to the absolute and Marx's privileging of labor (until it finally collapsed under the weight of positivism). In a loose variation on Kant's three Critiques, *Knowledge and Human Interests* differentiated three basic types of knowledge or cognitive inquiry — science, hermeneutics, and reflective critique — which in turn were correlated with interests in technical control, in practical understanding, and emancipation. Soon after publication of this study, the ascendancy of rationalism began. In several "postscripts" or epilogues to his earlier writings, Habermas introduced a sharp distinction or dichotomy between rigorous knowledge and pragmatic interests, or between the ordinary lifeworld and the domain of "discourses" wedded to rational validity claims. In the field of emancipatory critique, he similarly bifurcated "rational reconstruction" (a theoretical enterprise) and therapeutic experience. The primary focus of Habermas's subsequent work has been on discourses — which are rationally disciplined forms of communication — and on the rational reconstruction of various types of "competences" (cognitive, moral, communicative). Discourse analysis has led to the formulation of a discursive theory of knowledge as well as a "discourse ethics," tied respectively to the standards of "truth" and "rightness." Apart from probing cognitive and moral development, reconstructive inquiry has yielded a theory of "universal pragmatics" and a framework of "communicative action" and rationality (to mention only the most prominent titles of recent investigations).[17]

It is precisely in the fields of universal pragmatics and communicative interaction that the redemptive quality of contemporary critical theory is said to emerge. Basically, universal pragmatics seeks to pinpoint the general preconditions or "capabilities" required to undergird rational communication or discourse as such. In Habermas's presentation, rational communication implies or is premised on four general validity claims: the claims to truth, rightness, truthfulness, and comprehensibility. While truth claims govern the denotative or referential aspects of speech, that is, statements referring to "external nature" (or the external world), rightness claims apply to intersubjective relations, that is, to the normatively regulated domain of "society" (or the social world). Claims to truthfulness — not discursively redeemable — point to the speaker's "internal nature" (or inner world), while comprehensibility involves the transparency of the chosen medium of communication. Thus, universal pragmatics shows human speech to have a network of relationships: to outer and inner nature, to society, and to language itself. In Habermas's words, the model is that of "a communication in which grammatical sentences are embedded, by way of universal validity claims, in three relations to reality, thereby assuming the corresponding pragmatic functions of representing facts, establishing legitimate interpersonal relations, and expressing one's own subjectivity." Language itself in the model is conceived as "the medium of interrelating three worlds." The model was fleshed out in *The Theory of Communicative Action* into a general philosophical and sociological framework. In that study, communicative action is differentiated from a variety of more subject-centered and purposive activities, including "teleological" and "dramaturgical" actions. Communicative rationality in turn is rigorously demarcated from the sphere of "cognitive-instrumental rationality," that is, a calculative reasoning dedicated to the expansion of technical control. If at all, antidotes to divisiveness can only be found in the communicative domain. "This concept of communicative rationality," Habermas writes, "carries with it connotations based ultimately on the central experience of the unconstrained, unifying, consensus-producing force of argumentative speech — a speech in which different participants overcome their merely subjective views and, owing to the mutuality of rationally motivated convictions, assure themselves of both the unity of the objective world and the intersubjectivity of their life-context."[18]

The theory of communicative rationality also serves as launching pad for an attack — carried out with growing intensity — on the older Frankfurt School and its notion of reconciliation. According to Habermas, traditional philosophy — including "early" critical theory — was basically a monological enterprise, that is, one rooted in the category of "subjectivity" or subjective "consciousness"; drawing on Wittgenstein and other analytical thinkers, his own perspective promises a "paradigm shift" from consciousness to language and thereby a settlement of previously unresolved (and irresoluble) dilemmas. *The Theory of Communicative Action* initially sketches the background and motivations of the older Frankfurt School, before proceeding to a critical assessment. In Habermas's presentation, the concept of "instrumental reason" — the school's central focus — involved in essence a radicalization of Lukács's notion of "reification," a radicalization that expanded the latter notion from the domain of commodity exchanges to the broad range of cognitive rationality and progressive historical rationalization. From the perspective of Horkheimer and Adorno, all conceptual reasoning — including idealist dialectics — is bent on identifying and truncating otherness, thereby betraying "the utopian goal of cognition." Rationalization accordingly appears as an encompassing process — leading to the thesis of the "untruth" of the whole. The pacemaker of this total streamlining of the world is the cognitive ego or subject, a subject wedded entirely to the goal of self-preservation and using this as a warrant for unlimited domination — whose effects, however, prove to be self-destructive. In Habermas's words, "Horkheimer and Adorno understand 'control of nature' not merely as a metaphor; the label of 'mastery' or 'domination' serves as the common denominator for the control of external nature, the command over human beings, and the repression of one's own internal nature." In this manner, construed as conceptual-identifying thought, the concept of instrumental reason is meant to disclose the mechanism or "logic" governing the mastery of nature and human beings alike. According to the immanent dialectic of this logic, "victories over outer nature are paid for with defeats of inner nature," as well as defeats of (less rational) social groups. The dialectic of enlightenment and rationalization ultimately derives from "the structure of a reason that is instrumentalized for the sake of self-preservation" — an instrumentalization that marks every progress or advance simultaneously as a regress.[19]

As Habermas notes, this somber scenario offers a ray of hope — a ray cast basically by the notion of reconciliation. "This philosophy of history," he writes (with special reference to the "dialectic of enlightenment"), "yields a catastrophic view of the relation between spirit and nature, a relation distorted beyond recognition. Yet, we can speak of distortion only insofar as the original relation of spirit and nature is secretly conceived in such a way that the idea of truth is linked with that of a universal reconciliation — where reconciliation includes the interaction of humans with nature, with animals, plants, and minerals." In this notion of reconciliation, Habermas discovers first of all a tension with the Hegelian legacy: for Horkheimer and Adorno clearly distance their view from a grand conceptual or metaphysical synthesis (achieved on the level of objective or absolute spirit). As he states: "The dialectical reconciliation of the universal and the particular remains, in Hegel's own terms, metaphysical, because it does not give its due to the 'non-identical' dimension in the particular." In clinging to the notion of reconciliation, Horkheimer and Adorno thus both embrace and simultaneously bracket the idealist legacy of philosophy: the latter by rejecting synthesizing worldviews and the former by keeping alive the prospect of a philosophical overcoming of divisions in a new guise. Their work, we read, was paradoxically motivated by a dual conviction: on the one hand, the conviction "that 'great' philosophy (culminating and terminating in Hegel) could no longer of itself develop and systematically ground the idea of reason, the idea of a universal reconciliation of spirit and nature — because this idea had perished with metaphysical-religious worldviews"; on the other hand, the belief that philosophy — whose moment of realization (in Marx's sense) had passed — "nevertheless constitutes the only available memorial to the promise of a humane social life," that under its ruins (so to speak) lay buried "the truth from which thought could draw its negating, counter-reifying power." Given these two convictions or assumptions, the problem was how to correlate or harmonize their evident conflict or contradiction — a task Horkheimer and Adorno failed to accomplish, and inevitably so due to their underlying premises. For, Habermas asks, "how can the idea of reconciliation, in whose light alone Adorno is able to expose the shortcomings of idealist dialectics, still be explicated — if negative dialectics offers itself as the only (but discursively inaccessible) path of retrieval?"[20]

According to Habermas, the only hint or clue provided by Horkheimer and Adorno regarding the character of noninstrumental thought is the notion of "mimesis"; yet, under the spell of traditional philosophy with its implicit conceptualism, the notion cannot be coherently stated or developed — but only opaquely invoked like a quasi-natural (and nonrational) power. "As place holder for that primordial reason (which later was diverted from truth), Horkheimer and Adorno specify a capacity, *mimesis* — about which they can speak only as they would about a piece of unintelligible nature: they characterize the mimetic capacity, in which instrumentalized nature remonstrates silently against its plight, as an 'impulse.'" At this point, the dilemma of early critical theory comes starkly into view: the divisions produced by thought or reason are to be healed by something beyond the range of thought. In terms of that perspective itself, domination is to be recognized as "unreconciled nature even within thought." However, Habermas asks, even if thought were capable of such an idea of reconciliation, "how could it transform mimetic impulses into insights, discursively in its own element and not merely intuitively in speechless 'recollection'" — given that "thought is always identifying thought, tied to operations devoid of specifiable meaning outside the bounds of instrumental reason?" The paradox of early critical theory consequently rests in its nontheorizable claim: in the fact that Horkheimer and Adorno "would have to put forward a *theory* of mimesis, which in their own terms is impossible."

This impasse was not and could not be overcome in their work. Thus, instead of explicating "universal reconciliation" — as Hegel had done — as the "unity of identity and non-identity of spirit and nature," they are content to let the notion stand "as a cipher, almost in the manner of *Lebensphilosophie.*" This is particularly evident in Adorno's writings. More consistently still than Horkheimer, Adorno in the end no longer "wanted to show a way out of this *aporia.*" His *Negative Dialectics* was both an "attempt to circumscribe what cannot be said discursively" and a "warning against seeking refuge in Hegel at this point." Basically, the book was a mental "exercise": by reflecting once more on dialectics, it demonstrates what otherwise remains clouded, namely, "the aporetic status of the concept of non-identity." In this manner, Adorno cancelled every "theoretical claim."[21]

Moving beyond the critique of his predecessors, Habermas delineates his alternative solution — an alternative designed to rescue critical theory from its self-abandonment as "theory." In pondering the paradoxes and *aporias* of the older Frankfurt School, he says, we come to appreciate the reasons and need for a "paradigm shift" in contemporary social theorizing. Ultimately, he attributes the *aporias* of the older generation to its failure to make this shift and thus to gain access to new resources. "I want to maintain," Habermas writes, "that the program of early critical theory foundered not on this or that contingent circumstance, but from the exhaustion of the paradigm of the philosophy of consciousness. I shall argue that a change of paradigm to communication theory makes possible the return to the enterprise that was *disrupted* by the critique of instrumental reason, thus allowing the recovery of the *since-neglected* tasks of critical social theory." The paradigm change actually occurs on two levels: that of concrete action theory — where it involves a shift from purposive or "goal-directed" to "communicative" action — and that of cognitive thought or rationality; given the context of modern rationalization, the accent falls squarely on the latter. "What needs to be explicated today," we read, "is no longer cognition and the *mastery* of objectified nature as such but rather the intersubjectivity of possible consensual *agreement* (*Verständigung*) — at both the interpersonal and intrapsychic levels"; the focus of investigation thereby shifts "from cognitive-instrumental to *communicative rationality.*" In Habermas's view, the shift was initiated in the notion of mimesis — but was foiled by its intrinsic *aporias*. The "rational core" of the notion, he insists, can be recovered only once we abandon the paradigm of the "philosophy of consciousness" — based on subjects representing and producing objects — in favor of the paradigm of "language philosophy" centered on intersubjective understanding and communication, thereby "subordinating the instrumental-rational aspect to a more comprehensive *communicative rationality*." This change also permits a rational grasp of the issue of reconciliation. In some (isolated) passages, Adorno actually linked the issue with that of an "undamaged intersubjectivity"; but the latter can only be established and maintained "through the reciprocity of consensual *agreement* based on free mutual recognition."[22]

ABSOLUTENESS AND REDEMPTIVE RECONCILIATION

It seems to me the dispute among spokespersons of critical theory is not minor or marginal but touches the heart of the school's enterprise. If the somber scenario sketched by Horkheimer and Adorno is correct, then critical theory is enmeshed in a "crisis" of culture, indeed in a real crisis whose resolution can only dimly be gleaned and only partially be advanced through purposive-human means. On the other hand, if Habermas's version is accepted, then critical theory is part of the ongoing, critical self-correction of rational inquiry and culture — a self-correction routinely performed by scientific communities wedded to the principle of fallibilism and evidently required for cognitive and societal progress. The only question remaining in this case is what (if any) relation this principle of fallibilism has to the issue of reconciliation as formulated by Hegel and later by the early Frankfurt School. In my view, a major strength and attraction of that first generation resided in its resolute attachment to this question, notwithstanding the difficulties of its articulation. As previously indicated, this articulation can be questioned and faulted in many ways — a point I want to take up now. The central problem, as I see it, consists in the totalization of the "nexus of corruption," a feature which is closely linked with, and actually a corollary of, the expulsion of absolutes (chiefly Hegel's absolute spirit). On this score, the earlier Frankfurt School is actually more consistent than Habermas who, while also expelling absolutes, still maintains the possibility of harmonious development and social progress. Perhaps a brief glance back at Hegel may be helpful.

In Hegel's system, the absolute spirit designates that point where all human strivings, all forms of willfulness and subjective intentionality come to rest; after having undergone multiple kinds of alienation, having struggled along the "highway of despair" and suffered the "reversal of consciousness," human spirit in the end blends with the absolute spirit — which Theunissen quite correctly treats as a synonym for God (specifically the God of Christianity). It is this absolute alone — which as the end is simultaneously a perpetual beginning — that for Hegel heals and overcomes divisions and furnishes a warrant for reconciliation. Once this warrant is cancelled or removed, the world necessarily sinks into divisiveness and darkness, into a totalized nexus of corruption where aggression and willful caprice relentlessly perpetuate themselves in a web of domination. This, in large part, is indeed Horkheimer's and Adorno's scenario — at least on its most manifest, rhetorical level. Hence the dilemmas and *aporias* noted by Habermas and many other readers — which can easily be sharpened under the rubric of instrumental reason. If the world is totally corrupt and perverse, then this world must be destroyed and replaced by a completely new one through some kind of *creatio ex nihilo;* moreover, given the removal of absolutes, such creation can only be the work of human agents or producers. In this manner, reconciliation and redemption become the target of goal-directed activity, that is, of purposive fabrication, thereby blending imperceptibly into what William Connolly has called the "civilization of productivity." At the same time, being themselves part of the corrupt world, human agents can only perpetuate or re-create the state of corruption; thus, instrumentalism becomes inescapable and self-destructive.[23]

As it happens, Horkheimer's and Adorno's scenario is not one-dimensional in this sense, but contains another, more recessed level, precisely the level on which reconciliation becomes pertinent. As Habermas correctly observes, their work at this point secretly pays tribute to Hegel's legacy — although they do so in a new guise and a radically revised vocabulary. This change is subtle and multi-dimensional. In my view, the departure from Hegel is not solely due to left-Hegelian influences, that is, to the postulated move from theory to praxis (which remains entirely external to Hegel's notion of spirit). Although this may be part of the story,[24] there is also — I believe — a deeper and more cogent motivation: namely, the realization that the absolute in our time can no longer be couched in terms of a self-transparent "subjectivity" or a univocal "reason" or *Vernunft*. Horkheimer's and (especially) Adorno's writings give evidence of ceaseless experimentation, of persistent efforts to recapture or reformulate the defunct and yet not completely exhausted or disposable legacy. Some of the terms used in this search are "mimesis," "remembrance of nature in the subject," and "thought thinking beyond itself." No doubt, some of these terms are enigmatic — given the stark background of instrumentalism and the subject-object bifurcation. However, I do not agree with Habermas's charge of inarticulateness: while providing less than a clear road map (a strange demand in this case), early critical theory surely did more than simply let these terms "stand like a cipher." Mimesis is a case in point. In none of the reviewed writings is the term a synonym for a regressive naturalism or a lapse into natural impulses; instead, it denotes a reflective sublimation or "sublation" of nature in thought. As we read in *Negative Dialectics:* "To represent the cause of what it repressed — that of mimesis — conceptuality has no other way than to adopt something mimetic in its conduct, *without* abandoning itself." In this adoption or receptivity, philosophical thought is akin to aesthetics or the "aesthetic moment." Yet, Adorno adds, the affinity of philosophy and art does not simply support their confusion. The task of philosophy is rather "to sublate the aesthetic into real thought or thought of the real; the latter and play are its two poles."[25]

The last phrase prompts a few additional comments on mimesis. In Horkheimer and Adorno's usage, the term designates initially a childlike playfulness and delight in imitation — before conduct is disciplined by the rigors of adulthood and rational thought. In this sense, mimesis cannot permanently be maintained without regression. However, in the view of early critical theory, adulthood and reason cannot simply cancel or eliminate playfulness — without becoming instruments of repression and domination (of inner and outer nature). This seems to me persuasive and entirely compatible with reflective insight. The stark antipode of instrumentalism (or instrumental reason) is a conduct and mode of thought which is nonpurposive, non-goal-directed, not purposely intentional — which is precisely the domain of play or playfulness. With this notion of play, Horkheimer and Adorno recover a good deal of the spirit (if not the letter) of Hegel's legacy; while expelling the absolute on the level of "idea," they recover it on a different, quasi-sensual or quasi-material level — and quite necessarily so. One might say (and I would in fact claim) that instrumentalism can only be overcome by some such move, differently put: that without "absoluteness" in some guise instrumentalism is inescapable. To be sure, "absolute" at this point does not mean being removed or aloof, but rather being entangled in and permeating everything (which does not equal immanentism).[26] This entanglement, moreover, has a temporal dimension, by linking past and future, beginning and end. This is the good sense of the notion of a recollection or "remembrance of nature in the subject." For, without remembrance of this sort, reconciliation or redemption readily slide into the mold of purposive fabrication. In some fashion, reconciliation must already have happened and be happening continuously so as to elude the culture of productivity. In this case, however, we (human agents) are at best partners in and not producers of reconciliation.

This point can serve as transition to Habermas's perspective. As indicated, communicative action and rationality are offered as remedy or solution for the problem of divisiveness. However, there are ample reasons for doubting the viability of this remedy. In fact, it might be said that the "solution" only succeeds by dissolving the issue of reconciliation or by putting it out of reach. This aspect can be elucidated in several ways. First, it is clear that communication is restricted to the intersubjective domain (the so-called social world) and not meant to extend to the domain of nature. Ever since *Knowledge and Human Interests*, Habermas has stipulated a sharp distinction between understanding and empirical science, consistently maintaining (against Marcuse and others) that the only cognitively "promising" way of dealing with external nature is that of technology or technical control. This acceptance of control, however, cannot readily be confined or isolated from other domains; it certainly is not as such mitigated by communicative rationality. It is not only conceivable but current practice that human society collectively (at least in its large majority) concurs that exploitation of nature is in the common interest and required for further progress; even restrictions of control are advocated basically for the sake of long-range survival. This communicatively established or sanctioned control, however, reverberates beyond its initial target — first of all into the sphere of inner or "internal nature"; for, as we know at least since Freud, societal progress and rationalization are inevitably purchased at the price of instinctual repression. From there — and this was one of the main insights of the earlier Frankfurt School — the road is not far to social and political domination. For advances in rationalization and modernity necessarily divide more rational and less rational groups, the more modernized and "developed" and the less modernized or "underdeveloped." As Connolly observes soberly: "Modernity does not appear, in either its capitalist or its socialist form, to be a universalizable form of life. These civilizations of productivity depend upon the continued existence of areas with 'undeveloped' economies and ecologies." Thus, Hegel's judgment of the Greek world is repeated on a new plane: "It 'creates for itself in what it suppresses and which is at the same time essential to it, an internal enemy' — a third world."[27]

In large measure, the contagion of control can be traced to the dubious character of the proclaimed "paradigm shift": the shift from consciousness or subjectivity to language. Although reiterated emphatically, the change is actually disavowed at crucial junctures of Habermas's argument. Thus, the difference between "communicative" and "teleological" action is basically a difference of performative attitude or goal orientation, with action being directed in one case to efficiency of control and in the other toward understanding. As Habermas admits, every action is at its core teleological, that is, governed by purposive intentionality and goal-direction.[28] The same can be said about the distinction between "instrumental-cognitive" and "communicative" rationality. However, intentionality and goal-directedness can only be the attributes of agents or subjects — which shows the continued role of subject-philosophy (or the paradigm of consciousness). The same paradigmatic continuity is also evident in the theory of universal pragmatics. The four dimensions (of validity) listed above are clearly centered or positioned around the subject construed as speaker or performer of speech-acts. As Habermas himself writes, universal pragmatics involves "fundamental demarcations." According to this scheme, "the subject demarcates himself (1) from an environment that he objectifies in the third-person attitude of an observer; (2) from an environment that he conforms to or deviates from in the ego-alter attitude of a participant; (3) from his own (inner) subjectivity that he expresses or conceals in a first-person attitude; and finally (4) from the medium of language itself." The labels chosen to designate these four dimensions are "external nature, society, internal nature, and language." Not surprisingly, the continued invocation of subject-philosophy gives rise to various splits or divisions (other terms for "demarcations") — between human beings and nature, ego and alter, ego and id — which in turn promote various modes of mastery and control. Again, Habermas himself serves as witness to this fact. "A general theory of speech acts," he states, "would thus describe exactly that fundamental system of rules that adult subjects have to master so as to fulfill the conditions for the successful employment of sentences in utterances."[29]

Paradigmatic continuity is particularly evident in the field of language, seen as a "medium" of communication. Treated as a system of rules mastered by speakers or speaking agents, language appears as a pliant tool readily amenable to cognitive theorizing and propositional (or quasi-propositional) statements. In contrast with willful designs, communicative action and rationality are said to yield a transparent consensus couched in univocal terms or identical meanings — a notion presupposing a streamlined language stripped of intrinsic ambiguity. Thus, to the extent there is a "linguistic turn," it is at best a partial or half-hearted shift: one accentuating communication while bypassing the inner complexity of the field — what Hamann and others have called the "abyss" of language. In this respect, the earlier Frankfurt School has actually made a more resolute move toward language and away from traditional subject-philosophy. As Horkheimer observed already in *Eclipse of Reason*, "Philosophy must become more sensitive to the silent testimonies of language and plumb the layers of experience preserved in it." In this endeavor, philosophy could not simply trust streamlined concepts tailored to the principles of identity; neither philosophy nor language, he said, can be reduced to a "formula." Instead, without shunning concepts, thinking has to recover and sublate in language the traces and marks of experience: "Philosophy is at one with art in reflecting suffering through language and thus transferring it to the sphere of experience and memory." In his *Negative Dialectics*, Adorno links this memory of suffering with the dimension of "naming" or "names," that is, with the metaphorical and rhetorical character of (ordinary) language through which it inheres in the concrete world. "What remains to be thought instead," he writes, turning against traditional epistemology, "has linguistically its distant and vague archetype in the names which do not preempt their target through categories." Language, he continues, is not simply a sign system designed to serve "epistemic functions"; going beyond abstract categorial definitions it rather seeks to release or rescue "non-identity" from the "spell of its exile." For this end, philosophy enlists the resources of rhetorics (without collapsing into the latter). In his words: "Rhetorics represents within philosophy that which cannot be thought except in language. It asserts itself in the imperatives of concrete presentation through which philosophy transcends the communication of already known and fixed contents."[30]

In my own view, contemporary thought is indeed marked by a paradigm shift engendering a host of new philosophical problems; but it can be such a shift only as a move to language in the strong and comprehensive sense. While not excluding them from view, the shift cannot be contained within the bounds of communication and speech-act theory. First of all, as an intentional performance, speech-acting does not make sufficient room for listening. In his stress on performative "competence," Habermas consistently privileges speaking over hearing or listening — basically suspecting the latter as a carrier of heteronomy (or a danger to autonomous reason). However, apart from being required for ordinary dialogue, listening or receptive sensitivity is implied in language on numerous levels. Every word spoken or written evokes or carries in its wake a whole host of other words and phrases, that is, a whole range of synonyms, antonyms, and close and distant allusions. Thus, every speech act or communication resonates with the whole dense web of ordinary language — which accounts for the difficulties of interpretation. Moreover, every spoken or written word conjures up the unspoken and unwritten — what might have been and what has not been (perhaps never can be) spoken or written; thus, language or speech reverberates with its own silence, with what Horkheimer called the "silent testimonies of language" — to which he exhorted philosophy to become attentive. In large measure, this complexity of language is sedimented in metaphor, in the poetic-rhetorical and idiomatic texture of speech;

attentiveness to this fabric means basically a "remembrance of nature" (language's nature) in thought — which does not equal a simple fusion of reason and literature.[31] It is only through such remembrance and in terms of such language-thought that reconciliation can be sensibly articulated (if it can be articulated at all). Along the same lines, language alone today can claim absoluteness or assume the role of Hegel's absolute spirit — with the proviso again that absoluteness does not mean separation (nor reducibility to a conceptual formula).[32]

Such a view of language in its emphatic and unrestricted (or unpruned) sense — and replete with Hegelian resonances — has been articulated by Gadamer in the final part of his *Truth and Method*, devoted to the portrayal of an ontological, language-based hermeneutics. Like Adorno, Gadamer links language with "naming" and the rendition of concrete experience. As he writes: "The word is not merely a sign; in a sense that is hard to grasp it is also something almost like an image" or name manifesting experiential content. The latter is not initially "wordless" and then (so to speak) subsumed under a term or concept; rather, it is part of experience itself "that it seeks and finds words which disclose it." Together with Adorno, Gadamer also vindicates concrete-idiomatic language against its reduction to abstract categories and conceptual schemes; like the former, he perceives this reduction as an exercise of mastery or control (of logic over content). "The logical ideal of the systematic order of concepts," we read, "triumphs progressively over the living metaphoric texture of language on which all ordinary concept-formation depends. For only a grammar governed by logic will want to distinguish between the 'real' and the 'metaphorical' meaning of words."[33] In his portrayal of ordinary language, Gadamer eloquently invokes Hegel's legacy of "speculative" thought — although the latter, in his view, remained himself confined within the field of propositional statements without reaching the domain of linguistic experience as such. In a sense akin to Hegel's but on a new level, Gadamer observes, "language itself has something speculative about it" — namely, as the enactment of meaning or the happening of speech. Such a process is speculative "in that the finite possibilities of a word are linked with the intended sense in a direction toward the infinite." For to speak or to say something means "to correlate what is said with an infinity of the unsaid in a comprehensive synthesis of meaning which alone grants understanding."[34]

Against this background, the issue of reconciliation comes again into view — both in its philosophical and its religious or theological sense. For if language involves not only speaking but also listening to (others and) its speculative complexity, then thought can also recu perate the notion of a primordial naming or calling — which is not a fixed point but a perpetual beginning: namely, the word(s) through which things and creatures were called into being. From this event or in pursuance of it, the same calling reverberates through history, as a call to all humans to reconciliation and atonement — a call addressed to them "by their name." For Christians, this summoning reaches its fulfillment in Christ — who is nothing but the embodiment of this word or call and who, through his effective reconciliation, holds out the same promise to all believers and to humankind at large. In Gadamer's words, language is operative first in creation seen as "the word of God." Most importantly, however, the actual redemptive or reconciling deed — "the sending of the Son, the mystery of incarnation" — is itself "presented in St. John's prologue in terms of the word." As elaborated by medieval and later theology, Christ as Son is also the midpoint or "center of language," a notion in which "the mediation of the incarnation event achieves alone its full truth."[35] Yet, Christ's redemptive act was performed not for his own sake but for the sake of the world — upon which he calls not from the platform of a doctrine or abstract principle, but in his capacity as the exemplary "name," the name of names, in whom the concrete suffering of existence is manifestly inscribed. Both his own suffering and that of the world, in turn, are not ends in themselves, but urgent pleas for transformative mediation, for the healing of brokenness and divisiveness. Until his return, this plea has to be the heart of all human speech and action — which, however, cannot proceed without the grant of absoluteness and absolution. As Paul wrote to the Colossians: "For in him all the fullness of God was pleased to dwell, and through him to reconcile to himself all things, whether on earth or in heaven, making peace by the blood of his cross" (1:19–20).

NOTES

1. The passage continues by saying that Christ's redemptive act was meant to "reconcile us both to God in one body through the cross, thereby bringing the hostility to an end" (2:16). As used in these passages, reconciliation seems to be akin to "atonement" in the Old Testament (e.g., Lev. 16:20, Ezek. 45:17–20, Dan. 9:24).

2. See Hans-Georg Gadamer, *Reason in the Age of Science*, trans. Frederick G. Lawrence (Cambridge, Mass.: MIT Press, 1981), 27–29, 34–35 (translation slightly altered); Michael Theunissen, *Hegels Lehre vom absoluten Geist als theologisch-politischer Traktat* (Berlin: de Gruyter, 1970), 100. Among many other passages Theunissen cites Hegel's statement: "It is the general interest of philosophy to reproduce in thought the same reconciliation which we accept in faith." He also points to a (limited) Hegel revival in the confines

of Christian theology: e.g., Hans Küng, *Menschwerdung Gottes* (1970) trans. J. R. Stephenson as *The Incarnation of God: An Introduction to Hegel's Theological Thought as Prolegomena to a Future Christology* (New York: Crossroad, 1987). On Theunissen see my "Dialogue and Otherness" in *Critical Encounters* (Notre Dame, Ind.: University of Notre Dame Press, 1987), 209–23, also my introduction to his *The Other,* trans. Christopher Macann (Cambridge, Mass.: MIT Press, 1984).

3. See especially Max Horkheimer, "Traditional and Critical Theory" (1937), in *Critical Theory: Selected Essays,* trans. Matthew J. O'Connell et al. (New York: Herder and Herder, 1972), 188–243. Although adopting the notion of dialectics largely from Lukács, Horkheimer even then expressed doubt in the existence of a privileged emancipatory subject or class (i.e., the proletariat).

4. Max Horkheimer, *Eclipse of Reason* (first ed. 1947; New York: Seabury Press, 1974), 97, 101. The study was translated into German by Alfred Schmidt and published together with later essays under the title *Zur Kritik der instrumentellen Vernunft* (Frankfurt am Main: Fischer, 1967).

5. Horkheimer, *Eclipse of Reason,* 93–94, 105. Regarding the last point Horkheimer added: "In modern fascism, rationality has reached a point at which it is no longer satisfied with simply repressing nature; rationality now exploits nature by incorporating into its own system the rebellious potentialities of nature. The Nazis manipulated the suppressed desires of the German people" (121).

6. Horkheimer, *Eclipse of Reason,* 107–9, 126–27, 169. According to Horkheimer, neither monism nor dualism offer a satisfactory philosophical solution: "The real difficulty in the problem of the relation between spirit and nature is that hypostatizing the polarity of these two entities is as impermissible as reducing one of them to the other.... The assumption of an ultimate duality is inadmissible — not only because the traditional and highly questionable requirement of an ultimate principle is logically incompatible with a dualistic construction, but because of the content of the concepts in question. The two poles cannot be reduced to a monistic principle, yet their duality too must be largely understood as a product" (171).

7. Horkheimer, *Eclipse of Reason,* 174–75, 177, 179. On mimesis and mimetic impulses see 114–16, especially the comment: "In the present crisis the problem of mimesis is particularly urgent. Civilization starts with, but must eventually transcend and transvaluate, man's native mimetic impulses" (115).

8. Max Horkheimer and Theodor W. Adorno. *Dialektik der Aufklärung* (first ed. 1947; Frankfurt am Main: Fischer, 1969), 3, 9; trans. John Cumming under the title *Dialectic of Enlightenment* (New York: Seabury Press, 1972), xiii, 3. In the above and subsequent citations I have slightly altered the translation for purposes of clarity.

9. Horkheimer and Adorno, *Dialectic of Enlightenment,* 4, 8–10. As the authors add grimly: "Enlightenment behaves toward things like a dictator toward men: He knows them insofar as he can manipulate them.... The

essence of enlightenment is the alternative whose ineradicability is that of domination. Men always had to choose between their subjection to nature or the subjection of nature to the self.... Under the pressure of domination human labor has always led away from myth — into whose jurisdiction it has always relapsed under the spell of domination" (9, 32).

10. Ibid., 7, 14, 29.

11. Ibid., 24, 39–40, 42. Compare also their comment on the sense of remembrance: "The issue is not the conservation of the past but the redemption of the hopes of the past" (xv).

12. Theodor W. Adorno, "Erfahrungsgehalt" in *Drei Studien zu Hegel* (Frankfurt am Main: Suhrkamp, 1963), 90, 96–99.

13. Adorno, *Drei Studien zu Hegel*, 99, 102–4. A very different interpretation of the notion of the "rationality of the real," namely, along theological (and christological) lines, had been given earlier by Franz Rosenzweig in *Hegel und der Staat* (Munich and Berlin: Oldenbourg, 1920), 2:79.

14. Theodor W. Adorno, *Negative Dialektik* (Frankfurt am Main: Suhrkamp, 1966), 17–18, 36; trans. E. B. Ashton as *Negative Dialectics* (New York: Seabury Press, 1973), 8, 27–28. In the above and subsequent citations I have slightly altered the translation for purposes of clarity.

15. Adorno, *Negative Dialectics*, 6–7, 12. The above does not simply mean a substitution of multiplicity for unity and of particularity for universality. As Adorno adds: "Like Kant and the entire philosophical tradition including Plato, Hegel is a partisan of unity. Yet, an abstract denial of the latter would not befit thinking either. The illusion of grasping the manifold directly would mean mimetic regression and a lapse into myth, into the horror of diffuseness — just as unitary thinking, imitating blind nature through its repression, ends in mythical dominion at the opposite pole. Self-reflection of enlightenment is not its revocation" (158).

16. Adorno, *Negative Dialectics*, 19, 141, 179–80, 191. In a later passage, Adorno links negative dialectics with a (nonobjectivistic) materialism, finding in negativity (and the prohibition of images) an affinity of the latter with theology: "At its most materialistic, materialism concurs with theology. Its central aspiration would be the resurrection of the flesh — a notion utterly foreign to idealism, the realm of the absolute spirit" (207).

17. See Jürgen Habermas, "Zur philosophischen Diskussion um Marx und den Marxismus" (1957) in *Theorie und Praxis* (Neuwied: Luchterhand, 1963), 261–335; *Knowledge and Human Interests*, trans. Jeremy J. Shapiro (Boston: Beacon Press, 1971); "Introduction" to *Theory and Practice*, trans. John Viertel (Boston: Beacon Press, 1973), 1–40; "A Postscript to *Knowledge and Human Interests*," in *Philosophy of the Social Sciences* 3 (1975): 157–89; "Wahrheitstheorien," in Helmut Fahrenbach, ed., *Wirklichkeit und Reflexion* (Pfullingen: Neske, 1973), 211–65; "What Is Universal Pragmatics?" (1976) in *Communication and the Evolution of Society*, trans. Thomas McCarthy (Boston: Beacon Press, 1979), 1–68; *Moralbewußtsein und kommunikatives Handeln* (Frankfurt am Main: Suhrkamp, 1983), esp. 53–125; *The Theory of Communicative Action*, 2 vols., trans. Thomas McCarthy (Boston: Beacon Press, 1984, 1988).

18. Habermas "What Is Universal Pragmatics?," 67; *The Theory of Communicative Action*, vol. 1, *Reason and the Rationalization of Society*, 10 (in the above and subsequent citations I have slightly altered the translation for purposes of clarity).

19. Habermas, *The Theory of Communicative Action*, 1:373, 378–80.

20. Ibid., 1:373–74, 380–81. In another formulation of the conflicting assumptions the study states: On the one hand, early critical theory "shares with the tradition of great philosophy (which, in however refracted a manner, it continues) certain essential features: the insistence on contemplation, on a theory divorced from practice; the direction toward the totality of nature and mankind. . . . On the other hand, Horkheimer and Adorno regard the systems of objective spirit as ideologies; the latter succumb hopelessly to a critique which ceaselessly moves back and forth between subjective and objective reason" (383).

21. Habermas, *The Theory of Communicative Action*, 1:382–85. Habermas in this context levels strong accusations against Adorno, chiefly the charges of approximating Heideggerian views and of betraying the motivations of the very beginning of the Frankfurt School: "As opposed as the intentions behind their respective philosophies of history are, the later Adorno and Heidegger resemble each other in their position on the theoretical claims of objectifying thought and of reflection: remembrance of nature comes shockingly close to the recollection (*Andenken*) of being. . . . A philosophy that withdraws behind the lines of discursive thought to the 'remembrance of nature' pays for the evocative powers of its exercises by renouncing the goal of theoretical knowledge — and thus by abandoning that program of 'interdisciplinary materialism' in whose name critical social theory was first launched in the early thirties" (385–86).

22. Habermas, *The Theory of Communicative Action*, 1:366, 386, 390, 392. The polemic against the older Frankfurt School is continued in Habermas's more recent *The Philosophical Discourse of Modernity: Twelve Lectures*, trans. Frederick Lawrence (Cambridge, Mass.: MIT Press, 1987), chapter 5. However, the presentation there does not yield much for present purposes — in part because nearly half of the chapter entitled "The Entwinement of Myth and Enlightenment" is devoted to a discussion of Nietzsche (whose "regressive-archaic" outlook is designed to cast a shadow on the older Frankfurt School). According to the chapter, Horkheimer and Adorno radicalized modern enlightenment by unleashing a relentless "ideology critique" against enlightenment itself; thereby they became trapped in *aporias*, now called "performative contradictions": "The radicalization or totalization of enlightenment denounces the latter with its own tools. Adorno was quite aware of the performative contradiction inherent in totalized critique. His *Negative Dialectics* reads like a continuing explanation of why we must circle within this performative contradiction and indeed should remain there" (119). Again, there is the accusation of the atrophy of "theory": Horkheimer and Adorno choose the option of "stirring up, holding open, and no longer wanting to overcome theoretically the performative contradiction inherent in a totalized ideology critique. Since, on this level of reflection, any attempt to

formulate a theory would slide into an abyss, they eschew theory and practice determinate negation on an *ad hoc* basis" (127–28). In this manner they miss the alternative solution of communicative rationality: Like historicism, Horkheimer and Adorno "surrendered themselves to an uninhibited skepticism regarding reason, instead of weighing the reasons casting doubt on this skepticism itself. In this way, perhaps, they might have laid the normative foundations of critical social theory so deep that they would remain untouched by any decomposition of bourgeois culture (like the one happening then in Germany for all to see)" (129).

23. Regarding the "civilization of productivity" compare William Connolly, *The Politics of Ambiguity* (Madison: University of Wisconsin Press, 1987), 76–86.

24. There is, I believe, an element of left-Hegelianism in the departure from Hegel (but only on one level). Suspicious of idealism and a mere reconciliation within the sphere of "mind," Horkheimer and Adorno shift the accent to nonmental "reality" and praxis. However, this is a misunderstanding of the notion of (absolute) "spirit" — which, for Hegel, designated the very core or essence of reality. Exiled from the absolute, external "reality" and human praxis are not only unreconciled but indeed irreconcilable and unredeemable. For a critique formulated along similar lines see Theunissen, *Hegels Lehre vom absoluten Geist*, 24–36.

25. Adorno, *Negative Dialectics*, 1–15. Contrary to the above (and similar statements elsewhere), Habermas accuses Adorno of confusing reason and art, philosophy and aesthetics; see *The Theory of Communicative Action*, 1:384–85. The notion of mimesis, to be sure, is further developed in Adorno's *Aesthetic Theory*, trans. Christian Lenhardt (London: Routledge and Kegan Paul, 1984), 79–83, 166–71, 453–55; but even there "thinking" about art is not simply equated with art. The work clearly seeks to articulate a "theory," though not in Habermas's sense (who, hardly has a monopoly on the term).

26. The "absolute" is indeed removed from willfulness and purposive intentionality; but precisely in this way is it able to participate in everything in a nondomineering, sympathetic way. Compare in this context Klaus-M. Kodalle, *Die Erorberung des Nutzlosen* (Paderborn: Schöningh, 1988).

27. William Connolly, *Political Theory and Modernity* (Oxford: Blackwell, 1988), 133. The polemic against Marcuse is developed in "Technology and Science as 'Ideology,'" in *Toward a Rational Society*, trans. Jeremy J. Shapiro (Boston: Beacon Press, 1970), 81–122, and "Psychic Thermidor and the Rebirth of Rebellious Subjectivity," in Richard Bernstein, ed., *Habermas and Modernity* (Cambridge, Mass.: MIT Press, 1985), 67–77.

28. Habermas, *The Theory of Communicative Action*, 1:101.

29. Habermas, "What Is Universal Pragmatics?," 28, 66. The continuity of subject-philosophy in Habermas's theory — his tendency to replace "the subject" by a plurality of subjects — was noted by Theunissen early on; see his *Gesellschaft und Geschichte* (Berlin: de Gruyter, 1969). For a brief summary of the study's argument see my "Critical Epistemology Criticized," in *Beyond*

Dogma and Despair (Notre Dame, Ind.: University of Notre Dame Press, 1981), 251–53.

30. Horkheimer, *Eclipse of Reason*, 165–66, 179; Adorno, *Negative Dialectics*, 52, 55, 162–63. In turning to rhetorics, Adorno does not propose its complete fusion with philosophy: "Dialectics — literally: language as the organon of thought — means the attempt to rescue critically the rhetorical moment, that is, to approximate thing and expression mutually to the point of indistinction.... In dialectics, contrary to popular opinion, the rhetorical element is on the side of content" (56). In his emphasis on "naming" (and the mimetic element of language) Adorno shows his indebtedness to Walter Benjamin. On the latter's language theory, and Habermas's ambivalent relation to it, see Martin Jay, "Habermas and Modernism," in Bernstein, ed., *Habermas and Modernity*, 125–39, esp. 129–34. In my view, Habermas tends to confuse the mimetic and metaphorical element with expressiveness (of a speaker's inner life).

31. The charge of fusing philosophy and literature is leveled by Habermas chiefly against Jacques Derrida and his followers; see his *The Philosophical Discourse of Modernity*, chapter 7, with its excursus on the "Levelling of the Genre Distinction between Philosophy and Literature," 161–210. Habermas concedes that ordinary language is "ineradicably rhetorical" and that the "illuminating power of metaphorical tropes" radiates into more "specialized languages"; but he insists on the strict separation of metaphor from reason, of rhetorics from philosophy (or the subordination of the former to the latter): "Whoever transposes the radical critique of reason into the domain of rhetorics in order to blunt the paradox of self-referentiality, thereby dulls the sword of the critique of reason itself " (209–10). But where, if not from ordinary language, does reason derive its vocabulary? Strict separation seems to be predicated on the assumption of a purely mental language (which is disavowed by the "linguistic turn").

32. As Adorno writes, with some exaggeration: "Hegelian dialectics was a dialectics without language — although dialectics in its most literal sense postulates language; to this extent Hegel remained an adept of the prevalent mode of science. He did not need language in an emphatic sense since everything, including the speechless and opaque, was supposed to be spirit and spirit the comprehensive synthesis. This supposition cannot be salvaged." These lines should be read in conjunction with comments on the retrieval of (Hegelian) "infinity" and "speculation" on a new level: "An idea bequeathed to us by idealism — corrupted by it more than any other — needs to be rethought today: the idea of the infinite.... Even after breaking with idealism philosophy cannot do without speculation which was extolled by idealism and tabooed with it — though speculation needs to be taken in a sense broader than the overly positive Hegelian one." See Adorno, *Negative Dialectics*, 15–16, 163.

33. Hans-Georg Gadamer, *Truth and Method* (New York: Seabury Press, 1975), 377, 391. (In the above and subsequent citations, I have altered the translation for purposes of clarity.) The beginning of this logical ideal is traced to Aristotle. However, Gadamer also acknowledges another side in

Aristotle — where language appears as a mid-point between "naturalness" and logical artifact: "When Aristotle says of sounds or written signs that they 'signify' in becoming a 'symbolon,' this means that they do not exist naturally but according to convention (*kata syntheken*). But this is by no means an instrumental sign theory. Rather, the convention according to which spoken sounds or written signs mean something is not an agreement on a means (or instrument) of communication — which would always already presuppose language — but it is the basic concord on which human community and its agreement on what is good and just are founded" (390–91). In a telling footnote (p. 30, note 6) Gadamer adds that Aristotle's thoughts on language should be read "in the light of his Politics."

34. Gadamer, *Truth and Method*, 426. As Gadamer continues, this speculative quality is found "in an intensified way" in poetry or poetic language. Poetry is the most "absolute" or speculative form of language because it is least subject to control or least at our (instrumental) disposal. In all these respects Gadamer is very close to Heidegger's philosophy of language. On the latter compare Gerald Bruns, *Heidegger's Estrangements* (New Haven: Yale University Press, 1989).

35. Gadamer, *Truth and Method*, 379–80, 388. Regarding the speculative or absolute dimension of language, Gadamer's hermeneutics has also accorded a central place to the notion of "play" or (serious) playfulness; see esp. 91–99. On play compare also the essays "Lila" and "Play and Seriousness" in Roger Lipsey, ed., *Coomaraswamy, Selected Papers 2: Metaphysics* (Princeton, N.J.: Princeton University Press, 1977), 148–58.

6

Pluralism, Privacy,
and the Interior Self

Charles Davis

"Do not you believe that there is in man a 'deep' so profound as to be hidden even to him in whom it is?" The words are St. Augustine's in his *Expositions on the Book of Psalms* (1848, II: 194). The self for Augustine was, as Thomas Prufer puts it, a "transphenomenal abyss" (1963: 6). We enter the depths of that interior self helped by the light of God. "Being admonished by all this to return to myself," Augustine writes in the *Confessions*, "I entered into my own depths with You as guide; and I was able to do it because You were my helper. I entered, and with the eye of my soul, such as it was, I saw Your unchangeable Light shining over that same eye of my soul, over my mind" (1943: 137). For Augustine, to quote Thomas Prufer again, "The self is constituted in listening and speaking to God; it is no longer primarily constituted as a being in the world" (1963: 6). In Augustine we have the exemplary instance at the beginning of Western culture of the Christian experience of the interior self as standing alone in the presence of God. The individual has his or her self-identity in a relationship with God in interiority. In other words, the person is constituted as an interior or transphenomenal individual self by being present to God in inward solitude.

I myself have written in my book *Body as Spirit* about the problem created by the nonworldliness of that conception of the self. The Christian acknowledgment of the individual was a valuable contribution to the emergence of human freedom, and that individuality was achieved by the interiority of an inward relationship with God. But the interior self of Christian tradition does not merely transcend the world, but is also alienated from it, and the cleavage between the interior self and the phenomenal world has been harmful. It led eventually to the modern isolated ego, with its loneliness and promethean individualism. In *Body as Spirit* I was chiefly concerned with the refusal of bodiliness. Here I should like more directly to consider the relation of the individual, interior self to society. To do so, I will take up again Habermas's theory of religion, because in it he relates the history of religion to the question of social identity.

Habermas distinguishes four stages of social evolution in regard to ego and group identity (Habermas and Heinrich, 1974: 25–84; Habermas 1974: 91–103).

The first stage was that of archaic societies. Their structure was determined by kinship ties. These provided the basis for the elaboration of mythical worldviews. Analogies were made among all natural and cultural phenomena and expressed in mythical images by using kinship relationships as an interpretative schema. The myth thus produced an illusion of order by assigning a meaningful place to every perceptible element. Almost every contingency was interpreted away in that fashion. Archaic society was very insecure because of the underdevelopment of its productive forces and the lack of control over the environment. The insecurity was dissolved by the myth. Since in the world of myth all entities are analogues, human beings do not essentially differ from the things of nature, nor does the tribe stand out from its individual members or from nature. At this stage, therefore, problems of identity do not arise.

Problems come at the second stage, the world of the polytheistic religions of the early civilizations. These civilizations have a centralized political organization, either kingdom or city-state, which requires legitimation. Hence the polity has to be taken up into the religious narratives and made firm through ritual. At this stage, nature begins to be desacralized, and the political institutions receive a degree of autonomy in relation to the cosmic order. The effect is to open up an area of the unaccountable, where contingencies can no longer be interpreted away as with the myth of the previous stage, but where the individual has to act to bring the situation under control. It is at this stage that the gods assume human form and are conceived as actively and sometimes arbitrarily intervening in human affairs. The individual faced with unaccountable contingencies established patterns of interaction with the gods by devising new forms of religious action, such as prayer, sacrifice, and worship. What we therefore observe at this stage is the emergence of the individual in self-identity from the universal complex of other entities and, at the same time, the distinction of the particular concrete community from the universality of the cosmic order. Nevertheless, religious adherence is still identified with membership of a particular political community. For that reason, the particular community can become distinct from the universality of the cosmic order on the one hand and from singular individuals on the other, without that destroying the unity of the world centered in it and the social identity thus created. So, an equilibrium was achieved, a unity in difference, relating individuality, particularity, and universality. There was a limitation, however. The absolute right of the individual had not yet been established.

With the universal religions, from which Habermas takes Christianity as the exemplar, we reach the third state. "The one, the other-worldly, all-knowing and wholly just and gracious God of Christendom," writes Habermas, "leads to the forming of an ego-identity severed from all concrete roles and norms. This 'I' can know itself as a completely individuated being" (1974: 93). The individual standing before God becomes free and of infinite worth. Furthermore, because the commands of God are universal, the bearer of religion is no longer the particular political group, but the community of believers, to which all men potentially belong. Here, then, we have the emergence of the singular individual, considered of infinite worth, in a potentially universal community. However, the political systems of the time of the universal religions, which is the stage of the high civilizations, were class societies with extreme inequalities of power and wealth. For that reason they were in great need of powerful legitimation, but the universalism of the monotheistic religions militated against their giving such legitimation. "At this stage," says Habermas, "the religious meaning systems and the political imperatives of self-maintenance become structurally incompatible" (ibid.). Ideology entered in to ease this conflict. Its function was to cover over the dissimilarity between the collective identity as tied to the particular state and the individual ego-identity formed by the universal religious community.

That problem of identity is inherent in all the high civilizations, but it remained latent until modern times because of various mechanisms that mediated between the political order and religious universalism. Habermas mentions three such mediating mechanisms. First, the persistence of earlier identity formations, derived from myth and magic. Second, the distinction made between the members of the community of believers and those still to be converted. This distinction was used to justify the treatment of political enemies as though they were outside the boundary of the universal religious community. Third — and this was the chief factor — the dualism set up between divine transcendence, represented by the church, and the secular world, represented by the state.

In the modern era, which constitutes the fourth stage of social evolution, the mediating mechanisms have lost their efficacy. To take each of the three in turn. Protestantism eliminated many of the pre-Christian elements that had been incorporated into the Catholic order. The sifting out of anachronistic, pagan elements increased the pressure toward strongly universalistic imperatives and the individualized ego-structures corresponding to them. Again, with the breakup of the one Catholic Church into a multitude of confessions and denominations, membership of the community of believers ceased to be an exclusive and rigidly institutional attribute. The principle of toleration and the voluntary nature of religious association became generally acknowledged. Finally, Habermas takes note of the fact that recent theology has moved to overcome the traditional dualism between the church and the world by giving a this-worldly interpretation of salvation.

On that last point, Habermas, in commenting upon what he calls "the repoliticization of the biblical inheritance observable in contemporary theological discussion," argues that the idea of a personal God cannot be salvaged in the process, although he admits that the new interpretation does not mean "atheism in the sense of a liquidation without trace of the idea of God." What, then, does he think it means? He writes:

The idea of God is transformed [*aufgehoben*] into the concept of a *Logos* that determines the community of believers and the real life-context of a self-emancipating society. "God" becomes the name for a communicative structure that forces men, on pain of a loss of their humanity, to go beyond their accidental, empirical nature to encounter one another *indirectly*, that is, across an objective something that they themselves are not (1976a: 121; Habermas's italics).

The theologians in question might respond: Has Habermas probed the implications of that communicative structure deeply enough?

To understand Habermas's account of the history of religion, one must recall his thesis that the cultural life of societies is not a random process, but follows a rationally reconstructible pattern of development. His argument for this is an interlocking series of considerations. To speak in general terms, social systems are engaged in a double process of exchange. There is, first, the appropriation of outer nature, namely, the nonhuman environment, through production and, second, the appropriation of inner nature, which means human material, through socialization. The adaptation of inner nature to society in socialization is what is meant by cultural life. The adaptation or socialization is brought about through the medium of normative structures, in which human needs are interpreted and various actions allowed or made obligatory. Because normative structures are thus the means of socialization, the social integration of inner nature marches in step with normative claims that call for justification. But the discursive redemption of normative claims follows a rational sequence.

Since socialization is dependent upon normative claims and their justification, it itself follows a rational pattern. In other words, the cultural life of society is directional and embodies an irreversible sequence. The development of science and technology manifests, according to Habermas, an inner logic with rational sequences fixed from the outset, so that, as long as the continuity of tradition is not broken, cognitive advances cannot be forgotten and every deviation from the irreversible line of advance is experienced as a regression. Likewise, for him normative claims and their justification follow an inner logic, which creates an irreversible line of development, so that, as long as the continuity of tradition is unbroken, socially attained stages of moral consciousness cannot be forgotten and any deviation is experienced as a regression.

What, then, is the rationally reconstructible pattern of development in the cultural life of social systems? The question can be put in another way: What is the inner logic of the development of worldviews? There is an increasing demand for the discursive redemption of normative claims, which leads from myth through religion to philosophy and ideology and thence to critique. In the directional process the following irreversible trends are discernible: the expansion of the secular in relation to the sacred; the movement from heteronomy to autonomy; the evacuation of cognitive contents from worldviews, so that cosmology is replaced by a pure system of morality; the shift from tribal particularism to universalistic and individualized orientation; increasing reflexivity of the mode of belief (1976a: 11–12).

The last trend is the determining one. Döbert, a younger collaborator of Habermas, to whose work Habermas refers, interprets the history of religious consciousness as the development of a process of reflection through which human beings gain clarity in regard to themselves and free themselves from the domination of normative systems that impose themselves with a nature-like compulsion (1973: 140). Since the opposite of a nature-like compulsion of norms is a mutual agreement on norms, reached in a free reciprocal process of communication, Döbert suggests that the development of religion may be viewed as the evolution of communicative competence. The end-point of this development of religion as communicative competence is described by Peukert in summing up both Habermas and Döbert (1976: 228). Persons as subjects will have become competent to test and render perspicuous for one another assertions and behavioral expectations through a linguistically mediated process of reciprocal reflexivity. Thus, the final stage or ideal is the reciprocal transparency of persons in a process of communication.

To return now to the modern era as the fourth stage in Habermas's account of the evolution of social identity. The considerations I have been outlining should make understandable why Habermas contends that at this stage all that is left of the universal religions is the core of a universalistic morality. (The mystical components, grounded in a contemplative experience that is characterized by a withdrawal from action, cannot be taken up [*aufgehoben*] into ethics and have split off into a sphere of their own [1976b: 101]. The consequence of this clarification and purification of the universalistic structures originally introduced by the world religions is a cleavage between the ego-identity derived from universalistic structures and collective identity as bound up with a particular community. Habermas writes:

on the basis of universalistic norms no particular entity possessing an identity-forming power (such as the family, the tribe, the city, state or nation) can set up bounds to demarcate itself from alien groups. Rather, the "own" group is here replaced by the category of "the other" who is no longer conceived as an outsider because of his nonmembership (1974: 94).

Somehow particular citizenship or national identity has to be enlarged into a cosmopolitan or universal identity. But how? The whole of humankind is an abstraction. Unless there can be found an all-embracing collective identity on the basis of which individualized ego-identities can be formed, then universalistic morality and the ego-structures that go with it will remain a mere postulate, actualized only occasionally and then within the private sphere, without in a substantial fashion grounding social life.

Needless to say, Habermas does not see any solution in a return to religion. For him Christianity, though the most rational of the religions, is no longer viable after its confrontation with science and secular morality. But further, during the Christian era the opposition between the universalistic ego-structures and the particularism of the state was covered over, not resolved. He examines the solution offered by Hegel, who remains for Habermas a contemporary thinker precisely because he gave the impulse to reflection upon the problem of identity.

An adequate presentation of Hegel's solution would require an account of his general philosophy, because he viewed the problem of identity, namely the cleavage between the singular "I" and the particular society, in the context of the self-unfolding of absolute Spirit in nature and history.

But it must be enough here to say that Hegel defended the thesis that modern society finds its rational identity in the sovereign constitutional state, which, though particular, was for him the embodiment of universal morality. Few would disagree with Habermas when he argues against Hegel that the modern state cannot provide a rational identity, uniting the singular, the particular, and the universal. Two of the reasons he gives may be mentioned. First, the modern state remains a class structure; it does not embody the universalizable interests of the whole people, but organizes the domination of group interests over the whole. Second, recent developments, such as nuclear weapons, multinational corporations, worldwide communication, have rendered the sovereign territorial state anachronistic.

The failure of Hegel indicates for Habermas that the old social identity, centered in the state and both articulated and fixed in particular traditions and world-images, is now finally outdated and irrelevant. He goes on to outline a new identity, which he contends is possible in the complex societies of today and at the same time compatible with a universalistic ego-structure.

This new identity is not tied to state boundaries; it is not related to a particular territory or organization. It does not come from membership in some permanent collective body. It is grounded, Habermas says,

in the consciousness of universal and equal chances to participate in the kind of communication processes by which identity formation becomes a continuous learning process. Here the individual is no longer confronted by collective identity as a traditional authority, as a fixed objectivity on the basis of which self-identity can be built. Rather, individuals are the participants in the shaping of the collective will underlying the design of a common identity. (1974: 99)

He discerns in present societies processes of communication concerning norms and values. These processes are often not institutionalized politically, and are therefore in that sense subpolitical. But in fact they penetrate and affect the political system and political decisions. The consciousness of a universal and equal opportunity to participate in the social formation of norms and values is the basis for a new collective identity, uniting the singular, the particular, and the universal. This new identity of a still-emerging global society cannot be articulated in world-images. It presupposes the validity of universalistic moral systems, but these can be grounded simply upon the norms inherent in rational discourse. Habermas is here referring to his own analysis of the normative basis of communicative action. This leads him to say of the new identity:

Such identity no longer requires fixed contents. Those interpretations which make man's situation in today's world comprehensible are distinguished from the traditional world images not so much in that they are more limited in scope, but in that their status is open to counter-arguments and revisions at any time. (Ibid., 100)

I have already said enough about Habermas's dismissal of religion to make it unnecessary here to discuss his theory of identity from that standpoint. Instead, I want to take up what I consider his valuable insights on social identity into a theological context.

Does not what Habermas says about identity correspond to an experience undergone by an increasing number of Christians today? I mean the breakdown of the old Christian identity and the emergence of a new identity. Many, I think, no longer find their social identity as Christians in membership of a particular Christian church standing over against them as a collective body with a traditional authority. They still regard themselves as Christians, but their identity as Christians comes to them as participants with others in a continuous collective process of learning to be Christians. They are not Christians because they have joined themselves to a fixed, already existent Christian collectivity, with requirements for membership clearly defined so as to provide an objective basis for the Christian self-identity of individuals. They remain Christians, despite perhaps the irregularity, tenuousness, or even nonexistence of their connection with a particular church, because they continue to participate in the social process of shaping what it means to be a Christian at the present time. They are engaged with others in forming Christian norms and values in the context of the situation today.

Admittedly, most Christians still find themselves within one or other of the different Christian churches, just as everyone is still a citizen of a particular state. But the meaning of church membership as that of citizenship has changed. Citizenship in a particular state is no longer the basis for self-identity in contemporary society. We are participants in a worldwide process in which, with others from various countries as equal participants, we are striving for a new collective identity. Our fundamental social identity comes from our conscious share in shaping the new, emergent collective will. Our present citizenship is a point of entry into the wider process, a place from which we may act, and it may indeed recede right into the background if we are working with citizens from many countries in some international body or movement. It is likewise with church membership. It is no longer fundamental as a fixed, objective basis on which we define our self-identity as Christians. That is now given through participation in ongoing Christian history. At most church membership serves as a point of entry into the Christian process, a place from

which we may act, and it recedes more and more into the background
as we develop a network of relationships with others that ignore the
boundaries of particular churches. People sometimes hardly know
how to answer when they are asked whether they are members of a
particular church. The reason is simply that membership is no longer
a useful or relevant concept in defining social identity

As soon as social identity is seen as given by active and conscious participation in a history and not by membership of a fixed,
objective, authoritative collectivity, the question of pluralism and
religious diversity is thrown into a new light. I will begin with a
consideration of pluralism as a political factor (see Davis 1974). John
Courtney Murray defined pluralism as: "the co-existence within the
political community of groups who hold divergent views with regard
to ultimate questions concerning the nature and destiny of man"
(1954: 165). Pluralism in that sense may be called valuational pluralism, because divergent views concerning the nature and destiny of
humankind both arise from and lead to differing and incompatible
value judgements. The problem of pluralism for the political community and its common action lies in the divergent value judgements
governing decisions.

Pluralism implies disagreement and dissension within the political community. But one cannot speak of pluralism unless there is
one community. Pluralism, then, also implies unity, some consensus or agreement. The divergent groups form one community; they
agree to live together and cooperate in action for common goals.
Pluralism is not brute plurality. It means harmony amid religious
and valuational conflict.

Pluralism is of the very essence of politics. Herbert Richardson
distinguishes between nonpolitical and political societies on the basis
of the refusal of admission of pluralism. Political societies are structurally pluralist, in as much as they aim at a co-willing that unifies
divergent willings, while keeping their divergent plurality (*Religion
and Political Society*, 1974: 103). The exclusion of pluralism is thus
the suppression of the properly political dimension of society.

But how can a society deal in a rational manner with divergent
value judgments? Without a disastrous dehumanization, it cannot
evade the issue by ignoring values, though that is the direction taken
by contemporary technocratic society. Again, if those in power simply assert their own values and impose them in practice, there is a
destruction of human freedom and a virtual elimination of politics.
If neither evasion nor absolutism, what then? Herbert Richardson
makes what I consider a too-facile distinction between procedural
and teleological values, but his account does point in the right direction. There can be pluralism only when people agree to engage in

open and continuing discussion. "Civilization," wrote Thomas Gilby as quoted by John Courtney Murray "is formed by men locked together in argument. From this dialogue the community becomes a political community" (Murray 1960: 6). As I myself wrote in an essay on pluralism:

There should be a public deliberation about values, through which the implications and consequences of divergent value judgements are comprehensively displayed. The supposition is that open and adequate deliberation will favor the occurrence of correct value judgments on the part of men of good will and thus create a sound public consensus. A pluralist society allows dissent. It does not, however, exclude, but rather as a human society or community of meaning presupposes a consensus, created and maintained freely in open discussion. A public consensus will not eliminate dissent; indeed, as a freely created agreement, it presupposes and implies dissent. But dissent is identified as dissent with reference to the consensus, and a minimum of consensus is a condition for political argument. Political argument is not just the attempted provoking of assent to intellectually cogent reasoning, but a common process of deliberation, evaluation and decision. (Davis 1974: 247)

What Habermas, it seems to me, has added to considerations such as those is the insight that the particular political communities or states do not provide an appropriate embodiment of the common process by reaching agreement about norms and values. First, the existing states are all structures of domination, objectified disvalues, so that the pursuit of genuine values will be a rejection of the present political order. Membership of a state is, therefore, part of the contingent facticity of one's existence, not a definition of one's normative being as a moral and social agent. Second, all the determining social and political issues of today transcend the boundaries of particular states. Human history has become one in a conscious and active way, so that a social identity that is not anachronistic has to be grounded upon a collective reality wider than that of the particular state. There is, indeed, not yet a universal, global order, but there is the opportunity of participating in its emergence by evoking the inherently universal structure of communication to shape a new collective will, leading to an order beyond the present divisions. However much we may positively value a particular national heritage, possessing it as a fixed and finished whole cannot ground a rational social identity today. Instead, that heritage must serve as a source of a distinctive contribution to the common enterprise of forming a new, complex, and universal identity for people of all nations.

I am reminded here of Lonergan's concept of cosmopolis. In dealing with the problem of cultural decline, he argues:

What is necessary is a cosmopolis that is neither class nor state, that stands above all their claims, that cuts them down to size, that is founded on the native detachment and disinterestedness of every intelligence, that commands man's first allegiance, that implements itself primarily through that allegiance, that is too universal to be bribed, too impalpable to be forced, too effective to be ignored. (1958: 238)

"Cosmopolis," he adds, "is above all politics. So far from being rendered superfluous by a successful World Government, it would be all the more obviously needed to offset the tendencies of that and any other government to be shortsightedly practical" (ibid., 239).

I do not share Lonergan's confidence in detached intelligence as the cure for human ills. He sees cosmopolis as counteracting the tendency to identify the rational with the immediately practical or expedient. But even that tendency is met better by the active universalism of an interest in human liberation than by detached reflection. The worst expedients of the modern technocrats are cloaked by a claim to the detached objectivity of science. Intelligence is as biased or as universalistic as one's practical life; it is neither unfallen nor separately redeemed. Further, Lonergan has a low view of politics as merely concerned with the exercise of power and the sustaining of law and order. But a political community in the full sense comes into existence when persons engage in civilized debate concerning the ends of life and of society.

To put my point briefly: social change is not brought about by a change of consciousness alone, but by a concurrence of a change of consciousness and a change of structures. Cosmopolis registers the change of consciousness when it places our first allegiance beyond class or state. What needs to be added is active participation in the formation of new, universal structures. It is that active participation that grounds a new social identity.

In their writings, both Lonergan and Habermas, in my opinion, exaggerate the function of detached, discursive rationality as exemplified by science, at the expense of other forms of rationality. But the problem of pluralism cannot be met by communication solely at the theoretical level. That becomes abundantly clear when we turn to the question of religious diversity.

I have said that a basic Christian identity today is not grounded upon membership in a particular church, but upon participation in an ongoing, and therefore future-oriented, Christian history. I now want to argue that that account itself is a limited view. Christian identity is but one mode or manifestation of a more fundamental religious identity, which we share with people from other religious traditions, as all being participants in a single total history. That history is now entering a new phase, in which this fundamental religious identity, previously implicit and indeed blocked and denied, is now emerging.

That conviction is based on several different but convergent considerations (Smith 1976: passim). First, past religious history is not fully intelligible unless it is understood as a single history of human religiousness. Not merely are many developments similar across the different traditions, but also the actual histories of the different religious communities are much more intertwined than previous accounts, written from the viewpoint of a single tradition, have allowed. The point has readily been admitted in regard to the East and the overlapping of Confucianism, Taoism, and Buddhism in China, but Wilfred Cantwell Smith has shown how Christians and Muslims have to a large extent shared the same history. In a recent article he states:

my thesis is that both Christian history and Islamic history are to be understood in significant part as each a sub-sector of a history of human religiousness that is in principle, of course, world-wide and history-long, but for our present purposes must be seen as at least a context of development that we may call Islamo-Christian history. (1977: 519)

To apply that thesis to two particular phenomena: scholasticism and what we may call scripturalism. A true historical apprehension would see "Islamic thought and Jewish and Christian, more or less in that order so far as beginnings go, participating historically in a Mediterranean movement of thought called scholasticism" (ibid., 520). Again:

when seen on a world scale, Jews, Christians, and Muslims may all be understood, and understood more tellingly, as participating historically in the religious phenomenon of Scripturalism — initiating their participation in the Scripture movement at somewhat different stages in its dynamic development, with interesting and important differential results; but the phenomenon of Scripture in no one of the cases can be so fully and accurately understood as when apprehended in all (ibid.).

Second, religious exclusiveness is itself a particular development that arose at a particular time and place and would now seem to have come to the end of its historical usefulness. Smith writes:

It has certainly been true for some time now and for considerable parts of the world that men have their life religiously in independent, even isolationist, communities, separated from each other not absolutely, of course, but in principle, and even considerably so in practice. Our new study of mankind's religiousness, however, is investigating the fact that this situation arose in human development. In *The Meaning and End of Religion* I have suggested that it arose at a given time and place in Western Asia, in that fascinatingly creative period between Alexander and Muhammad — and has since established itself, and has spread, though not to all the world: to India quite late, and to China virtually never. We in the West have come to take it so utterly for granted that religious life should be lived out in separated and bound-aried communities, that we have given less attention than it deserves to the great question of how this came to be and what it implies. Yet one is begin-ning to discern perhaps a total history of man's religiousness, constituting a pattern in which the rise of the separated religious communities constitutes a meaningful episode. (1976: 109)

Third, there is discernible today a convergence of religious tra-ditions, which is in a fair way to transform all of them. That does not mean that all religious traditions are saying the same thing or that there is no religious truth or that anything goes in matters of religion. The history of religion is not just a history of authentic religious experience and achievement, but of religious aberration. A work of discernment and purification is needed, and this will in-clude judgements of truth or falsity, though it must be remembered that such judgments have to take account of the figurative nature of religious expression.

What, however, is implied by this development is the end of or-thodoxy, in the sense of a religious identity mediated through the fixed, objectified contents of a particular religious tradition. There may indeed be invariant elements, but it is not possible to forestall future history and draw a clear line between the invariant and the variable elements. Thus, as I wrote elsewhere:

It is possible that the Christian tradition has a central, decisive contribution to make in world history. However, to put forward a *prior* claim of that kind savors of ethnocentricity and cultural imperialism. It also runs up against serious difficulties of hermeneutic or epistemological principle, because in effect it attempts to bypass the mediation of history and *praxis* in our coming to the truth. Only in the actual process of the emergence of world order shall we be able to discern the precise role of existing elements. (1976: 103)

I conclude, then, that basic religious identity — at least for some of us — is not given by belonging to a particular religious tradition, but by active participation in the present shaping of a universality to be realized in the future. Present working for a yet-to-be-realized uni-versality can already unite people of different positions (Habermas 1974: 103).

The structure of communication now growing among the re-ligious communities with their traditions is not just a matter of theoretical or doctrinal discussion. It is a sharing of life. People are learning to live together, to listen to one another's stories, to in-terpret and become familiar with alien symbols, to respect different customs and join in the rites of others. There are different degrees of sharing. Sometimes, as often in the past, an element from one tradition is assimilated into other traditions so fully that its origin is forgotten, though it may well be substantially modified in the process. At other times, the sharing takes place in a manner that does not destroy, but perhaps heightens the sense of difference. There is developing religiously what Herbert Richardson, with reference to politics, calls a "polyconsciousness," namely, a more highly differentiated consciousness with a greater capacity of bearing plurality within itself. "A person," he writes, "living in a political society must possess more power of empathy; he must be an Empathetic Man. Such empathetic persons are able to identify imaginatively with those who are different from themselves and, in this way, to bear a higher degree of inward contrariety" (*Religion and Political Society*, 1974: 113).

It must be added that religious pluralism, when placed in the context of universal communication, is not an evil to be eliminated, but the appropriate expression of the transcendence of the religious object, of human freedom and of the historical mediation of human truth and value. The universalistic structure of religious identity as I have outlined it does not anticipate the removal of plurality but articulates a unity of communication in the lasting differences of historical experience and remembrance and consequently of traditions, though these remain under a constant process of development and revision. Traditions with their diversity will never be replaced by the abstract universality of formal rational discourse.

Though Habermas would no doubt disagree, I see the basic religious identity I have described as coinciding with the new social identity he has analyzed, though articulating it at a deeper level. Previously, in agreement with Peukert, I argued that communicative action had implications demanding religious expression. In a similar way, I contend here that the new universal identity now emerging is a new articulation, beyond particularism and orthodoxy, of the religious identity of the past, not its abolition without remainder.

According to both Hegel and Habermas, it was monotheism, particularly in its Christian form, that led to the emergence of the singular individual. Standing before God, the "I" became a completely individuated being, possessing an unconditional or infinite worth apart from any particular concrete role. The singular individual, therefore, had his or her social identity in a potentially universal community of believers rather than from the state. When Habermas, however, turns to the problem of identity in modern society, he does not take up Hegel's concern for the modern estrangement from the Absolute. I also find nothing in Habermas's account of the new social identity to replace the function of monotheism in grounding a singular ego-structure. Participation in communication processes for the formation of norms and values is a basis for a universalistic ego-structure, transcending the particularism of enclosed groups. But such a universalistic ego-structure does not of itself imply the unconditional worth of the individual. Are we then simply to relinquish the Christian stress upon the individual self? After all, the doctrine of an individual self, distinct from God but constituted in relationship with God, is not shared by the nontheistic religious traditions.

Political theology is in part a protest against the virtual confinement of religion since the Enlightenment to the private sphere of the individual and the family. Metz, for example, proclaimed a program of deprivatization (*Entprivatisierung*). He presented political theology in contrast to existentialist, personalist, and transcendental theologies, which for him have compounded the tendency to privatization. As a theologian Metz began his career as a disciple of Rahner and an interpreter of his transcendental theology. Rahner's theological anthropology takes the transcendental experience of the subject as its starting-point and context of meaning. Metz turned away from this toward a theological eschatology, for which the political subject was the starting-point and context of meaning (Mann 1969–70).

There are, I think, several distinct issues entangled here. I should like to try to unravel them.

Religion as a private affair or privatized religion may be taken to mean a religious outlook and practice solely concerned with the personal values of private life. The social and political factors of life in the world are left unexamined. These are considered as outside one's personal life, even though they constitute the world in which one has to earn one's living. Religion, however, is a personal matter. Its concern is with my attitudes and my behavior as immediately bearing upon my personal relationships with the other members of my family and with people I personally meet. The function of religion is to encourage values and behavior that promote harmony in interpersonal relationships and to foster generosity and helpfulness. As for the misfortunes of life, these are to be met with patient endurance, supported by the thought of the transitoriness of this life and the rewards of the next. At the same time, a genuine sense of the transcendent may frequently prevent this kind of religion from becoming entirely self-enclosed, and a thrust toward the transcendent remains there as a potentially disturbing element. Within the context of privatized religion, however, the sense of the transcendent is chiefly nurtured through individual prayer. The devout strive to develop an interior or spiritual life by setting aside time for mental prayer and practicing other spiritual techniques.

Clearly such a religion is too limited in range to counteract the injustices of existing society or to create a free society. For that reason the whole concept of an interior or spiritual life has fallen into disrepute among some. But what has happened here both in privatized religion and in the reaction against it is a confusion between the interior self and the private self.

The interior self emerges as a result of a differentiation of consciousness, which was first achieved when the individual self was constituted in relation to God. The subject or self with God was differentiated as an interior world over against the external world. Later the relation with God was dropped or ignored, and Christian interiority became modern subjectivity. In either case, the interior self is the subject as distinctly aware of his or her individual being and activity as a conscious subject.

The private self, in contrast, is the self as acting within the private sphere, even when not particularly self-aware. The private sphere consists in those relatively unorganized segments of life, notably the family, still existing in the interstices of bureaucratically administered society. In the trend toward the totally administered society, the family and the related areas of individually chosen personal activities fall more and more under the indirect or hidden control of bureaucratic bodies, such as those that constitute the entertainment industry. Further, because of the dependence of the private sphere upon the public, the sense of freedom in one's private life is to a large extent illusory. Nevertheless, the private sphere does remain a place where people feel a release from the relentless rational routines and compulsions of their working lives.

To confine religion to the private sphere, so that it serves as a therapeutic counterbalance on Sunday to the grinding rationality of the rest of the week, with the church as the rallying point for the suburban escape of family life from factory and city, is blatantly to distort it. But the effect upon religion is derivative. It is chiefly human beings who are crippled when offered personal fulfillment only in the private sphere, so that their freedom is effectively curtailed to a consumer and recreational freedom. Human persons are in that way being refused the full realization of their subjectivity, which comes only in building a truly human society in a free and equal communication with other human persons. Thus, the call for the deprivatization of religion and theology would be more adequately expressed as an element in a demand for the deprivatization of the personal life of human subjects.

The underlying problem here is positivism and the Romantic compromise with positivism. What is at work in the present polarity between public and private spheres is a positivistic identification of rationality with the supposedly value-free, formal rationality of the empirical analytic sciences. That identification excludes any rational grounding of norms and values, so that the ethical and the religious are put outside the realm of the rational and assigned to prerational conventions or irrational free decisions. Romantic and, at a later date, existentialist theologies and philosophies have compromised with positivism, insofar as they too have placed faith and moral decision beyond reason and rational assessment. The polarization between the scientifically (or, more accurately, scientistically) rational and the existential as irrational is reflected in the present configuration of public and private. What is admissible in the public sphere must be justifiable through the value-free procedures of science and technology, which means that public affairs are, or at least should be, in the hands of experts. Values are relegated to the private sphere, because they are not subject to rational grounding or control. I myself once heard a sociologist argue that the discussion of values had no place in a university, because no hard knowledge on them was available; they should be discussed over beer on a Friday night at the faculty club. There are some who see the pocket of irrationality, represented by the private sphere, as eventually overcome when improved techniques enable the irrational to be fully controlled rationally.

The deprivatization advocated by political theology, if not illusory, must be the overcoming of the polarity between the rational and the existential, between public knowledge and strategic action on the one hand and private faith and voluntary involvement on the other. Political theology cannot be simply the inclusion of a concern with social and political issues into a structure of theological thought that remains privatistic. It must articulate and defend a wider concept of rationality than that of the positivists, so that norms and values, moral and religious, can be recognized as subject to the procedures and criteria of an intersubjective communication and a prudential or practical rationality. Political theology must become critical theology, in order to be a public theology, operative within the public sphere. That indeed implies that moral and religious assertions are always open to counterarguments and revisions. Theology, however, does not become political by using social and political issues as material with which to exercise and articulate an utterly private, incommunicable, and therefore socially impotent, existential conviction. It does so by entering and submitting itself to public discussion.

The overcoming of the polarity between the public and private spheres does not however mean the suppression or desuetude of interiority. On the contrary, it will be the liberation of the interior self. The interior self is the self-conscious subject in possession of his or her individuated being and activities and thus through self-possession is free. Such a self is the political subject *par excellence*, capable of entering into the communication process among free participants that constitutes the political life of society as distinct from its mere administration. There is no politics without individuated persons or interior selves and, on the other hand, the self remains undeveloped unless it enters into political relationship with others. By politics I mean the collective shaping of norms and values in free communication, not the struggle for and distribution of power in society.

It is a mistake to confuse the acknowledgment of the unconditional worth of the individual with the individualism of bourgeois society. Bourgeois individualism reduces human beings to their economic relationships and, in doing so, puts them in competition with one another. This ignores all differences among men and women except one, and that one is basically a merely quantitative variation in the amount of property. Society is organized on the principle that human beings are replaceable units, shaped to fit into a limited number of functional slots. There is no place for the immense variety of individual qualities and personal creativity, for that would disturb the system. Individualism is thus not respect for the individuated being of the free person, but simply the human unrelatedness of men and women when organized solely in terms of economic competition. Paradoxically, therefore, individualism means conformity not individuality.

For that reason, a recent writer, Ronald Massanari, has suggested that the theologies of play or imagination — he has in mind the writings of Harvey Cox, Sam Keen, David L. Miller, and others — should be counted among the theologies of liberation. These "playful theologies" are concerned with the liberation of the white American middle-class male from the dominant myth of his oppressive society. He writes:

In the dominant "myth" great emphasis is placed on individualism as part of its ideal. But a closer look shows that individualism is really a closed conformity to the ideal of the "myth." In actual fact the individualism of the "myth" is the death of the individual. Its affect [sic] is militant conformity. When playful theology refers to the individual it is not bound to the conformities of the "myth." It undercuts the very form of individualism found in this monovision of the dominant class, thus potentially liberating the individual to be a creative, self-inventing person. (1977: 202)

The theologies of play as liberation theologies thus urge us to see play as well as work, celebration as well as routine, imagination as well as reason as part of politics when understood in a fully human way. The joyful festivities promoted by religion and the imaginative richness of its symbolic ritual and art are wrongly dismissed as anodynes; they are rather signs of a full humanity. The somber and humorless seriousness of much Marxism is one of the clearest signs that some important element has been missed.

Is not that element perhaps the element of transcendence? Can the interior self in the sense of the individuated and self-possessed human subject be constituted and sustained otherwise than in a relationship to the transcendent? Herbert Richardson maintains, as I have previously mentioned, that political society in the sense of a structurally pluralist society rests upon faith in the transcendent, a faith that prevents the establishment of any official religion and excludes the absolutizing of any single set of temporal goals. Further, he sees the uniqueness of every person as one of the ways in which transcendence has been given expression in the Judaeo-Christian tradition. "To affirm the uniqueness of persons means not simply that God transcends and is uniquely different from every other person, but that all created persons transcend and are uniquely different from one another" (*Religion and Political Society*, 1974: 117). He adds: "This means that there must exist a realm of personal relation and human privacy that stands quite free from scientific — or even social — manipulation" (ibid.).

This suggests another and deeper concept of privacy than the one previously examined. For me — I am not attributing this thesis to Richardson — personal privacy at its most intimate coincides with the mystical element in religion. By the mystical element I mean the experience and subsequent conviction that at its deepest core the reality of my individual self becomes one with Ultimate Reality. I have chosen a general formulation. I have made it clear elsewhere (Davis 1976: 59–86) that I do not consider negligible the difference between a mystical oneness that preserves the distinction of a personal God and the individual human being and a mystical oneness that identifies the self and Ultimate Reality without distinction. I also think that theism has made possible the emergence of the individual self in a way that other forms of religion have not. Nevertheless, the mystical element as found in all the major religions establishes for each person a private space where that person's intimate being opens out on to a reality that transcends history, the temporal order, and society; where, therefore, time is intersected by eternity. In doing so, it liberates the human person into a subjective freedom beyond the conventions of any particular social order.

Clearly, in one sense, that mystical element is apolitical. As transcendent, it is not enclosed within the political order. But I suggest that it is eminently political in as much as it is the deepest source and ground in politics. In releasing human persons into individual freedom as subjects, it makes possible the process of communication among free and equal participants, which is the essence of emancipated politics. The preservation of genuine politics against the encroachment of administration by experts depends upon the continued survival of the individual in our society. But if the human subject has no transcendent and indefeasibly private core, it is hard to see why the individual as a social factor should not be abolished as an obsolete historical form as the scientific control of social systems becomes comprehensive and more efficient.

To adapt, then, a remark of Horkheimer, without the mystical element politics is mere business. If it ignores that mystical element or fails to integrate it with the rational, political theology will be insufficiently critical in its assessment of the present situation and will end by being just one more coat of varnish over post-Enlightenment theology, instead of its replacement.

REFERENCES

Augustine, Saint. 1848. *Expositions on the Book of Psalms*, vol. 2. A Library of the Fathers. Oxford.

———. 1943. *Confessions*. Trans. F. J. Sheed. London: Sheed and Ward.

Davis, Charles. 1974. "The Philosophical Foundations of Pluralism." In *Le pluralisme: Symposium interdisciplinaire / Pluralism: Its Meaning Today*. Montreal: Fides.

———. 1976. *Body as Spirit: The Nature of Religious Feeling*. New York: Seabury Press.

Döbert, Rainer. 1973. *Systemtheorie und die Entwicklung religiöser Deutungssysteme. Zur Logik des sozialwissenschaftlichen Funktionalismus*. Frankfurt: Suhrkamp.

Habermas, Jürgen. 1974. "On Social Identity." *Telos,* no. 19 (Spring): 91–103.

———. 1976a. *Legitimation Crisis*. London: Heinemann.

———. 1976b. *Zur Rekonstruktion des Historischen Materialismus*. Frankfurt: Suhrkamp.

Habermas, Jürgen, and Dieter Heinrich. 1974. *Zwei Redon*. Frankfurt: Suhrkamp.

Lonergan, Bernard. 1958. *Insight: A Study of Human Understanding*. London: Longmans Green.

Mann, Peter, O.S.B. 1969–70. "The Transcendental or the Political Kingdom: Reflexions on a Theological Dispute." *New Blackfriars* 50 (1969): 805–12; 51 (1970): 4–16.

Massanari, Ronald. 1977. "The Politics of Imagination: Playful Theologies as Theologies of Imagination." *Cross Currents* 27: 199–204.

Murray, John Courtney. 1954. "The Problem of Pluralism in America." *Thought* 29.

———. 1960. *We Hold These Truths: Catholic Reflections on the American Proposition*. New York: Sheed and Ward.

Prufer, Thomas. 1963. "A Protreptic: What Is Philosophy?" In *Studies in Philosophy and the History of Philosophy*, vol. 2. Washington.

Religion and Political Society. 1974. Jürgen Moltmann, Herbert W. Richardson, Johann Baptist Metz, Willi Oelmüller, M. Darrol Bryant. Ed. and trans. The Institute of Christian Thought. New York: Harper & Row.

Smith, Wilfred Cantwell. 1976. *Religious Diversity: Essays.* Ed. Willard G. Oxtoby. A Harper Forum Book. New York: Harper & Row.

————. 1977. "Interpreting Religious Interrelations: An Historian's View of Christian and Muslim." *SR: Studies in Religion / Sciences Religieuses* 6, no. 5 (1976–77): 515–26.

7

Theologia Crucis and the Forensically Fraught World: Engaging Helmut Peukert and Jürgen Habermas

Gary M. Simpson

"Helmut Peukert's *Science, Action, and Fundamental Theology* is almost the first — it could be the best — serious application of Jürgen Habermas's theory of communicative action to recent developments in theology" (David Rasmussen on the dust jacket). Even by itself that claim makes justifiable a careful consideration of Peukert's proposal. Systematically and within the structure of his proposal, Peukert turns to Habermas because Habermas figures in centrally at the point of convergence of the fundamental problems of science, human action, and theology.[1] James Bohman has put it simply: "the basic idea behind this work is to develop a fundamental theology from the theory of communicative action" (xxiii) and to develop it in the dimensions of subject, society, and history "all at the same time" (Peukert: 127, 140, 215, 241). Peukert enlists Habermas with a double strategy. On the one hand, "he does not simply apply the concepts of the theory of communicative action already developed by Habermas; rather, he asks whether the conception of rationality developed in this theory must not ultimately have a theological dimension if it is to be consistent and

This article originally appeared in the *Journal of the American Academy of Religion* 57, no. 3 (1989): 509–41. It is reprinted with permission.

coherent" (Bohman: xii). On the other hand, "at the very least, such a reconstruction of the 'rational core' of theological statements would provide a contemporary access to the Christian tradition" (Bohman: xii).[2]

Peukert advances two theses:

First, I want to assert that the Judeo-Christian tradition is concerned with the reality experienced in the foundational and limit experiences of communicative action and with the modes of communicative action still possible in response to these experiences. Second, I want to assert that a fundamental theology can and must be developed as a theory of this communicative action of approaching death in anamnestic solidarity and of the reality experienced and disclosed in it (Peukert: 215).

My long-term project vis-à-vis Habermas assumes a whole-hearted concurrence with this first thesis.[3] Furthermore, my analysis is circumscribed by a broad concurrence with Peukert's basic idea, with the dimensions to be addressed, and with his double strategy.

The major claim[4] of this essay focuses on Peukert's second thesis and is bound up with Bohman's insight concerning a "certainly significant" turning point in Peukert's proposal (Bohman: xiii). Namely, Peukert "clearly sides" with Karl Apel's more Peircean concept of the "unlimited communication community" rather than Habermas's ideal "speech situation" (part 1). This siding is enhanced by privileging Christian Lenhardt's theologically constructed paradox of anamnestic solidarity and by grounding the Christian response to this paradox in a theology of the resurrection.[5] Taken together, this threefold movement determines the overall thrust of Peukert's proposal (part 2).[6] By way of response, I will reconstruct Habermas's critical exchange with his own Frankfurt School heritage and contend that in that exchange he articulates an extreme intensification of the limit experience of communicative action which Peukert's analysis prescinds (part 3). This limit experience, which I will call "the forensically fraught world," provides a contemporary access to a fundamental problem of the Christian tradition. Habermas's formulation, which Peukert prematurely prunes away, must now be grafted back. This can be accomplished with the help of two insights developed by the critical theorist Alvin W. Gouldner. This grafting will find its theological response — via theses — in a political *theologia crucis*. Grounded in a political *theologia crucis* is the innovative Christian experience and praxis of reconciliation. The experience and praxis of reconciliation represents the ultimate response to the limit experience of the forensically fraught world (part 4).

1. HABERMAS AND APEL:
A CERTAINLY SIGNIFICANT SIDING

The systematic-theological background for Peukert's dialogue with Habermas is the "paradigmatic significance for the development of a fundamental theology" (Peukert: 250) of the approaches of Bultmann, Rahner, and Metz. Peukert is indebted to Bultmann's existential analysis of death as a focal category even as he criticizes Bultmann's individualistic reductionism in this analysis. His "perspective" on Rahner's transcendental-hermeneutic transformation of Catholic theology highlights the intersubjectivity implicit in Rahner's thesis of the unity of the love of neighbor and the love of God. From Metz's theology Peukert borrows the insight that theology necessarily should be society-oriented and should include a historical-eschatological dimension. However, just as Peukert's analysis of the history of the philosophy of science culminated in the "basic problem" of intersubjective communication, so also his analysis of these three fundamental theologies points to the following:

a basic problem in common, as yet unsatisfactorily clarified — namely, that of intersubjective communication, or, in other words, communicative action. This problem has a sort of steering function for fundamental theology and thus for the determination of a fundamental conception as a whole (250; also 162).

Enter Habermas!

Peukert's interest in Habermas's theory of communicative competence lies in the conception of the ideal speech situation as the normative core of both theoretical and practical discourse.[7] For the purposes of this essay, I will assume that Peukert's presentation is congruent with Habermas's and will move into a presentation of his critique of the *aporia* that faces Habermas's theory.

Peukert stresses that he has "arrived at a decisive point" in his proposal when he investigates the criteria for distinguishing between a true consensus and a mere convention and how these criteria can be grounded.

To begin with, one could call to mind various kinds of criteria. But even a criterion such as "the reliability of observations" or "the adequate interpretation of the results of experiments" must in turn be decided upon in a discourse. Even if one's intent were to refer back to the truthfulness of the partner or to the correctness of methodological rules, one is still obligated to explain such claims discursively. However, if the claim of a discourse to call "true" a statement about which one has reached an agreement could only then in turn be decided again in a discourse about this discourse, infinite regress is unavoidable. On the other hand, it would be absurd to hold that any given factually attained agreement is valid as a legitimation for truth or correctness of statements. This would entail giving up the search for any grounding of validity claims (186).

According to Peukert, this situation leaves "no alternative but to seek the criteria for the legitimation of validity claims in the structure of reciprocal-reflective communication" (186).

This situation leads Peukert into a consideration of the oft-discussed transcendental-empirical, ought-is paradox. He accepts Habermas's solution to this issue as do I (Habermas 1987a: 321–60; Simpson 1983; Benhabib: 225, 238–43, 255–75, 287–97, 304–9, 325–27). It is my strong contention, however that at this point in his proposal Peukert fails to take a crucial analytic step and that this omission is detrimental for the outcome of his proposal. He seems to recognize the empirical conundrum of "no alternative" to an "unavoidable" "infinite regress" and yet he does not press for a theological analysis of this extreme limit situation that results from the ideal speech situation. In part 3, I will proffer a preliminary analysis of this situation, but before doing so it is important to gain a clear picture of the direction in which Peukert proceeds and its theological outcome.

Rather than a theological analysis of the ideal speech situation and the resulting empirical limit situation, Peukert simply changes the venue to another transcendental presupposition for communicative action and its resulting empirical conundrum.

The idealizing supposition of such a[n ideal speech] situation in the practice of communication has *yet another dimension*. The conversation in which validity claims are decided upon argumentatively cannot in principle be limited. *Anyone who brings forth arguments, anyone who in any way enters with the intention of entering into communication, must be accepted as a partner.* The supposition of the ideal speech situation thus implies an *unlimited communication community*. Hence, in principle, in any communicative act the entire human species is implied as the final horizon of the communicative community. (187; emphases added)[8]

What Peukert does not state in this quotation is that this is the systematic juncture at which, as Bohman puts it, Peukert "clearly sides here with Apel's more strongly transcendental interpretation" of communicative action (xiii). That this "yet another dimension" is an insight borrowed from Apel Peukert makes undeniably clear beginning just two pages later (189–93). Whether or not Apel's articulation is "*more strongly* transcendental" than Habermas's, I will leave as an open question in this essay. It is, at least, "another dimension," i.e., the historical dimension; and it is within this dimension that Peukert seeks to uncover "an elementary *aporia*" (202) that can be cracked open theologically and only theologically. The question still remains: is it the *only* elementary *aporia* that can be and must be cracked theologically and only theologically?

Peukert preliminarily states his problematic in the form of a question:

> But how can what has come to be factually be shown to be rational or rejected as irrational?... The decisive point seems to lie in the question of how, in a situation of conflict or in a period of historical transition, a revision of the previous language and system of norms may be found that heretofore did not exist but nonetheless should be rationally justified. (196–97)

In order to penetrate the historical dimension of this problematic, Peukert takes a deliberate detour first through a controversy with "decisive significance" between Walter Benjamin and Max Horkheimer and second through a "thought experiment" proposed by Christian Lenhardt. Entering these detours with a critical eye will support my major claim that Peukert's introduction of "another dimension" represents a change of venue from Habermas's transcendental criterion and that this change of venue dismisses a most extreme limit situation of communicative action from being considered theologically.

2. BENJAMIN AND LENHARDT:
A DOUBLE DETOUR TOWARD RESURRECTION

Peukert considers the discussion between Benjamin and Horkheimer regarding a closed or unclosed past to be "one of the most theologically significant controversies of our century" (206). As a result of this controversy, Peukert interprets Benjamin's thought as an "attempt, writ large... to bring together historical materialism and theology, and to do so in such a way that historical materialism returns to elementary problems dealing with history and attempts then to indicate a common depth structure" (208). Primarily, Benjamin is concerned to develop a theory of the writing of history that does not renounce the elementary solidarity with the generations of the oppressed. Peukert holds that the generations of the oppressed, "the innocently annihilated" (171, 214, 230–35, 239, 244), must be a key constitutive of the unlimited communication community. The innocently annihilated in particular have been denied partnership and subjectivity and, therefore, must be rescued in a targeted, preferential way.

Peukert notes that Benjamin, in response to Horkheimer's charge that he was theological, suggested that "emphatic memory [*Eingedenken*]"[9] was the precise way "completely nontheologically" to "modify" and "transform" a previously closed past (207). Peukert focuses on Christian Lenhardt's concept of "anamnestic solidarity" as the "most clearly designated" (Peukert: 208) way "of entering into communication (187) for the innocently annihilated. Lenhardt explains this concept by means of a typology of the past innocently annihilated generation, the present oppressed generation that struggles for liberation, and the future generation that achieves liberation. The innocently annihilated generation "owe[s]" nothing to anyone; it already suffers for the sake of a better future for other generations. The generation of those struggling for liberation receives the suffering of the innocently annihilated generation as a gift to the struggle and works for the liberated happiness of the future generation in order to satisfy its debt to the annihilated generation. What is the situation of the future generation? On the one hand, if this future liberated generation through remembrance keeps solidarity with the innocently annihilated, thereby paying its debt to past generations and retaining the universal solidarity that is necessarily constitutive for identity, then how can this liberated future generation be considered "happy," since it maintains this extremely unhappy memory? In this case the price of liberation is an unhappiness which cannot be real liberation. On the other hand, if in order for liberation to be happiness it must forget the extreme unhappiness of the past innocently annihilated generation, then how can it be considered liberated while severing its solidarity with the innocently annihilated through amnesia? In this case the price of liberation is the loss of universal solidarity which is constitutive for a liberated identity. "Anamnestic solidarity marks, then, the most extreme paradox of a historically and communicatively acting entity;... the condition of its very possibility becomes its destruction" (209).[10]

This analysis brings Peukert to the second basic thesis of his overall proposal: the response to the "paradox of an existence that refuses to extinguish the memory of the victims of history in order to be happy" is "ultimately theological" (210). Peukert argues that the theological response to the paradox of anamnestic solidarity must be grounded in the historical experience that the Christian tradition calls the resurrection of Jesus.[11]

The Gospels and the entire Christian proclamation are unequivocal...that God resurrected Jesus from the dead.

The experience of the resurrected Jesus signifies for others the opening of the possibility of existing in solidarity oriented toward God.

The act of the resurrection of Jesus makes possible faith in this resurrection. As anamnestic solidarity with Jesus...faith in the resurrection of Jesus is at once universal solidarity with all others. And as anamnestic solidarity, it is universal solidarity in the horizon of all humanity and of one unified history; it constitutes one humanity in the unconditional solidarity of communicative action that anticipates the completion of salvation for all. (226–67)

In his theology of the resurrection, Peukert does not forthrightly and systematically address crucial questions. Is not the intent of the rescue of the innocently annihilated that these innocently annihilated might now be subjects in community rather than "refuse in history" (206)? Furthermore, is not a constitutive requirement of their being subjects in community that they indeed be partners in communication? Finally, is not partnership in communication enacted precisely by bringing forth arguments, by giving an account of those arguments, *and* by way of response listening and replying to arguments that are brought forth?[12] This situation immediately raises again the issue of the dynamics of speech as communicative argumentation and ultimately poses the question of the distinction *and* relationship between solidarity and reconciliation vis-à-vis a universal community. As I will argue in part 4, these issues can only be addressed adequately to the extent that fundamental theology is grounded as a *theologia crucis*.

3. PRUNING AND ITS PROBLEMS: ANAMNESTIC SOLIDARITY AND LIKENESS

The culminating theological thrust of Peukert's proposal unintentionally truncates the question of the subjectivity of the resurrected innocently annihilated ones by overlooking the dependence of their subjectivity on intersubjective accountability rooted in speech as communication. This happens because Peukert fails to engage in a theological analysis of the kind of communication that would occur even within the universally inclusive community for which he argues, the kind of communication that Habermas describes with his transcendental criterion of the ideal speech situation. Even though Peukert prunes Habermas's criterion before it is probed for its theological depth dimension, there still are "faded inscriptions"[13] in his proposal that can be deciphered in order to address this issue. Refurbishing these faded inscriptions will take us beyond the paradox of anamnestic solidarity as "the most extreme intensification of the basic experience preoccupying the Jewish and Christian tradition" (Peukert: 230).

The survival of these faded inscriptions is related to one of my preliminary theses: Bohman correctly notes that Peukert "sides" with Apel's transcendental criterion, resulting in an eventual pruning of Habermas's criterion. Also Bohman correctly notes that this siding is "certainly significant." It is necessary, however, to provide an analysis of this siding since this siding is not accomplished "clearly," as Bohman says, but rather implicitly and ambiguously. On the one hand, Peukert states that he will "note at important junctures how this [Habermas's] approach differs from others [notably from the Erlangen School and from Apel]" (184). On the other hand, he states: "In the various analyses different vocabularies have been developed, most of which serve to distinguish the various attempts at analysis *rather than to make substantive distinctions*" (184, emphasis added). He then states that he will "adopt Habermas's terminology" because "it comes closest to reaching the dimensions most appropriate to the problem at hand" (184). The ambiguity regarding his siding with Apel arises because he adopts Habermas's terminology throughout while simultaneously siding with Apel's transcendental criterion of "the unlimited communication community" as "the utmost ideal achievable in modern times" (202). By employing Habermas's terminology to side with Apel's criterion and thereby the problematic which that criterion addresses, Peukert surreptitiously jettisons Habermas's criterion and problematic with regard to the overall thrust of his proposal.

Systematically, on the one hand, the siding with Apel means that Peukert focuses on the praxis-oriented problem of humanity's universal solidarity in the face of the counterfactual, temporal annihilation of innocent victims. On the other hand, this siding with Apel marginalizes and obscures another praxis-oriented problem: the kind of intersubjective communication that would provide the normative foundations for social evolution, society, and subjectivity. Peukert's privileging of Lenhardt's typology follows closely on the heels of his siding with Apel. Categorically, on the one hand, this siding results in privileging the categories of innocently annihilated, universal solidarity, anamnestic solidarity, and resurrection. Within the proper framework, this privileging is highly laudable and remains one of the key insights — though not the only one — of liberation theology. This privileging is absolutely necessary, even while remaining insufficient, for any future Christian theology. On the other hand, in the culminating thrust of Peukert's proposal the systematic privileging of these categories results in an accompanying, gradual and surreptitious fading — almost to the point of disappearance — of the categories of *Mündigkeit*, reciprocity, argumentation, self-reflexivity, critique, self-critique, systematic distortion, and crucifixion. As I will argue in more depth later, these one-sided tendencies need not be the case.

It is my strong claim that the problematics that have led Habermas to formulate his transcendental criterion of the ideal speech situation cannot be simply pruned and jettisoned in a kind of quantum leap to "another dimension." Nor do I think that the historical dimension intensifies the *aporia* of communicative action so that the problematics of the ideal speech situation are rendered either preliminary or of less significance for theology. The problematic of the distinction between a truthful consensus and a mere convention, which has arisen within the contexts of Habermas's many disputes,[14] is intimately connected with the subjectivity of those who are rescued from the refuse heap of history. Their subjectivity, to the extent that it remains deeply dependent on their partnership in communication, means having not only the right to speak for themselves — that much at least — but also and especially the privilege and right to hear and respond to a just and true critique rather than to the annihilating injustice perpetrated upon them. Furthermore, their partnership in communication means having the privilege of being accountable even for the mortifying arguments that they bring forth against their annihilators who deserve them.

It is precisely the dependence of participatory subjectivity on a particular genre of intersubjective speech and the significance of this dependence for the distinction between a truthful consensus and a mere convention that has led Habermas to a detailed analysis of argumentation. At the heart of this analysis of argumentation lies his oft-made reference to the forensic metaphor of the courtroom, the "court of appeals" (Peukert: 116).

To sum up.... Thus the rationality proper to the communicative practice of everyday life points to the practice of argumentation *as a court of appeal* that makes it possible to continue communicative action with other means when disagreements can no longer be repaired with everyday routines and yet are not to be settled by the direct or strategic use of force. (Habermas 1984: 17–18, emphasis added)[15]

The human community can never get beyond nor should it ever upon appeal regress below the communicative courtroom. In all communication and in every community no matter how universal there remains at least the possibility of an appellate transition — a turning-up-the-volume or an upping-the-ante — to the courtroom of argumentation. Truncating this possibility in any way is the ultimate distortion.

Peukert accurately describes Habermas on this score and both explicitly and in faded inscriptions seems to subscribe to this situation as "at the same time the central thesis of the whole of theology" (Peukert: 171). He does this when he couples solidarity with "reciprocity" as "elementary determinations" (202);[16] when he argues that "the constitution and transformation of reality" is "bound to a medium" of reflexivity (138); when he notes that "argumentation" is "the most clearly and systematically reconstructed paradigm" (190); and when he argues that in the dialectic between factual and critical genesis "there must be a constant return ... to ever-renewed testing ... as the necessary structure of a rational treatment of history" (197).

On the one hand, Peukert agrees with Habermas; on the other hand, it is difficult to figure out precisely why he just prunes this limit situation from theological analysis. Does his avoidance of theologically confronting this limit situation arise out of a mendacity due to a perception that the Christian tradition has little resource with which to respond to this situation? The primary source of this conjecture is that "decisive" point in Peukert's analysis that we looked at in part 1 above (see Peukert: 186). How he nuances the particular paragraph which we examined seems to indicate an embarrassment of sorts at having to admit that, when it comes to grounding truth, there is no alternative to an "unavoidable," discursive "infinite regress," save giving up the search altogether. May it not also be that he nuances this paragraph too one-sidedly with the terminology and perspective of theoretical philosophy and formal logic and thereby this extreme conundrum looks just plain uninteresting to a praxis-tuned political theology? Perhaps if the limit situation of an unavoidable infinite regress, or better "ongoing testing" (Habermas 1987a: 199, 206, 321, 347), were reconstructed from the perspective of practical philosophy, then this conundrum would appear theologically charged.[17] It is just for this reason that in part 4 I will enlist Alvin Gouldner's articulation of critique.

In an earlier discussion, Peukert makes a similarly nuanced reference that the "claims to be raised for a theory of communicative action ... leave the impression that one is asking for the impossible" (166). In this context he notes that Apel's "transformation of philosophy" means precisely that "we must withdraw from the illusion that absolute reflection is possible for communicative practice and its reflective self-enlightenment" (166). On the one hand, that absolute reflection is in fact not possible, with that I heartily agree. On the other hand, that absolute reflection is asked for and even demanded, necessarily and absolutely demanded if truth, truthfulness, and correctness are to be pursued, to that I also heartily subscribe. There remains a necessary and absolute, impossible demand for the sake of truth, truthfulness, and correctness, and within this demand itself lies the "formal anticipation of the correct life" (Peukert: 191), "of leading a genuine life" (Habermas 1983: 109).[18] This intersubjective situation denotes the most fundamental limit experience, though not the only one, preoccupying the Jewish and Christian traditions precisely because even God submits God's self to the demand of communicative reflection and reflexivity. For Christian theology this situation can only be expressed as a fundamental *theologia crucis*, as I will argue later.

Habermas's most radical diagnosis of this extreme limit experience of human interaction comes, appropriately so from the perspective of the demand of reflexivity, in his critique of his own predecessors, Horkheimer and Adorno.[19] He argues, in a rather thick paragraph even by Habermasian standards, that behind their "myopic perspective" to get "beyond" the forensic situation of "critique" and "justification" "rightly intertwined" there resides a "purist belief" and "intention" — a "purism" — in which they "remained caught" (1982a: 30). Habermas retorts that there remains an "everlasting impurity" within human interaction, no matter how universal, that makes the presupposition of the ideal speech situation "necessary" and "inescapable." The "always already" of the transcendental criterion is always already bound to the "always already" of the pragmatically based everlasting impurity.

But they [participants in discourse] know, or at least they are able to know, that even that presupposition of an ideal speech situation is only necessary because convictions are formed and contested in a medium which is not "pure" nor removed from the world of appearances in the manner of platonic ideals. Only a discourse which admits this everlasting impurity can perhaps escape from myth, thus freeing itself, as it were, from the entwinement of myth and Enlightenment (1982a: 30).[20]

Much of the time this fundamental insight appears somewhat muted because Habermas expresses it most often through the term "counterfactual" (1982b: 235–36; 1976: 348–49; 1987a: 206, 404–9). The communicative court simultaneously is necessitated by and surfaces in a counterresponse to the factual everlasting impurity, what Alvin W. Gouldner aptly calls "the universality of internal contradictions" in all their historical particularity (Gouldner 1973: 425–28, 449; 1976: ix–xvi; 1980: 8–16, 30 n. 13, 169–73, 252–53).

Peukert evades a theological analysis of this extreme tension between the ever-renewed testing of the ideal speech situation and the everlasting impurity in the pragmatics of speech, and he does so via a kind of hyper-acceleration to "another dimension." At one point he does this by noting that "to justify means to universalize" (Peukert: 193). However, even within a universal community there must be testing. Universalizing does not exempt critique and justification; on the contrary, the very need and necessity for universalizing arises so that intersubjective, reflexive critique and justification can proceed, so that the courtroom can proceed. In one faded inscription Peukert too seems to suggest something similar, namely, that the pursuit of truth, truthfulness, and correctness "always occurs in the horizon of a community which is universal *and within which* [!] claims upon actions and orientations must be tested and established" (194, emphasis added). Yet, the overall thrust of Peukert's theological proposal depreciates this situation. Why is this the case?

Peukert fixates on the necessary but *per se* insufficient problematic of temporality and universality, and this fixation hinders him from engaging in a more penetrating analysis of the resonance between universality and justification (Habermas 1982b: 246–47). Systematically, this results from treating the paradox of anamnestic solidarity not only as "a common depth structure" (Peukert: 208) between historical materialism and theology or as the "point of departure" for theology (235, 239) — both of which are certainly valid and fruitful apologetic approaches — but also as a kind of steering mechanism or central sinew for the whole thrust of a fundamental theology (230, 244).[21]

In an important sense, the very categories that Peukert uses become subsidiary steering components that shore up the main steering rudder and further impede a more radical diagnosis of the limit situations of communicative action that arise in the resonance of universality with critique and justification.[22] Severed from the resonance of universality with critique and justification, anamnestic solidarity *as* the controlling category can lead to a rather dangerous situation. With the help of insights developed by the feminist critical philosopher Seyla Benhabib, I will proffer a perspective on Peukert's controlling category of anamnestic solidarity.

Anamnestic solidarity is a conflation of anamnesis and solidarity, of "a remembering existence in practical solidarity" (Peukert: 239), and, therefore, it can be probed in its separate movements. Peukert informs us that anamnesis is a category that he adopts from Benjamin as well as from Metz. While there is a difference between anamnesis as remembrance and mimesis as imitation, Benhabib's analysis of mimesis yields an instructive critique that is productively applicable to the concept of anamnesis.[23]

Benhabib's critique of mimesis is developed within her discussion of Horkheimer and Adorno. Because Horkheimer and Adorno remain trapped within "the work paradigm of human activity" — in distinction from Habermas's paradigm shift to intersubjective, communicative action — for them "the fundamental relation is that between humans and nature" (Benhabib: 200). For Horkheimer this relation to nature is articulated via Marx's understanding of labor, while for Adorno the relation to nature is articulated via the idea of aesthetics. While they reject the Marxian moral optimism attached to the work model of action, their model of mimetic activity is "a reversal but not a true negation of the work model of activity" (Benhabib: 189). Benhabib argues that the work model of activity in its Hegelian form resorts to the "externalization into nature" of a single subject, Spirit; in its Marxian form to the "objectification of nature" by a collective subject, humanity; and in its mimetic form to the "internalization of nature" by the isolated subject.

For Adorno, mimesis surpasses mere mimicry, which results in the suppression of the self by the other, by giving oneself over to the other via contemplation. But Benhabib persists in her suspicion that mimesis, functioning as an encompassing fundamental category, remains too tied to idealism and its philosophy of the subject and identity (*merito!*).

Yet what distinguishes this [contemplative] act of giving oneself to the other from an act of narcissism? How can we ever establish that this act of contemplative giving into the other is not merely a *projection* on the part of the self onto the other attributes that the self would gladly acknowledge to be its own? Why isn't mimesis a form of narcissism? (221)

Benhabib argues that "mimesis is best actualized in the sphere of relations to another like ourselves" (387; also see Habermas 1984: 382–90; also Moltmann: 26–28). Peukert seems to recognize this danger of likeness in reference to anamnesis when he notes that a "basic problem [is]... divinizing the one who is remembering — the historian" (Peukert: 311). My problem with him on this score is that he has relegated this comment to a footnote without any further systematic consideration or theological analysis. That would not be so damaging if it were not for the fact that this untreated "basic problem" is intimately connected to the controlling category. Benhabib's analysis of mimesis and likeness indicates that even revolutionaries are susceptible to the lure of likeness (180–82). The lure of likeness is ultimately most dangerous to the innocently annihilated ones if their subjectivity is dependent primarily on the remembering of revolutionaries.

Peukert employs the category of solidarity as a version of "transsubjectivity," a concept that he takes up in his discussion of the Erlangen School's treatment of history. He remarks:

If one agrees with the principle of transsubjectivity as a basic principle, it is naive not to establish this transsubjectivity in its historical dimension from the start. My intent is not to investigate this thesis in its entirety, or even the total structure of such a reconstruction, but rather to analyze more precisely the decisive point of the proposed procedure in its microstructure. (197, emphasis added)

The "if," along with the other nuances of this remark, implicitly indicates that he essentially agrees with the principle of transsubjectivity and promotes this principle through the category of solidarity. Solidarity can be readily correlated with transsubjectivity because both can be conceptualized in a historical dimension. This correlation makes it apparent why solidarity is so compatible with anamnesis, which is also obviously diachronic.[24]

Because Peukert employs "solidarity" as a version of transsubjectivity, Benhabib's perceptive critique of transsubjectivity can be fruitfully explored within this essay. She correlates transsubjectivity with the tendency to privilege a collective singular subject of history from Hegel to Marx to Horkheimer to Adorno, and even to Habermas.[25] She enumerates four presuppositions of the philosophy of the subject in which the model of transsubjectivity, its history, and its activity constitute three of the four presuppositions. Briefly stated, the transsubjective subject "externalizes" (Hegel) or "objectivizes" (Marx) or "recollects" (Adorno) or "generalizes" (Habermas) itself. Because transsubjectivity (solidarity) remains tied to the philosophy of the subject and to the work model of activity, it undermines the fundamental plurality of communicative intersubjective action (68–69, 140–41). To these insights I would add that because transsubjectivity (solidarity), like mimesis and anamnesis, expresses and presupposes likeness, it hereby defocalizes the inescapable, pragmatic basis of everlasting impurity that cuts across every transsubjectivity and into every solidarity. With Peukert's coupling of anamnesis and solidarity as *the* steering category, a discourse on likeness could come to dominate.

With a similar concern in mind, Lenhardt borrows an insight put forth by Horkheimer and puts his finger on a trap that can befall even revolutionaries in their — and my — own *per se* necessary and laudable task of judging the contemporary situation with a view toward future-oriented, emancipatory practice.

Our linear progress-conscious minds are wont to consider relevant only that kind of historical consciousness that helps us build an allegedly new world. Progressivists of all ages and shades, and this includes Marxists, were interested in developing a historical consciousness solely for the instrumental purpose of arming themselves for evolutionary or revolutionary change.... Perhaps the task of the historian is not to provide us with ammunition and lessons to learn but simply — or not so simply — to lend an ear to the plaintive voices of ancestors, thus creating a basis for anamnestic solidarity. (Lenhardt: 141)

This insight is recognized by Peukert as well when he notes that the self-critique of self-deception is undertaken intersubjectively so that "self-deception does not become the destructive deception of others" (201). It is for this reason that I had emphasized earlier that those rescued through the resurrection must be rescued in such a way that their subjectivity remains ultimately grounded in the inter-subjectivity of the communicative court rather than in anamnestic solidarity alone. I take this to be the reason why Lenhardt too employs the forensic metaphor, "plaintive voices," when he seeks to provide a grounding, a "basis," for anamnestic solidarity. Only in this way are those rescued safeguarded from being subtly instrumentalized for the otherwise necessary tasks of the evaluation of the contemporary situation or of future-oriented emancipatory praxis or of the constitution of one's own identity.

Anamnestic solidarity becomes a legitimate category for an emancipatory theory and thereby a legitimate moment of emancipatory practice only as it becomes a subsidiary category under the umbrella of communicative argumentation. Indeed, as a movement subsidiary to communicative argumentation, it is necessary! This is necessary because "simply — or rather not so simply" upping the ante to the courtroom cannot result in a fixation *solely* on the courtroom to the minimizing in any way of other future-oriented emancipatory practice. There are, contrary to Lenhardt, lessons to be learned and innovative emancipatory changes to be effected. Yet, the most innovative and emancipatory praxis in our era continues to be the concrete establishment and maintenance of communicatively saturated lifeworld interrelationships and socio-political structures.[26]

The pruning of Habermas's transcendental criterion in favor of Apel's, the privileging of Lenhardt's paradox of anamnestic solidarity,[27] and the focus on a theology of the resurrection[28] all combine to make Peukert's fundamental theology too susceptible to the dangers of likeness and identity. It is my strong contention that the communicative courtroom of argumentation, of critique and justification, is on center stage in all of history and in all the particularity of everyday life. Therefore, it must be given fundamental theological status. Because of this all the solidarity that we can and must muster, also anamnestically, must always maintain a sharpened consciousness of the universality of empirical, internal contradictions and of the susceptibility of both solidarity and anamnesis to identity-orientedness.[29] The maximalizing of emancipatory praxis together with the minimalizing of mere conventional activity necessitates a fundamental theology developed around the continual resonance between the courtroom as critique and justification and emancipatory praxis within all three dimensions.[30]

4. GRAFTING AND ITS GIFTS:
HABERMAS AND *THEOLOGIA CRUCIS*

The Forensically Fraught World

Thesis: Habermas's transcendental criterion of the ideal speech situation actualized as the communicative court of argumentation must not be pruned from the life-giving root of fundamental theology, and this means that the limit experience to which theology must respond is deeply embedded in the empirical circumstances of, what I claim is, a "forensically fraught world."[31]

Commentary: It is the necessary anticipation and the potential ubiquity of this forensically fraught world within everyday life that Habermas has made the bone of contention in his discussions on every turn: from his earliest critiques of positivistic science and of Kant, Hegel, Marx, Pragmatism, and Freud with his insistence on "language" as that which "raises us out of nature" and makes humans human to his dialogues with Popper and Gadamer and Luhmann and Kohlberg; from his more recent interpretive attempts to include the sociological insights of Durkheim, Weber, Lukács, and Parsons within the horizon of communicative rationality to his more critical encounter with his immediate ancestors such as Horkheimer, Adorno, Benjamin, and Marcuse. This same insistent contention continues to be at the heart of his more recent encounters with the neo-conservatives and with the Nietzscheanly rooted Foucault, Derrida, Lyotard, and Rorty (1987a). In all these discussions the conceptualization of a forensically fraught world rules out of order either the monologic reduction of the pursuit of validity or the exclusion of reason altogether from the pursuit of validity or a capitulation to complexity that retreats from the very pursuit or the collapsing of disclosures of meaning with validity or the myopic, nihilistic blindness to the existence of any validity and the accompanying retreat to taste; or any combination of the above. These alternatives all fall off the path of the forensically fraught world and some are even seductive for Habermas (McCarthy 1985).

The question that I have been posing to Peukert throughout this essay is whether, in siding with Apel, in adopting Lenhardt's thought experiment, and in focusing on the resurrection, he has not been unduly seduced away from the forensically fraught world, from *theologia crucis*, and from Jesus' ministry and mission of reconciliation. His retreat from a forensically fraught world represents a collapsing of praxis-generated disclosures of innovative meaning with validity and critique.[32] This collapse runs the risk of a continuation (and increase!) of identity thinking and action in an anamnestic and transsubjective mode and the tragic consequences that can accompany this possibility. Only a concerted insistence on and argument for a forensically fraught world can avert these tragic consequences. Habermas's articulation is the contemporary high ground of that argument and thus the most fruitful partner for a fundamental political theology that maintains a similar insistence.

The refusal to withdraw from, and indeed the radical promotion of, a forensically fraught world does in fact lead to a most extreme and intensified limit experience. With the promotion of a forensically fraught world, Peukert's recognition of the empirically unavoidable infinite regress can be reconstructed from the point of view of practical philosophy so that a more in-depth theological probing of this situation can be undertaken.

In a variety of different contexts, Alvin Gouldner has articulated just such a forensic reconstruction of the limit situation of critique and justification. He also seeks to locate empirically the historically developing embodiment of this forensically fraught world of critique and justification in a particular culture.

The culture of critical discourse (CCD) is an historically evolved set of rules, a grammar of discourse, which (1) is concerned to *justify* its assertions, but (2) whose *mode* of justification does not proceed by invoking authorities, and (3) prefers to elicit *voluntary* consent of those addressed solely on the basis of arguments adduced. CCD is centered on a specific speech act: justification. (1979: 28; also 1965: 168–74; also 1970: 3–18, 481–512)

It is because the embodiment of the forensically fraught world in a particular culture of critical discourse exposes deep empirical internal contradictions that Gouldner, perhaps like no other social theorist, focuses on the grave and internecine consequences of the forensically fraught world. The forensically fraught world is constitutively linked with the intersubjectivity of the death of the other and the self. This link can be seen in the following quotation that culminates in a powerful metaphor.

The grammar of critical discourse claims the right to sit in judgment over the actions and claims of any social class and all power elites. From the standpoint of the culture of critical discourse, all claims to truth, however different in social origin, are to be judged in the same way. The claims and self-understanding of even the most powerful group are to be judged no differently than the lowliest and most illiterate....

Notice, then, that CCD treats the relationship between those who speak it, and others *about whom* they speak, as a relationship between judges and judged.... To participate in the culture of critical discourse ... is thus a subversion of that [the already established social] hierarchy. To participate in the culture of critical discourse, then, is a political act.

The essence of critical discourse is in its insistence on reflexivity [judges becoming subject to their own judging]....It is therefore not only the present but also the anti-present, the *critique* of the present and the assumptions that it uses, that the culture of critical discourse must also challenge. In other words: the culture of critical discourse must put its hands around its own throat, and see how long it can squeeze. CCD always moves on to auto-critique, *and* to the critique of *that* auto-critique. (1979: 59–60)[33]

While Gouldner admits that the historically developing, cultural embodiment of the forensically fraught world "may also be the best card that history has presently given us to play," he argues that there remains dialectically a "dark side" that gives ample reason for "no celebration" (1979: 7–8). His ambivalent assessment corresponds with the ambivalent nuance that I intend by using the word "fraught."[34] There is a very real sense that this forensically fraught world is something that human community yearns for because humanity cannot live and thrive without it. Yet, the more fully the forensically fraught world is embodied empirically in the life-world and in systemic structures and in their reproduction, the more human community cannot live with this forensically fraught world, either. The embodied promotion of the forensically fraught world of critique and justification serves increasingly to expose the universality of internal, empirical contradictions, the pragmatically based everlasting impurity. It is the empirically ambivalent fraughtness of the forensic world that necessitates that fundamental theology be articulated as a political *theologia crucis*.[35]

Theologia crucis

Thesis: The promotion of the forensically fraught world necessitates the development of fundamental theology as a political *theologia crucis* since on the cross God also submits to and becomes dependent upon the forensically fraught world.

Commentary: Jürgen Moltmann's political *theologia crucis* is the best — though not the best possible — of the more prominent contemporary proposals of *theologia crucis* within a First World context. This is the case because he integrates three components: the God-against-God dimension of the crucifixion, the forensic framework of the crucifixion, and a socio-political reference for *theologia crucis*.[36] First, Moltmann interprets Jesus's crucifixion in reference to a tripartite conflict brought on as a consequence of his ministry (126–59). Jesus is in conflict with the Romans, the Jews, *and* with God.[37] While it is not unusual for many, if not most, contemporary interpreters to view Jesus's death as a conflict with the Roman authorities and/or with the Jewish authorities, Moltmann takes the conflict of Jesus on the cross into the heart of God. "The theology of the cross must take up and think through to a conclusion this third dimension of the dying of Jesus in abandonment by God...[as] something which takes place within God himself" (152). If the crucifixion is not understood as something within God, then it is too facilely interpreted only as an injustice perpetrated by the Romans and/or the Jews resulting from a misunderstanding on their part. Moltmann stresses that the cross as a conflict between God and God prevents such a popular but truncated conceptualization of the cross (149–52). God cannot simply be enlisted in support of the innocently annihilated Jesus vis-à-vis his unjust executioners, a support that is then confirmed, fulfilled, and redeemed in the resurrection.

Second, Moltmann not only takes the crucifixion into the heart of God but he does so forensically. The tripartite conflict of the cross is a tripartite trial of the cross between Jesus and the Romans, the Jews, *and* God. Furthermore, as the first point implies, this cruciform trial is not between the Romans and/or the Jews on the one side and Jesus and God on the other. Rather, the cruciform trial that takes places as "something within God himself" is a trial of "God against God," a "theological trial between God and God" (152). The forensically fraught world demands radical reflexivity and on the cross God submits to this most extreme and mortifying limit.[38] It is within this threefold forensic framework that Jesus is crucified as rebel, blasphemer, *and* God-forsaken.

It is the ubiquity of a forensically fraught world with its promotion of radical reflexivity that necessitates interpreting the cross as a theological trial between God and God. This trial between God and God surfaces already within Jesus's ministry, a ministry that Peukert rightfully interprets through the conceptualization of communicative action. The ubiquity of the forensically fraught world surfaces in Moltmann's theology in his understanding of "righteousness" that is both empirical and eschatological-apocalyptic (173–77).

In so far as Jews and Gentiles are involved in the crucifixion of Jesus, faith in the righteousness of the crucified Jesus regards itself as bearing public witness in the universal trial concerning the righteousness of God, a trial which is the ultimate motive force of human history. (134)

And again:

Only on a superficial level is "world history" a problem of universal history, by the solution of which a meaningful horizon can be found for the whole of existence. At the deepest level the question of world history is the question of righteousness. And this question extends out into transcendence. (175: see also 61, 68–69, 168, 226, et al.)

Rudolf Siebert makes a critique of Peukert's student, Edmund Arens, who "is particularly hestitant [sic] to deal with the negativity of God mythologically expressed in his 'wrath.' . . . Political theology must take this negativity of God seriously" (Siebert: 422). Siebert seems to hold this same critique of Peukert (Siebert: 430–31, 457–59), a critique to which I subscribe because it cuts to the heart of Peukert's deficiency. While Peukert at times comes close to explicating the ministry of Jesus in its connection with the negativity of God, he finally withdraws from this understanding. For instance: "Thus the dispute about a specific mode of communicative action is at the same time a dispute about the reality *of* God" (Peukert: 224, emphasis added). If the word "of" were instead "within," then Peukert would not be subject to Siebert's rightful critique. The dispute about a specific mode of communicative action is at the same time, and finally on the cross, a dispute about the reality within God or a dispute about the reality of God against God.[39]

I remain dissatisfied with the notion of the "negativity of God" that is employed mystically by Siebert as well as in other ways by Douglas Hall, Carl Braaten, and Paul Tillich. My dissatisfaction arises because that terminology is not as sufficiently forensically saturated as I think is empirically indicated, biblically warranted, and systematically necessitated. A determinate enlistment of Habermas's conceptualizations can help to correct this deficiency. Such a determinate enlistment would also show more precisely than does Moltmann that the forensically fraught world is the thread that links together Jesus as rebel, blasphemer, and God-forsaken and thus the causative undercurrent of his death, an undercurrent that goes back to his ministry. A conceptualization of the resurrection from the dead, which is beyond the scope of this essay, will have to show the resurrection's significance in relation to this forensically fraught, intersubjective notion of death.

Third, Moltmann rightfully seeks to develop political theology as a *theologia crucis*.

Theologia crucis is not a single chapter in theology, but the key signature for all Christian theology. . . . The theology of the cross is a practical doctrine for battle. . . .

In political terms, its [Luther's *theologia crucis*] limit lay in the fact that while as a reformer Luther formulated the *theologia crucis* in theoretical and practical terms against the medieval institutional church, he did not formulate it as a social criticism. . . . The task therefore remained of developing the theology of the cross . . . as social criticism. (72–73)[40]

The socio-political penetration of *theologia crucis* cannot be formulated in a once-and-for-all relationship since socio-political realities are highly diversified both diachronically and synchronically.

That almost obvious insight stands behind D. Hall's clarion call for an "indigenous" theology of the cross. Moltmann, of course, knows this fact and gives a very suggestive indication of the direction that this indigeneity might take in a contemporary Western context.

If the Christ of God was executed in the name of the politico-religious authorities of his time, then for the believer the higher justification of these and similar authorities is removed. In that case political rule can only be justified "from below." ... Political rule is no longer accepted as God-given, but is understood as a task the fulfillment of which must be constantly justified. The theory of the state is no longer assertive thought, but justifying and critical thought.... A critical political theology today must take this course of desacralization, relativization and democratization. (328)

In light of this suggestion it can be claimed that because the radical intensification of the limit situation of the forensically fraught world is taken up by the cross into God, then the forensically fraught world must be brought to bear ubiquitously and into the empirical particularities of the lifeworld and the systemic structures. There then can be no socio-political context which is or can be neutralized, immunized, or isolated from the forensically fraught world.[41] In this vein Moltmann notes: "The new 'political theology' and 'political hermeneutics'...become more radical when they seek to reclaim from the biblical tradition the awareness of a trial between the eschatological message of Jesus and social and political reality" (326).

It therefore remains obligatory for a practiced socio-political *theologia crucis* to enlist vigorously the empirical analyses being developed from the perspective of the investigation and promotion of the forensically fraught world.[42] Moltmann has not yet done this to my satisfaction and perhaps cannot do it integratively without first articulating his political *theologia crucis* more directly in conjunction with communicative action. It is to Peukert's unsurpassable credit that he took the initiative to intensively investigate communicative action in light of fundamental theology.

The Ministry of Reconciliation

Thesis: A practiced socio-political *theologia crucis* pursues the Christian hope *ultimately* as a ministry of reconciliation.

Commentary: In the context of this essay the polemical edge of this thesis resides in the praxis of reconciliation as ultimately surpassing solidarity. The praxis of reconciliation aligns itself more closely to a forensically fraught political *theologia crucis* than does the praxis of solidarity which itself dare not in any way be depreciated with regard to its necessary endowment to the praxis of reconciliation.[43]

With this alignment, the praxis of reconciliation takes more deeply into itself the universality of empirical, internal contradictions than does the praxis of solidarity.[44] The praxis of reconciliation, therefore, more focally highlights the necessity of reflexive critique and repentance as a radical life of repentance for all parties than does the praxis of solidarity, as well as more fully pursues a universally inclusive community. In this way, the praxis of reconciliation more carefully counters the seductions of identity thinking and activity than does the praxis of solidarity (that is, a solidarity which is unfettered from forensic fraughtness).[45] This carefulness of the praxis of reconciliation is also its fragility.

The ministry of reconciliation in the empirical, pragmatic circumstances of human socio-political life counters the cooptational and exploitative intentions of the powerful to the extent that this ministry and praxis is grounded and continually tested by the forensically fraught world of the cross. The constitutive interpenetration of the praxis of reconciliation with the forensically fraught world of critique and the cross is what delivers the promotion of reconciliation from being functionalized as a "cover-up, the sin of sins" (Stendahl: 87). James Cone, perhaps more adamantly than any contemporary theologian, has paraded the cooptation of reconciliation as a thematized issue for public scrutiny (74–76). In Jan Lochman's reconstruction of reconciliation, he seeks to counter the "false ideology of reconciliation" by constitutively coupling reconciliation with liberation (105–12).

It is only by grounding reconciliation forensically in critique and the cross that the ministry of reconciliation can be conceived *at all* in reference to murder and to murderers.

With the question of righteousness in history...the message of the new righteousness which eschatological faith brings into the world says that in fact the executioners will not finally triumph over their victims. It also says that in the end the victims will not triumph over their executioners. The one will triumph who first died for the victims and then also for the executioners, and in so doing revealed a new righteousness which breaks through the vicious circles of hate and vengeance and which from the lost victims and executioners creates a new humanity....[Here] can one speak of the true revolution of righteousness and of the righteousness of God. (Moltmann: 178)

There is much more that can and must be said about political fundamental theology and communicative action, but these three components at least can be advanced by way of response to Peukert's proposal to view the paradox of anamnestic solidarity as the most basic limit experience of communicative action and a theology of the resurrection as the most fundamental Christian response to that experience.

NOTES

1. I take Peukert's analysis of the modern history of the philosophy of science and its culmination in the theory of communicative action to be essentially correct and, therefore, I will not address this aspect of his work.

2. I do not concur with Dennis McCann's critique that Peukert has carried off a "raid" on Habermas. A raid implies a strategy of "hit and run" and would in fact be "strategic action" in the deplorable sense (Habermas 1984: 285–95, 322–37). What makes strategic action so reprehensible is running away from reciprocal understanding and the argumentive-communicative situation, and engaging in systematically distorted communication, and thus avoiding accountability. Peukert has not done this!

Roman Catholics in particular have entered into dialogue with Habermas. However, Quentin Skinner notes the convergence between Habermas, with his Protestant heritage, and Luther, "above all...in the 'redeeming power of reflection'" (38) (*merito!*) I, myself a Lutheran, owe a considerable debt to Lutheran theologian Robert W. Bertram, who introduced me to the critical theory of society and the particular direction of my enlistment of it for critical public theology.

3. In view of the valid critique by Arthur Cohen, I am wary of the expression, "Judeo-Christian tradition." It retains a dialectical force — of solidarity, on the one hand, but of subtle cooptation on the other.

4. It is salutary to take note of Habermas's recommendation regarding philosophy and its claims to truth. "It prefers a combination of strong propositions with weak status claims" (1987a: 409).

5. Bohman also notes that this theology of resurrection has its ecclesiological correlate in the *communio sanctorum* that Apel finds at work in Peirce's notion of the community of inquirers (Apel: 28, 204 n. 24).

6. The notion of an "overall thrust" vis-à-vis isolated and/or non-systematically integrated statements, references, or theses is an important aspect of my response to Peukert's proposal. I would argue that my reading of the overall thrust of his proposal can be substantiated by noting how others, such as Rudolf Siebert (1985), read his overall thrust.

7. Peukert's proposal predates Habermas's full-blown presentation of communicative action and thereby does not address his conceptualization of system and lifeworld or his theory of modernity that thematizes the linguistification and liquefaction of the sacred. These two areas in particular must now be taken into consideration when developing the fundamental themes for an indigenous political theology in conjugation with communicative action (see Simpson 1989).

8. May not Peukert's transition to the historical dimension be taken prematurely due to an urgency to defend his teacher, Metz? The opening for this suspicion lies in Bohman's review of "the most direct lineage of Peukert's

book" (ix). As Bohman notes, it is in "the historical dimensions" that Metz challenged Habermas's "disconsolately" reconstructed version of the Enlightenment project (x). For this reason Bohman states: "The present volume is his [Peukert's] most sustained response ... to secure Metz's programmatic and suggestive insights" (xi).

9. The translation of *Eingedenken* can express different nuances. Peukert's "emphatic memory" does not capture the nuance or the *"ein."* I will return to this point in part 3. See David Ingram's translation of *Eingedenken* as "thoughtful identification" (80).

10. Before investigating "what sort of theology" (210) can respond to the paradox of anamnestic solidarity, Peukert urgently makes the point that, given the "paradigmatic, most extreme limit situation" (212) represented in this paradox, there can be no recourse to "a wider, even more comprehensive theory at the same level." I concur with him on this point. There can be no meta-reflection in order to respond to the most extreme empirical paradox of communicative action (213). I thereby share his articulation of the relation between theory and praxis. What I do not share with Peukert, and what can only become clear through the remainder of this essay, is his analysis of what precisely constitutes the most extreme limit situation and thereby the theological and historical innovative response to this limit situation. Furthermore, to the extent that Peukert's critique of a meta-theory overcoming religion is directed at Habermas — he does not specifically name Habermas as his target — he would be mistaken. Habermas also shares Peukert's theory-praxis relationship. Habermas's point is not that some meta-theory is overcoming religion, but rather that a particular historical praxis, which is both articulated and promoted by his theory of communicative action, is overcoming religion.

11. I deliberately use the word "response" when describing how Peukert views the relationship of the resurrection to the paradox of anamnestic solidarity. The question arises whether or not Peukert claims that the resurrection is a "solution" to the paradox of anamnestic solidarity. While he never entertains "solution" language, he does assert that the resurrection "saves" from the paradox (232–38). Peukert does not, of course, view the paradox of anamnestic solidarity only as a paradox in theory or conceptuality but also as an experienced, practical, historical, paradox. Perhaps this much can be said: if the resurrection can be understood as a "solution," it too would have to be understood as an experienced, practical, historical "solution."

In this essay I will not undertake an analysis of Siebert's critique that Peukert's "deficiency consists in the merely 'assertive' character of their [Peukert and his student, Edmund Arens] *aporia*-solution" (Siebert: 472). For Peukert's use of "assertion" see (223–27, 313 n. 26).

12. I take this situation to be central for Habermas from the beginning and at the root of his metaphoric use *and redefinition* of the Kantian term *Mündigkeit*, which is usually translated in Habermas's work as "responsibility and autonomy" (1971: 314ff.). Habermas makes himself very clear — though in a theoretical mode of explication — on this issue of the relationship

between subjectivity, participation in communicative argumentation, hearing critique, accountability, and self-critique (1987c: 74–76). See McCarthy (1982: 59).

From the point of view of Christian systematic theology my notion of "being rescued to be partners by bringing forth, giving account, and responding to arguments" would have to be sustained biblically and creedally by looking at, among others, Jesus' parables and metaphors of the Last Judgment as well as at the meaning of Jesus' own ongoing intercessorial praxis of "sitting on the right hand" of the Creator as that praxis is connected with the praxis of the Spirit and the Church.

13. This is Christian Lenhardt's pithy phrase (Lenhardt: 134).

14. Among these disputes have been: with positivism, critical rationalism, historical hermeneutics, systems theory, "postmodernists," as well as with his own heritage in the Frankfurt School. See even his face-to-face conversation with Herbert Marcuse (1978).

15. See also, for instance, (Habermas 1987a: 40). An additional line of investigation might be to look into the use of forensic metaphors by the earlier Frankfurt School writers. For instance, one of Peukert's longest quotes of Horkheimer includes the phrase "a supernatural court of appeals" (Peukert: 209).

One of Habermas's key insights, which is integral to his concept of argumentation as a court of appeals, is his understanding of "the everyday" (1987a: 311–16, 322–23, 339–41). While beyond the scope of this particular analysis, an investigation of this insight would be important for a full-fledged conceptualization of "the forensically fraught world."

16. See my conceptualization of "reciprocity" as the core structure of communicative action and its connection to a forensic metaphor (1983; 1987: 42–45).

17. Habermas also argues that the moral-practical domain has "a certain priority over" the cognitive-epistemic and expressive as the ground of accountability (1987c: 76).

18. See note 34 below for an example of how Habermas articulates what is here referred to as the "impossible demand."

At this point I would also preliminarily include the whole expressive domain of authenticity or truthfulness. In order to develop this conceptualization sufficiently the whole issue of aesthetic rationality or aesthetic harmony (Habermas 1986: 199–203; 1987a: 314, 418) — the relation of aesthetics and reason, of aesthetics and the redemption of validity claims — must be entered more fully than I have yet done. This is of course a recent hot spot of debate within the growth industry of Habermasian literature. See, e.g., Martin Jay (133–39), Albrecht Wellmer, and David Ingram.

It seems to me that the issue of aesthetic rationality also intersects with some of the debates within theology that have been stimulated by contemporary proposals such as G. Lindbeck's, R. Thiemann's, S. Hauerwas's, et al. I increasingly remain discomfited by these proposals because of their failure to focally articulate the reciprocal intersubjectivity of critique and justification among communities. David Tracy's *The Analogical Imagination* also deals in depth with these issues but is a decidedly different approach from the other above-mentioned theological proposals.

19. See Habermas (1982a). See Peter Hohendahl for an instructive interpretation of Habermas's "Entwinement" article, though Hohendahl does not deal with the thick concluding paragraph to which I will refer. See also Habermas's clarifications regarding "self-reflection in the sense of critique and self-reflection in the sense of universalistically oriented rational reconstruction" (1982b: 229) and the way in which he has attempted to have "the Kantian meaning of 'critique'... attain a position of honour within the Hegelian-Marxist tradition" (1982b: 232).

Not surprisingly Habermas discusses the extreme limit situation posed by critique at other places where he reflects on his relationship to his own Frankfurt School tradition (1983: 101–12 131–72).

20. Habermas takes pains to stress that "It must be made clear that the purism of pure reason is not resurrected again in communicative reason" (1987a: 301). He states: "Once participants enter into argumentation, they cannot avoid supposing, in a reciprocal way, that the conditions for an ideal speech situation have been sufficiently met. And yet they realize that their discourse is never definitively 'purified' of the motives and compulsions that have been filtered out. As little as we can do without the supposition of a purified discourse we have equally to make do with 'unpurified' discourse" (1987a: 323).

The translation and/or version of the final paragraph of this article as it appears in *The Philosophical Discourse of Modernity* (1987a: 130) is slightly different from the earlier English version in *New German Critique*. On the one hand, the later version in *The Philosophical Discourse of Modernity* leaves out the phrase "everlasting impurity"; on the other hand, this version represents an important clarification of Habermas's theory of religion (see Simpson 1989).

21. As I will make clear more specifically in part 4, Thesis 1, I am suggesting that the Marxist notion of critique is a more fruitful "common depth structure" to explore between Marxism and theology than is anamnestic solidarity, which is Benjamin's, Lenhardt's (Lenhardt: 146–52), and Peukert's suggestion. This is the case precisely because critique is a more fundamental limit experience of communicative action to which Christian theology, experience, and praxis respond. See note 35 below.

22. Not only does Peukert refer to the "dilemma" into which the choice of certain categories can lead (314 n. 34), but Lenhardt too notes that the employment of categories can result in "unwittingly covering up" certain problem areas. This is the case with Peukert's choice of anamnestic solidarity as the main steering category and central sinew of his proposal. See also Alvin Gouldner's account of the relationship of critique and "focalization" (1976: xiv, 9, 55, 204, 280–84) as well as his account of the dialectic between critique and apologetic (1976: 278–85).

23. Benhabib's critique is applicable also because, as Habermas notes (1987a: 68), Horkheimer and Adorno employ the concept of mimesis in order to explicate further the notion of *Eingedenken*.

24. In Benhabib's critique of Hegel she notes how Hegel combines trans-subjectivity and memory (31–32).

25. I hope in a future essay to develop Benhabib's critique of Habermas on this score. Habermas also, of course, speaks against the transsubjective notion of a macro-subject (1987a: 357–60).

26. See Habermas's argument on "ideal and reality" (1982b: 235ff).

27. Habermas (1982b: 246–47) registers his agreement that anamnestic solidarity is a "postulate" that follows from the universalistic "logic" of practical discourse and therefore is a limit situation vis-à-vis this abstract logic. Empirically speaking, however, the "relation" that must be established is that of "*participants* in practical discourses." This status of participants in practical discourse hinges on "the force of reconciliation" that anamnestic solidarity "lacks." He again registers his deep appreciation of Benjamin's notion of anamnestic redemption of past injustices — and of Peukert's articulation of Benjamin — that "can at least be virtually reconciled" even though they "cannot of course be undone" (1987a: 15). While it is likely that in both these cases Habermas uses the concept of reconciliation to mean something like the mere reversal of the "brutal contingency...[and] power of facticity" that death wields (Habermas 1986b: 103), I invest a fuller significance to "reconciliation" than a mere reversal of mortal contingency. Does not "the force of reconciliation" depend also upon the status and relationship of all the participants in the communicative court of argumentation once the brute facticity of death is overcome?

28. I take Douglas Hall's critique that resurrection theology is a capitulation to a kind of positivistic optimism and his argument for the necessary development of an indigenous theology of the cross to have its import at this point (121–23, 138–45, 210–13).

29. Benhabib notes that while identity philosophy and theory can be overcome via the paradigm shift to communicative intersubjectivity, the pragmatic basis and "compulsion" of identity activity remains inescapable. Identity activity can either run wild or be "limited" but it cannot be eliminated. On the one hand, she is correct; on the other hand, her conceptualization must be related dialectically to the feminist critique of the prevailing theological view of sin as the prideful overextension of the self's identity. Future conceptualizations of sin must take this critique into itself. Coupled with the traditional focus on an overextending identity is a collapsed identity both of which violate, though in obverse directions, an authentic identity grounded in reciprocal intersubjectivity.

Habermas notes that "The probability of conflict-free [cultural] reproduction by no means increases with the degree of rationalization of the lifeworld — it is only that the level at which conflicts can arise is shifted" (1987a: 348).

30. Habermas does precisely this when he focuses on "the communicative context of a universal historical solidarity" (1987a: 15). He stresses that "critical testing and a fallibilist consciousness even enhance the continuity of a tradition that has stripped away its quasi-natural state of being...[and]

even strengthen solidarity in life contexts that are no longer legitimated by tradition" (1987a: 347).

31. There are numerous, often overlooked, instances in which Habermas makes use of forensic metaphors to fashion the overall thrust of his work. For instance, in the opening sentence of *Knowledge and Human Interest* he uses a forensic metaphor to characterize the whole modern philosophical enterprise. "If we imagine the philosophical discussion of the modern period reconstructed as a juridical hearing, it would be deciding a single question: how is reliable knowledge (*Erkenntnis*) possible" (3). See also, for instance, Habermas's pithy warning against using the "hermeneutical insight into the *prejudicial* structure of understanding to rehabilitate *prejudice*" (1985: 315; my emphasis; see also Habermas 1987b: 310–14).

My use of the term "world" would have to be further developed in relation to Habermas's ontological restructuring of that concept borrowed from the work of Karl Popper (Habermas 1984: 75–102; 1987a: 313–14). Habermas's prioritizing of the moral-practical world over the objective and expressive worlds is also applicable to my notion of forensically fraught worlds.

32. Because Peukert's overall proposal crosses over into collapsing praxis-generated disclosures of innovative meaning with validity, there is a sense in which he converges with other theological proposals such as Barth's, Lindbeck's, Thiemann's, Hauerwas's, et al. These proposals have a tendency to fixate on disclosures of meaning without constitutively connecting these disclosures to the court of validity. This is precisely the force of Habermas's recent critique of both Derrida and Rorty (1987a: 166–67, 197–210, 312–13, 319–21, 334–35). What does need to be stressed is the precise significance that praxis-generated disclosures do have relative to the communicative court. They are crucial because they most often convene the court by bringing suit against conventional disclosures. However, from then on they must participate fully in the historical, communicative process of raising, redeeming, and responding to validity claims. I take this to be exactly the self-understanding of feminist theology, for instance.

33. In virtually all of Gouldner's analyses, he, like no other social theorist of whom I am aware, focuses on the linkage of reflexive critique with the intersubjective experience of death, on critique as "internecine." See, for instance, Gouldner 1970: 414–34, 482–84, 507–10, and 1973: 457–59.

In "tracing the origins and transformation of critique" Benhabib often sounds like Gouldner with her focus on the reflexivity of critique. "Criticism privileges an Archimedean standpoint.... It leaves its own standpoint unexplained, or it assumes the validity to its standpoint prior to engaging in the task of criticism.... The Marxian method of critique presupposes that its object of inquiry is reflexive" (Benhabib: 33). Unfortunately, she does not make the connection between reflexive critique and the intersubjective experience of death that Gouldner does. This connection is crucial for an adequate conceptualization of the limit situation of the forensically fraught world and a practice-oriented *theologia crucis* that responds to this experience.

It comes, therefore, as no surprise that the constitutive connection between liberative praxis and the reflexivity of critique is upheld most forthrightly by those most deeply entrenched in liberative movements, i.e., in movements that seek to liberate people from premature death. See, for instance, Jose Miranda (1–16) and James Cone (1982).

34. The word "fraught" can mean simply loaded or weighted and thus not necessarily express an ambivalent nuance. However, as the standard dictionaries note, "fraught" has also absorbed into itself the ambivalent nuance, which I intend, due to its frequent use in phrases such as "fraught with peril" and "fraught with pain."

Habermas has an excellent discussion of Durkheim's conceptualization of ambivalence vis-à-vis the sacred (1987c: 49–52, 75–76). Durkheim's conceptualization here is reminiscent of Rudolf Otto's understanding of the holy as *mysterium tremendum et fascinans*. Otto's concept in turn reminds one of Martin Luther's standard formula that begins his explanations to the Ten Commandments: We should *fear and love* God that... Habermas, however, when he explicates the phylogenetic transition from the sacred to communicative action, does not thematize adequately enough the ambivalent character of communicative action. More recently he has introduced a clearer focus on this crucial factor. For instance: "In the restlessness of the real conditions of life, there broods an ambivalence that is due to the dialectic of betrayal and avenging force.

"In fact, we can by no means always, or even only often, fulfill those improbably pragmatic presuppositions from which we nevertheless set forth in day-to-day communicative practice — and, in the sense of transcendental necessity, from which we *have to* set forth. For this reason, sociocultural forms of life stand under the structural restrictions of a communicative reason *at once claimed and denied*" (1987a: 325; also 338).

It is Habermas's past deficiency in this regard that has led me to incorporate Gouldner's work. Perhaps Gouldner centrally thematizes this situation where Habermas has not because Gouldner brings the issue of death focally into his critical social theory especially vis-à-vis critique and self-critique where Habermas has not.

35. Part of my major claim is that Habermas, Gouldner, and Benhabib, by focusing on the Marxist notion of critique rooted in the reflexivity of the communicative court, offer a common depth structure between theology and Marxism that is other than and more fundamental than the common depth structure that was first suggested by Benjamin and adopted by Lenhardt and Peukert. See also Paul Connerton's "Introduction" in Habermas 1976: 15–21, for his account of critique as the depth structure of Marxism.

36. This claim can, of course, be more fully redeemed only by entering into an analysis of other theologies as well as an analysis of theologians who offer more general critiques of *theologia crucis*, such as Francis Fiorenza. Furthermore, a more engaging encounter with grassroots Third World "fresh formulations of the theology of the cross [would] perforate our Western cultural curtains" (Schroeder: 13).

37. Thanks to post-Holocaust era investigations into the varieties of Judaism, it is now common to acknowledge that Jesus was not in conflict with all of the Jews or with all of the Romans for that matter and that his dis-

tinctiveness from various Jewish groups was over a variety of issues and to various degrees. Additionally, the early church's effort to search the Hebrew Scriptures for prototypes of Jesus's divine mission shows that Jesus was not thought to be in conflict with all of the future-oriented, promissory actions of God.

38. That this is the case for God implies that this must be the case also for humans in their communicatively constituted subjectivity, also and especially for those who are annihilated innocently if they are to be subjects and not refuse.

39. Some of Peukert's own statements about the prophets (219–20) approach but do not enter this depth dimension.

40. Moltmann's critique of Luther is partially correct yet remains too one-sided. He evaluates Luther only vis-à-vis the Peasants' War. A more circumspect analysis of how Luther brings his *theologia crucis* to bear upon the socio-political realities of his day not only would justify a more nuanced interpretation of Luther but would also be instructive for a contemporary political *theologia crucis*. See, for instance, Robert W. Bertram's reconstruction of Luther's critique of Thomas Müntzer.

41. That there can be no locus of socio-political life that can be immunized from critique and justification is a focal concern of both McCarthy (1982: 78) and Nancy Fraser.

42. See for instance, the essays in *Critical Theory and Public Life*, ed. John Forester; also John F. Forester (1989), Russell Hanson, and Richard Sennett.

43. Victor Furnish links reconciliation "with the very heart of his [Paul's] gospel" (218). Furnish makes this link by connecting reconciliation to justification though he does not trace any sinews to Paul's theology of the cross. For the interconnections between reconciliation, justification by faith, and *theologia crucis* see Paul Hinlicky. My differences with Hinlicky's notion of omnipotence must remain beyond the scope of this essay.

44. Richard Rorty severely chides Habermas for taking "the cultural need" for reconciliation "too seriously" (167) due to Habermas's being "so preoccupied with the 'alienating' effects" of the progressive changes that have created modern communities of solidarity (169). I, on the other hand, applaud Habermas's focalization on alienation and suggest that this concern also lies behind his statement that Horkheimer and Adorno with their retreat to mimesis are only "circling around" the idea of universal reconciliation (1984: 282–83, 372–86).

45. Moltmann's reflections on the distinction between and relationship of a dialectical epistemology and an analogical epistemology can be interpreted in a similar fashion. "The analogical principle of knowledge is one-sided if it is not supplemented by the dialectical principle of knowledge.... The epistemological principle of the theology of the cross ... does not replace the analogical principle of 'like is known by like,' but alone makes it possible" (27).

REFERENCES

Apel, Karl-Otto. 1981. *Charles S. Peirce: From Pragmatism to Pragmaticism.* Amherst: University of Massachusetts Press.

Benhabib, Seyla. 1986. *Critique, Norm, and Utopia.* New York: Columbia University Press.

Bertram, Robert W. 1987. *"Confessio:* Self-Defense Becomes Subversive." *Dialog* 26: 203–5.

Bohman, James. 1984. "Translator's Introduction." In *Science, Action, and Fundamental Theology*, vii–xxii. By Helmut Peukert. Cambridge, Mass.: MIT Press.

Cohen, Arthur. 1971. *The Myth of the Judaeo-Christian Tradition.* New York: Harper & Row.

Cone, James. 1977. "Black Theology on Revolution, Violence, and Reconciliation." In *Christian Declaration on Human Rights*, 64–76. Ed. Allen O. Miller. Grand Rapids: William B. Eerdmans Publishing Co.

———. 1982. "Black Theology and the Black Church: Where Do We Go from Here?" In *A Covenant Challenge to Our Broken World*, 260–63. Ed. Allen O. Miller. Atlanta: Darby Printing Company.

Fiorenza, Francis. 1975. "Critical Social Theory and Christology: Toward an Understanding of Atonement and Redemption as Emancipatory Solidarity." *Proceedings of the Catholic Theological Society of America* 30: 63–110.

Forester, John. 1985. *Critical Theory and Public Life.* Cambridge, Mass.: MIT Press.

———. 1989. *Planning in the Face of Power.* Berkeley: University of California Press.

Fraser, Nancy. 1985. "What's Critical about Critical Theory? The Case of 1985 Habermas and Gender." *New German Criticism* 35: 97–131.

Furnish, Victor. 1977. "The Ministry of Reconciliation." *Currents in Theology and Mission* 4: 204–18.

Gouldner, Alvin W. 1965. *Enter Plato.* New York: Basic Books.

———. 1970. *The Coming Crisis of Western Sociology.* New York: Basic Books.

———. 1973. *For Sociology.* New York: Basic Books.

———. 1976. *The Dialectic of Ideology and Technology.* New York: Seabury Press, Continuum Books.

———. 1979. *The Future of Intellectuals and the Rise of the New Class.* New York: Seabury Press, Continuum Books.

———. 1980. *The Two Marxisms.* New York: Seabury Press, Continuum Books.

Habermas, Jürgen. 1971. *Knowledge and Human Interests.* Trans. Jeremy J. Shapiro. Boston: Beacon Press.

———. 1976. "Systematically Distorted Communication." In *Critical Sociology*, 348–62. Ed. Paul Connerton. New York: Penguin Books.

———. 1978. "Theory and Politics." *Telos* 38: 131–40.

———. 1982a. "The Entwinement of Myth and Enlightenment: Re-reading *Dialectic of Enlightenment.*" *New German Critique* 26: 13–30.

————. 1982b. "A Reply to My Critics." In *Habermas: Critical Debates*, 219–83. Ed. John B. Thompson and David Held. Cambridge, Mass.: MIT Press.

————. 1983. *Philosophical-Political Profiles*. Cambridge, Mass.: MIT Press.

————. 1984. *The Theory of Communicative Action*, vol. 1. Boston: Beacon Press.

————. 1985. "On Hermeneutics' Claim to Universality." In *The Hermeneutics Reader*. Ed. Kurt Mueller Vollmer. New York: Continuum Publishing.

————. 1986a. "Questions and Counterquestions." In *Habermas and Modernity*, 192–216. Ed. Richard J. Bernstein. Cambridge, Mass.: MIT Press.

————. 1986b. "Taking Aim at the Heart of the Present." In *Foucault: A Critical Reader*, 103–8. Ed. David Couzens Hoy. New York: Basil Blackwell.

————. 1987a. *The Philosophical Discourse of Modernity*. Cambridge, Mass.: MIT Press.

————. 1987b. "Philosophy as Stand-in and Interpreter." In *After Philosophy: End or Transformation?*, 296–315. Ed. Kenneth Baynes, James Bohman, and Thomas McCarthy. Cambridge, Mass.: MIT Press.

————. 1987c. *The Theory of Communicative Action*, vol. 2. Boston: Beacon Press.

Hall, Douglas. 1976. *Lighten Our Darkness: Toward an Indigenous Theology of the Cross*. Philadelphia: Westminster Press.

Hanson, Russell. 1985. *The Democratic Imagination in America*. Princeton: Princeton University Press.

Hinlicky, Paul. 1987. "Christ Was Made to Be Sin — Atonement Today." *Currents in Theology and Mission* 14: 177–184.

Hohendahl, Peter. 1985. "Habermas' Critique of the Frankfurt School." *New German Critique* 35: 3–26.

Ingram, David. 1987. *Habermas and the Dialectic of Reason*. New Haven: Yale University Press.

Jay, Martin. 1986. "Habermas and Modernity." In *Habermas and Modernity*. Ed. Richard J. Bernstein. Cambridge, Mass.: MIT Press.

Lenhardt, Christian. 1975. "Anamnestic Solidarity." *Telos* 25: 133–54.

Lochman, Jan. 1977. *Reconciliation and Liberation: Challenging a One-Dimensional View of Salvation*. Philadelphia: Fortress Press.

McCann, Dennis. 1981. "Habermas and the Theologians." *Religious Studies Review* 7: 20.

McCarthy, Thomas. 1982. "Rationality and Relativism: Habermas's Overcoming of Hermeneutics." In *Habermas: Critical Debates*, 57–78. Ed. John B. Thompson and David Held. Cambridge, Mass.: MIT Press.

————. 1985. "The Seducements of Systems Theory." *New German Critique* 35: 27–53.

Miranda, José Porfirio. 1977. *Being and the Messiah*. Maryknoll, N.Y.: Orbis Books.

Moltmann, Jürgen. 1974. *The Crucified God*. New York: Harper & Row.

Peukert, Helmut. 1984. *Science, Action, and Fundamental Theology: Toward a Theology of Communicative Action.* Cambridge, Mass.: MIT Press.

Rorty, Richard. 1986. "Habermas and Lyotard on Postmodernity." In *Habermas and Modernity.* Ed. Richard J. Bernstein. Cambridge, Mass.: MIT Press.

Schroeder, Edward. 1985. "Lessons for Westerners from Setiloane's Christology." *Mission Studies* 11, no. 2: 13.

Sennett, Richard. 1980. *Authority.* New York: Vintage Books.

Siebert, Rudolf. 1985. *The Critical Theory of Religion.* Berlin: Mouton Publishers.

Simpson, Gary M. 1983. *Reciprocity and Political Theology.* Ann Arbor: University Microfilms.

———. 1987. "Whither Wolfhart Pannenberg? Reciprocity and Political Theology." *Journal of Religion* 67, no. 1: 33–49.

———. 1989. "The Linguistification (and Liquefaction?) of the Sacred: A Theological Consideration of Jürgen Habermas's Theory of Religion." *Exploration* 7: 21–35; also as "Die Versprachlichung (und Verflüssigung?) des Sakralen. Ein theologische Untersuchung zu Jürgen Habermas' Theorie der Religion." In *Habermas und die Theologie.* Ed. Edmund Arens. Düsseldorf: Patmos.

Skinner, Quentin. 1982. "Habermas's Reformation." *New York Review of Books,* October 7: 35–38.

Stendahl, Krister. 1974. "Reconciliation." *Currents in Theology and Mission* 1, no. 3: 85–90.

Wellmer, Albrecht. 1984. "Truth, Semblance and Reconciliation." *Telos* 62: 89–115.

8

Rationality and the Limits of Rational Theory: A Sociological Critique

Robert Wuthnow

The attractions of critical theory are many. It poses the important question of how the conditions under which we live — the conditions of an international capitalist system that has become an ever-expanding totality based on technical reason — are shaping our very capacity to think and to make wise choices about our collective destiny. At a time when many other strands of social theory appear to be caught up in the narrow servicing of this totality, the attractions of a theoretical approach that promises fresh insights, an escape, and perhaps even a guide into the uncharted waters beyond our present domain are indeed great. Little wonder, then, that scholars and social activists alike — with concerns as different as analytic philosophy and environmental politics, international relations and cultural sociology, feminism and public theology — have gravitated toward the weighty texts of Habermas and others of the Frankfurt School.

And yet the job of learning from critical theory, and of seeking from it guidelines to direct the tasks of critical scholarship in these wider arenas, must itself be undertaken critically. The program of the Frankfurt School, like the cultural assumptions it seeks to transcend, is inevitably a product of its times and of the specific intellectual heritage it has chosen for its own. Our reading of critical theory must also take into account the dynamics of our own purposes, our own institutional locations, and the broader climate of issues that concern us. Within the framework of critical theory there are, of course, strong assumptions that must be understood and examined — in the spirit of critical inquiry itself — in order to make our own discourse about it as self-reflective as possible. There are in addition, I believe, substantive and methodological lessons that can be learned from examining closely the contributions of critical theory: lessons that may point beyond some of its own assumptions and have value for an even wider variety of theoretical approaches concerned with the important tasks of cultural criticism.

I want to focus here particularly on the manner in which modernity and tradition have been understood in critical theory, and on the ways in which rational communicative action has been conceived. Having raised problematic issues in each of these areas, I then want to take a more constructive tack, building primarily on the importance that critical theory attaches to language, and discussing some of the facets of this emphasis that seem to be in need of special attention in any effort to assess the implications of critical theory for public theology: issues concerning the polysemy of language, the polymorphousness of the lifeworld, the mediation of rationality, and the resacralization of culture.

In pursuing these issues I shall concentrate primarily on Habermas's two-volume work, *The Theory of Communicative Action*, by no means being able to do justice to its complexity and insights, but drawing from it as one of the most extensively argued, responsive to the sociological tradition, and of course recent contributions of the Frankfurt School.[1] My remarks reflect my own particular vantage point as a sociologist of religion, and thus will draw more on issues of language and theory that have begun to attract cultural sociologists in recent years, rather than on any of the various perspectives that might be advanced from the standpoint of philosophy, social ethics, or theology. I shall, however, emphasize assumptions and forms of argument in Habermas's work that may be transferable to critical studies of a wider variety. In doing so, I depart at the outset from one of Habermas's own strongly stated assertions, namely, that all the major lines of theoretical inquiry in the social sciences (other than his own) are fundamentally flawed because they present a limited picture of the modernization process. Whether that is so may be decided on the narrower grounds on which Habermas actually defends this assertion. Nevertheless, the prospect of critical studies learning from Habermas's method, while retaining their own diverse perspectives, seems considerably more likely than does the prospect of cultural criticism marching in lockstep with Habermas leading the parade. Before launching into more specific issues, it will be helpful

to have in mind a brief overview of the broader critical agenda that
Habermas has attempted to develop.

THE PROGRAM OF CRITICAL THEORY

The Theory of Communicative Action brings critical observations to bear
on those areas of life that we in Western democracies have especially cherished, perhaps because these are the areas into which we
have increasingly retreated in search of our own identities, freedoms,
individuality, and sense of meaning: the realms of family, religion,
entertainment, formal and information communication, the arts,
reading, our private escapes, our private lives. Not only have these
realms served as the final bastions in which to protect our sense of
who we are as individuals, but they have also provided the primary
wellsprings from which expressive and critical genres of communication have flowed. Together they constitute the everyday lifeworld
of the individual; collectively, they also constitute the institutional
realms in which traditional values are preserved, in which creative
reflection on the pathologies of one-dimensional capitalism can take
place, and the freedom to muse and discuss the issues that interest
us most can be found.

Habermas, however, does not romanticize this lifeworld. His
interest lies instead in developing a highly abstract theoretical framework in which the problems of the lifeworld can be comprehended
systematically and in the same analytic terms as the forces that have
begun to threaten the lifeworld. These forces, which Habermas often
summarizes in the phrase "monetarization and bureaucratization,"
present a powerful threat, he claims, not only (or even primarily)
because of the political and economic forces that drive them, but
because the most sophisticated theoretical frameworks that social scientists have developed to make sense of these forces have prevented
us from seeing the complexity of their effects on the lifeworld. Indeed, the basic problem is one of language: an arrangement within
our categories of thought that blinds us to the connections between
the various realms of our existence — a bifurcation of speech at the
theoretical level.

This emphasis in Habermas's work, which of course has roots in
the longer tradition of Frankfurt-style critical theory (especially in
Adorno and Horkheimer), creates a particularly strong link between
the interests of abstract sociological theory and more particular efforts to engage in cultural criticism, such as those in the literary
and theological communities. In contrast to the work of more orthodox Marxists, or even many economic and political analysts on

the left and on the right, Habermas brings the discussion of our contemporary malaise out of the realms of technical public policy debates and into the spheres in which reflection on basic public and private values is taking place. It is, therefore, a theoretical perspective toward which a number of theologians have gravitated in recent years: it has become a platform from which to launch critical forays against the meritocracy of experts who presumably view the world through the single-visioned lens of scientific-technical-instrumental rationality.

Before turning to some of the more problematic features of this formulation, there are, I believe, several positive contributions that deserve to be emphasized. At the relatively more concrete historical levels of his discussion (which Habermas, in an ironic turn of the tables vis-à-vis the standard empiricist complaint against social theorists in American sociology, refers to as the more "conjectural" aspects of his analysis), Habermas stresses the impact of two overriding tendencies in modern Western societies: capital accumulation and state bureaucratization. These become the concrete expressions of his more general discussions of money and power. Both the lifeworld as we presently experience it and communicative action as it might possibly be experienced are situated within the context of these dominant societal tendencies. This specification of the main institutional parameters of modern societies has, in fact, been one of the more constant features of Habermas's work over the past two decades. It is, to be sure, not at all unique to his work, deriving as it does from neo-Marxist and Weberian discussions of advanced capitalism and state socialism. Nevertheless, it posits a layer of institutional reality that has often been neglected in critical studies concerned with vague notions of "democracy," "civil religion," the "public square," and the like.

A closely related feature of Habermas's argument that bears underscoring is its emphasis on the crises and pathologies of *both* capitalist and socialist societies. At the extremes, capital accumulation and state bureaucratization of course serve to identify the dominant modes of social organization in capitalist and socialist societies respectively. But both tendencies are, in Habermas's view, present in both kinds of society. Indeed, capital accumulation and state intervention interact constantly to correct the various problems that arise from fluctuations in the world economy and from the unforeseen contingencies associated with central planning. Unlike much of the literature that has emerged in recent years from neoconservative quarters in defense of an idealized version of capitalism against the scourge (or at least inefficiency) of Soviet-style socialism, therefore, Habermas's perspective is oriented toward identifying the sources of problems such as alienation, identity deformations, and privatization in both systems.[2]

It is also worth noting that Habermas's discussion of these problematic tendencies in modern societies is grounded in a broader view of the relation between history and theory than his forebears at Frankfurt inherited from Marxism. He observes, in tracing his own lineage within the development of critical theory, that the emphasis on reason, mind, morality, and other ideals found in the work of Adorno and Horkheimer was contingent on theoretical assumptions that, in turn, were guided by Marxist understandings of the historical evolution of the means of production. Specifically, the Frankfurt School believed it could separate the truth content of these ideals from their delimited, bourgeois, ideological manifestations because of the joint impact of the concrete movement of capitalist forces of production and the consciousness of this movement that Marxist theory provided. Habermas writes: "Without a *theory* of history there could be no immanent critique that applied to the manifestations of objective spirit and distinguished what things and human beings could be from what they actually were."[3] Yet he goes on to observe that this very philosophy of history was sufficiently fragile that the program of Horkheimer and Adorno was destined to fail. They thought the further development of capitalist forces of production would unmask ideology and leave truth revealed, whereas in fact their own empirical investigations during the 1930s and 1940s pointed increasingly to the conclusion that culture of all kinds was becoming enmeshed within the authoritarian structures of capitalism and only instrumental reason was expanding.

The paradoxical feature of this discussion is, of course, that Habermas himself still, at one level, seems to reflect the very historicist reasoning that he criticizes in Horkheimer and Adorno. Like them, he places his own discussion of the problems of the lifeworld squarely within the historical progression of capitalism that underlies the transition from tradition to modernity and beyond. Like them, he also legitimates his own claims to having seen farther or more clearly than his forebears on the basis of an evolutionary conjuncture that has made greater theoretical insight possible. Indeed, he states in the very last sentence of *The Theory of Communicative Action* that his insights have been made possible by the same penetration of monetarization and bureaucratization into the lifeworld that he has attempted to reconstruct: "It may be that this provocative threat, this challenge that places the symbolic structures of the lifeworld as a whole in question, can account for why they have become accessible to us."[4]

Unfortunately, this is a tantalizing thought that is left dangling —

the opening perhaps to yet another theoretical treatise at some point in the future. It does, however, raise both the more general and the more specific questions about the relation between historical movement and critical theory that need to be faced. The general question is whether cultural criticism in the Marxist tradition is to some degree inevitably contingent on some formulation of societal evolution; the specific question, whether Habermas has been effective in reformulating this contingency in such a way that his own diagnoses are any less likely to fail than those of Horkheimer and Adorno. The answer to the former is perhaps implicit in the answer to the latter.

CRITICAL THEORY AND THE TRAJECTORY OF HISTORY

What Habermas has attempted to accomplish, it appears, is a further decoupling of critical theory from assertions about the actual trajectory of history in capitalist societies. This tendency has, of course, been evident among Marxist theorists from the beginning: ambivalence about historical determination is evident in Marx's own writings, and the relations between history and the theoretical reconstruction of history become more complex in Kautsky, and then in Lukács, and of course in Horkheimer and Adorno. The dilemma within Marxist theory has always been how to escape a purely idealistic or utopian vision of the future, on the one hand, by grounding this vision in assumptions about the movement of capitalism itself, while, on the other hand, avoiding specific deterministic statements that run contrary to the actual variability of social change and put Marxist theory itself in jeopardy of empirical disconfirmation.

Habermas, it appears, has effected only a partial resolution of this dilemma. He has been most successful, by virtue of his capacity to specify a number of different levels of theoretical abstraction, at distinguishing evolutionary processes at several interconnected but distinct levels of abstraction. For instance, his usage of terms such as "monetarization" and "bureaucratization" clearly designates a level of conceptual abstraction that lies somewhat closer to historical events themselves than does his usage of terms such as "action-coordinating mechanisms" and "autonomous subsystem imperatives." To this extent, empirical observations can be distinguished from more abstract conceptions of societal evolution. The price, however, has been paid primarily in Habermas's failure, at least in the eyes of many of his critics, to specify a vision of an alternative to the present — an image of rational communicative action — that is not idealistic and that does not seem unattainable. Put simply, Habermas's vision of rational communicative action remains much less satisfactory than does his analysis of the problems of modernity. Indeed, it is perhaps because the one has yet to be related to the other within the framework of a single systematic theoretical formulation that Habermas so frequently falls back on an implicit notion of historical movement in his selection of words. Lacking a strong, internally legitimated set of connections running from the crises of advanced capitalism to the desired sphere of communicative action, he relies on metaphoric imagery that connotes movement from one to the other.

My point in raising this issue is not to call for a more systematic relating of Habermas's critique of the present with his vision of a preferred alternative. It is rather to suggest that cultural criticism, at least within the context of a culture that is itself deontological, may be constrained to rely on metaphoric images of change. In fact, the lesson for Marxism may be the same as that which has been learned in theological reformulations of the eschatological vision. In neither case can the kingdom of God be set over against the present vale of woe in terms of an actual historical progression. The imagery of becoming, of hope and redemption, of an envisioned community that becomes its own self-fulfilling prophecy, nevertheless remains powerful.

If the metaphor of historical movement plays an important rhetorical role in Habermas's critical theory, it also imposes a distinctive view of the relation between past and present. Although Habermas advances fundamental criticisms of the present and of modernity in general, the dependence of his theory on a sense of cultural evolution forces him to take an even more negative view of the past. He harbors a deep and unqualifiedly negative view of tradition — a view that he has, on occasion, defended vigorously on theoretical grounds. It is, however, more in his uncritical selection of language that Habermas's sentiments betray themselves. Indeed, his choice of words suggests repeatedly that tradition is impure, defiled, repugnant, and to be gotten beyond as quickly as possible.

The main problem with Habermas's conception of the past and of the cultural material left over from the past is that he views it only as a point of comparison with the present. His discussion of the mythic worldviews of archaic societies, for example, is not meant to illuminate features of the past that might need to be reincorporated into contemporary culture but to show how modern conceptions of rationality operate. Myth cannot be thought of as an ongoing feature of the present, or even as a mode of discourse that can temper the harshness of modern rationality. One is relegated to the distant past; the other is made to characterize the entire present. In short, myth and tradition become stylized elements of Habermas's dialectical form of argumentation. They present an extreme contrast against which to compare rationality; therefore, those features of myth that differ most distinctly from rationality are emphasized at the exclusion of other elements. As Habermas asserts, mythical worldviews "present an antithesis to the modern understanding of the world."[5]

In reading Habermas we must, therefore, be careful not to reify categories that serve primarily an argumentative purpose, making them part of our own taken-for-granted worldview, rather than seeing them as tools of discourse. Habermas's intention is to create an argumentative space from which to gain perspective on the distinctive, but generally taken-for-granted, assumptions of modern rationality. His method is to construct systematic contrasts between rational and mythic worldviews. Doing so allows him to thematize characteristics of the rational lifeworld in a way that what was once invisible becomes, as it were, visible.

RATIONAL COMMUNICATIVE ACTION

Habermas's conception of an as-yet-to-be realized state that contrasts with the conditions he criticizes in the culture of advanced capitalism — this conception of rational communicative action — is also a rhetorical device that depends on setting up a series of connected parallel oppositions. Like his discussion of myth and rationality, the contrasts he draws between a flawed present and an idealized future depend on a preconceived notion of cultural evolution. In his recent work he has formulated the concept of rational communicative action as a cognitive structure that defines a range of learning processes. In describing these learning processes he again distinguishes them sharply from any connotation that might be tainted with the residues of tradition. They are not, he asserts, "concrete ideals immanent in traditional forms of life."[6] In other language, we might say that these learning processes are not end-states to be striven after, but ways of thinking. They constitute the limitations and possibilities available to us for engaging in communication about end-states, but leave open what these end-states may be. In this sense, Habermas has indeed abstracted to a higher level the "other" that he sets up in judgment against the contemporary. No longer is this other defined in substantive terms, as in the case of Marx's classless society; it consists instead only of possibility — the cognitive potential by which we might decide on any number of collective goals.

Habermas takes for granted as the starting point of his discussion of rationality the post-Kantian orientation of twentieth-century philosophy: that philosophy must concern itself centrally with reason, and that the analysis of reason must take place without reference to a divinity beyond the world or even "the ground of a cosmos encompassing nature and society."[7] He rejects the possibility of discovering an ontological system in which the principles of reason can be grounded. The quest for rationality, therefore, cannot result in a totality or metaphysical system, but must remain open — in the sense of engaging the empirical and historical sciences in continuous dialogue and taking a self-reflective stance toward its own historical development. The concept of reason is thus tempered at the same time that it is broadened to incorporate a wider vision of reality. It does, nevertheless, set the limited context in which all of Habermas's work must be understood. He starts with a worldview that assumes utter secularity and yet places ultimate faith in the value of rational argumentation.

The principal alternative to communicative action is, therefore, not an ontological system of divine truth, but instrumental reason. The main lines of demarcation separating the two can be summarized as follows: instrumental rationality is marked by an empiricist orientation toward the external environment; it is concerned chiefly with adapting to this environment and manipulating it; it takes the external environment for granted as a world of preexisting facts (that is, adopts a "realist" view); communicative understanding, in contrast, emphasizes the central experience of argumentative speech (the *logos*); focuses on the ways in which consensual, intersubjectively shared definitions of the objective world are attained; and thereby takes a phenomenological orientation toward reality that questions its objective existence and regards it more as a collectively constructed phenomenon. On these grounds, communicative understanding sides squarely with the phenomenological, hermeneutic, and interpretive approaches that have in more recent years come to dominate the social and historical sciences as opposed to the positivist and empiricist orientations of the physical and biological sciences and many of the applied or technical disciplines.

Having drawn the initial lines of contrast in this manner, Habermas is in a strong position to make an attractive case on normative grounds for the advantages of communicative rationality. Seeing the objective world as a socially constructed reality is, for example, a liberating perspective. In debunking its objectivity, as Peter Berger and others have shown, one gains mastery, command, a sense of being able to choose and create, rather than having merely to adapt.[8] In addition, communicative rationality interposes an important prior step before questions of policy and problem-solving can be addressed, namely, examining the broader presuppositions that underlie collective definitions of goals and problems. Rather than focusing on, say, the problem of perfecting a more accurate missile guidance system, attention can be directed to the broader assumptions that define this weapons system as an important issue in the first place, thereby opening up possibilities for alternatives to be considered. Beyond this, communicative rationality holds forth the opportunity to reconcile conflicting interests and outlooks. Disagreements can be traced backward, as it were, to find their sources in different conceptions of reality; understanding the communicative process itself can contribute positively to the task of building consensus. Communicative rationality also posits the possibility of overcoming much of the alienation and privatization that plagues modern society. The person who engages in communicative action is one who abandons purely subjective orientations and emphasizes intersubjectively recognized validity claims. This person harbors no sentiments that stand in the way of the collective good; such sentiments are openly placed on the table for collective scrutiny. Rather than living tenuously in a lifeworld characterized by private ambition and self-interest, therefore, it becomes possible to live genuinely in community.

There is, however, a tension in Habermas's conception of rational communicative action. The tension stems from his attempt to derive both instrumental rationality and communicative rationality from common roots, and it finds expression most clearly in his failure to distinguish clearly the parameters that make communicative rationality *rational* from those that make it *communicative*. Observe, for example, that Habermas begins his discussion of communicative rationality by asserting the significance of a "cognitivist version of rationality" concerned with descriptive knowledge; he also regards communicative action principally as action concerned with the "employment of propositional knowledge in assertions."[9] Indeed, "communicative rationality," without explanation, becomes "communicative understanding," and issues of argumentation squeeze out action entirely. No explicit attempt is made to contrast rational communicative action with other kinds of communication or even to distinguish noncognitive from cognitive modes of communication. From the beginning, the tendency is thus present for normative defenses of communicative action, as well as discussions of the phenomenological character of communicative action in the lifeworld, to be forced arbitrarily into categories of cognitively rational argumentation.

To be sure, Habermas recognizes that rational argumentation serves only as a starting point — a kind of metaphor — for a broader understanding of the varieties of communication that may take place in the lifeworld. Still, this metaphor supplies a standard of action that clearly restricts the lifeworld to something less than life itself. For example, Habermas specifies only three kinds of action in the lifeworld that he is willing to credit with rationality. First, putting forward an assertion and being able to defend it with appropriate evidence when criticized. Second, following an established social norm and being able to defend this action by relating one's situation to legitimate social expectations. And third, expressing a desire, intention, or feeling and being able to defend this expression to critics by drawing "practical consequences from it and behaving consistently thereafter."[10] Common to all three are the assumptions (a) that rationality arises somehow primarily in the presence of critics, (b) that one must be prepared to defend his or her actions whenever criticism arises, (c) that the character of an adequate defense rests on argumentation, and (d) that argumentation also implies some degree of self-conscious acceptance of "established" norms and patterns of behavior. Consistency, practical consequences, legitimacy, and argumentation become the hallmarks of rationality. In a centrally planned society, a corporate bureaucracy, or a setting governed by legal norms these criteria indeed may constitute desirable bases for communicative action. But the appropriateness of such criteria to highly systematized situations appears in itself to represent a restriction of the lifeworld to such situations. Where, one may legitimately ask, do matters of personal freedom, willful violations of established norms, pluralism, and nonreductive modes of expressivity enter the picture?

The question can perhaps be put even more forcefully: does not expressive communication lose something of its very essence in having to be defended against critics in terms of some standard of rational argumentation, effectiveness, or consistent appeal to social conventions? Habermas admits the existence of such expressive behaviors, but he wants them to be subject to canons of collective rationality. Indeed, he goes so far as to discredit them if they are not. Such idiosyncratic, innovative expressions, he says, actually conform to rigid patterns:

Their semantic context is not set free by the power of poetic speech or creative construction and thus has a merely privatistic character. The spectrum ranges from harmless whims, such as a special liking for the smell of rotten apples, to clinically noteworthy symptoms, such as a horrified reaction to open spaces. Someone who explains his libidinous reaction to rotten apples by referring to the "infatuating," "unfathomable," "vertiginous" smell, or who explains his panicked reaction to open spaces by their "crippling," "leaden," "sucking" emptiness, will scarcely meet with understanding in the *everyday* contexts of most cultures.... Anyone who is so privatistic in his attitudes and evaluations that they cannot be explained and rendered plausible by appeal to standards of evaluation is not behaving rationally.[11]

Perhaps so, but on the basis of this argument alone, Habermas has not succeeded either in ruling out the importance of such behavior or in incorporating it systematically into his own conception of the lifeworld. Why, after all, must expressive, poetic, privatistic expressions be reduced to the extreme deviant case of a preference for the smell of rotten apples? Why, even if one accepts this preference as an appropriate example, must its bearer play Habermas's game of defending himself against skeptical inquisitors in the first place? And why, should he decide to play the game, must he adopt the language of psychoanalytic neuroses rather than defying Habermas's very conventions by opting for metaphorical-poetic speech or by locating his preferences within the idiosyncratic experiences of his own lifeworld?

It will be necessary to return to the issues raised by these questions after considering other aspects of Habermas's approach more carefully. Here, let it suffice to suggest only that a critical and unresolved feature of Habermas's discussion lies at the intersection of rational-cognitive communicative action and the more expressive or idiosyncratic forms of communicative action that also constitute the lifeworld. The fact that Habermas's conception of communicative action is restricted to rational-cognitive forms of argumentation in no way diminishes the importance of what he has to say about rationality. Certainly there is a place for greater self-understanding of the components of rational communication. A theory that claims to salvage the lifeworld from the onslaught of monetarization and bureaucratization, however, must also do a better job of relating rational communication to the lived experience of the lifeworld itself.

THE REDISCOVERY OF LANGUAGE

The primary emphasis in Habermas's work that renders these criticisms of his theoretical language subject to the terms of his own theoretical framework is, as I have suggested, his elevation to primacy of the social role of language. The essential civilizational problems we face are no longer, in his view, purely materialist but consist of acquiring greater understanding of the components of rational communication. In this framework, culture ceases to be epiphenomenal and cultural criticism requires a deeper level of reflectivity about the very elements of which it is constructed.

The conception of language that we find in Habermas is, moreover, conditioned by a considered understanding of the main lines of epistemological reflection that have contributed to the development of a new appreciation of culture in the social sciences in recent years. Even in the trajectory of Habermas's own work, the evidence of this deepening understanding is readily apparent. In earlier formulations his views of cultural evolution, for instance, remained indebted to an ill-defined mixture of Marxism and Parsonian systems theory in which culture floated above the world of social relations as a kind of autonomous *geist*. Once he began to confront the contributions of Chomsky in linguistics, Levi-Strauss in cultural anthropology, and Searle in the philosophy of language, his work began to register a stronger, more concrete, and more behaviorally nuanced view of culture. In his initial attempts to specify a systematic program of universal pragmatics around a conception of the validity claims implicit in speech acts, he elevated culture to a central theoretical location. At this juncture, however, the broader discussion of linguistic conditions of validity remained narrowly construed as problems of syntactic comprehensibility. In subsequent reformations, this dimension of the pragmatic schema has been largely dropped, while greater attention has been paid to the role of language in all forms of validation and argumentation. The main contributions of this recent work can be identified along four principal axes.

First, Habermas has insisted on the nonreducible character of the symbolic realm and has defended this position with reference to an increasing number of philosophical arguments. He has taken pains most particularly to distinguish the symbolic world from the physical world of external nature, on the one hand, and from the subjective world of internal mental states, on the other hand. The symbolic realm, he argues, becomes objectified beyond any of the intentions that its producers may have held as individuals, and yet, insofar as it is a human production, it cannot be understood in the same terms as objects that exist within nature. The symbolic realm is thus a world constituted by its own "internal meaning connections."

Second, Habermas has emphasized increasingly the collective or social dimensions of language. What distinguishes the symbolic realm from both the physical and the subjective realms is its dependence upon — as well as its constitutive role within — social interaction. Although Habermas quibbles at points with a purely realist view of the physical world, he appears content for the most part to posit, at least for purposes of classification, the possibility of truth claims that lie outside the constraints of social construction. Thus, for example, the reality of gravitational forces might be experienced by jumping from a cliff — quite independently of socially constructed definitions of a theory of such forces or views of the situation itself. By the same token, symbolism is for Habermas essentially a vehicle of communication, rather than a symptom of mental states. Even when the content of communication takes an expressive form that is devoted to conveying internal thoughts and feelings, these expressions must conform to conventions of discourse as well as socially acceptable norms in order to communicate effectively.

Third, the symbolic realm has in Habermas's recent work become linked more closely and systematically with the phenomenological foundations of experience in everyday life. He has, for example, drawn more extensively from Alfred Schutz and from George Herbert Mead to suggest the extent to which everyday experience depends on symbolic constructions. Because of his overriding concerns with rational communication (as we have already suggested), Habermas still tends to force the discussion of symbolism into cognitive and propositional terms that separate it from the world of everyday experience. Yet his interest in specifying the ways in which systems of technical knowledge have colonized the lifeworld has also necessitated a clearer conception of the broader ways in which symbolism and the lifeworld interact.

Finally, Habermas has made greater efforts to distinguish more systematically among the various types (or uses) of symbolism. Again, much of his discussion forces the varieties of symbolism into categories that may function best as models of rational argumentation. In order to delineate the parameters of rational communication, he has nevertheless offered commentaries on expressive, aesthetic, and poetic forms of symbolism as well.

The main criterion against which Habermas's discussion of language must be judged, however, is not its point of departure, namely, its concern with rationality, its emphasis on thematized validity claims, and its implicit reliance on a Parsonian schema of norms and values. The criterion of assessment must instead be whether this point of departure is adequate for the *goal* toward which Habermas's discussion is directed — the goal of providing a critical theoretical perspective on the growing rationalization of the lifeworld. Against this standard, several features of Habermas's discussion appear problematic.

His interest in language rests from the start on the assumption that knowledge has a propositional structure that consists, in practice, of statements being made about speakers' beliefs. Working forward from knowledge to the propositional structure of statements, of course, constitutes a plausible progression. Working backward, however, from statements and propositions to a view of language as it constitutes the lifeworld is demonstrably inadequate. Only in the broadest sense of the term "statements" can the use of language in the lifeworld be limited to expressions of knowledge.

Beyond this, the specific context in which Habermas frames

his defense of a focus on statements demonstrates that his understanding of this term is not in fact meant in the broadest sense. Indeed, he draws a parallel between linguistic utterances of knowledge and goal-directed actions. Drawing on his earlier analysis, via Searle, of the components implicit in promises, Habermas suggests that statements about knowledge rest on the same kind of validity claims as goal-oriented actions: both constitute a form of promising that can be subjected to scrutiny. There is, he observes, a parallel between "know-how" and "know-that."[12] But this formulation, it would appear, already presupposes the limited view of rationality that Habermas wishes to examine as it penetrates the lifeworld. Know-how, know-that, and goal-oriented action clearly point toward instrumental action geared toward manipulating an environment assumed to be external and objective. Indeed, the very concept of truth that forms the core of Habermas's analysis of the rationality of truth claims is biased in this direction: "As *truth* is related to the existence of states of affairs in the world, *effectiveness* is related to interventions in the world with whose help states of affairs can be brought into existence."[13]

This conception of language also depends on a questionable criterion of objectivity. In attempting to specify a kind of language that can be subjected to criticism, Habermas limits his analysis to statements that have "a relation to the objective world (that is, a relation to the facts)" by which he means further a relation that depends on a "transsubjective validity claim that has the same meaning for observers and nonparticipants as it has for the acting subject himself."[14] This specification, of course, reflects Habermas's more general discussion of the pragmatics of validity claims.[15] From that discussion, however, it seems doubtful (a) that a statement's relation to the "facts" is consistent with its relations either to its speaker or to the meanings accorded it by its observers; (b) that the meaning of a statement is ever likely to be "the same" for speakers and observers; and (c) that the meaning of any statement can be ascertained by an external observer with any degree of accuracy or richness of description. Thus, even if one were willing to accept Habermas's emphasis on rational validity claims, it seems doubtful that this specification would hold up under empirical scrutiny.

The upshot of these difficulties is that Habermas's discussion of rational discourse is itself an indicator of the limited validity of such discourse for communicative action within the broader context of the lifeworld. Specific criteria of rationality appear elusive. Words such as "knowledge," "facts," "objectivity," and "meaning" are themselves products of discourse; their validity claims require unmasking. The critical task of a sociological theory based on universal pragmatics must, therefore, include an examination of the validity claims of rationality itself.

As a start, the conditions of validity specified by a theory of universal pragmatics must (as Habermas has done elsewhere) be raised to a higher level of abstraction that permits analysis of utterances of all kinds, not only those taken on a priori grounds as rational statements. The particular validity claims implicit in various kinds of utterances can then be subjected to separate analyses. Claims about presumed relations to the world of facts can be distinguished as alternative conceptions of truth, and these claims can be bracketed from claims concerned with sincerity, legitimacy, and comprehensibility. The purpose of an analysis of this kind would not be to subject statements to criticism according to preconceived norms of rationality, thus heightening the penetration of the lifeworld by such norms, but to clarify the conditions of meaningfulness essential to a more open sphere of communicative action. An agenda such as this remains true to the broader canon of "criticizability" that Habermas establishes as a goal for sociological theory, but it poses critical questions about speech acts within the domain of communication to which they are most appropriate, rather than forcing all such utterances to conform to standards of goal-oriented, objectifiable rationality.

As it stands, Habermas's discussion of validity claims of course provides a useful foundation for a higher order examination of the limits of rational discourse. The source of Habermas's own inclination to restrict the broader conception of language that arose from his courtship with speech-act theory and universal pragmatics can be traced, as the foregoing has suggested, primarily to his quest for cognitive rationality in the communicative sphere. But at a more general level the validity claims that render any act of communication meaningful can be understood as relations between the speech act itself and various conditions of the context in which it occurs — relations that are dramatized by features of language itself. Thus, for example, if a speaker utters the statement "I believe that God exists," a relation of sincerity between the speech act and the speaker is dramatized by the phrase "I believe." In this general framework, language retains much of its richness: its form and implicit content bear on the communicative process as well as its propositional content; it can serve any purpose and take any form, including highly truncated nonpropositional symbolic utterances; and it occurs in a multifaceted environment of facts, norms, intentions, and other language rules.

The desire to move toward a more rational understanding of the communicative process, however, leads Habermas to conceive of language more narrowly in terms of his root metaphor of argumentation. In this conception, validity claims no longer consist of the more implicit relations specified in speech-act theory but become thematized. They now take on explicit propositional form that can be used to defend statements against critics who challenge them argumentatively. No longer does one validate one's utterances through the implicit construction of language usage itself; one now turns the norms of language usage into objects of reflection and formulates explicit reasons to vindicate why one said what was said. This additional step, moreover, is not taken only by the analyst who wishes to construct a metatheory of language usage; it is normatively specified for actors in the lifeworld itself. By thematizing the arguments underlying their validity claims, they gain the capacity to communicate more effectively: mistakes are corrected, learning processes advance, and greater mastery of the communicative situation is achieved.

Stated this way, the question of whether Habermas's emphasis on rationality does justice to the character of language becomes visibly apparent. Communication advances, in his view, by being subjected to the criticizable language game of rational argumentation. Rather than being able to rest content with the statement "I believe in God," our hypothetical member of the lifeworld must thematize what he or she means by "believe" and must argue with critics about the propositional content of any such validity claim. Similarly, a not-so-hypothetical poet can no longer assert poetically that "my love is like a red red rose," but must thematize a logical statement about the character of simile in relating a personal attribute to the world of nature and must be prepared to defend the poetic usage of simile against alternative norms of reality construction. Here, the issue is clearly whether the gains that accrue from rational argumentation of this kind make for greater possibilities of poetic expression, or whether such argumentation, much like vivisection, destroys the object it seeks to understand. More generally, the issue raised runs to the heart of Habermas's ambivalent quest for rational mastery. Is not the goal of rational mastery as much an extension of instrumental reason when it is applied to the self-objectified world of language as it is when it is applied to the empiricist's world of nature?

RESACRALIZING CULTURE

Implicit in much of the foregoing is an argument about the need to define the limits of rationality more clearly and to mark off zones of the lifeworld that are protected from rationality claims and have legitimacy of their own. Following Durkheim, we might call this a requirement for sacralization — or in the context of modern secularity, "resacralization" — in the sense of constructing symbolic boundaries that sharply set off the sacred from the profane. This resacralization of culture can be understood as a rediscovery of multidimensionality over against the one-dimensionality of technical reason — not in resurrecting a dualistic worldview, let alone a three-tiered conception of the universe, but in setting apart arenas of action in which holistic meaning, transcendence, and even nonrationalized expressions of hope, unity, reconciliation, and redemption can survive. The question of course is whether such an ambition runs entirely counter to the agenda of a theory of rational communicative action, or whether some insights can be derived from this perspective.

Beyond the criticisms that Habermas has usefully made of monetarization and bureaucratization and the road signs his work has erected that point toward a fuller appreciation of the importance of language, the place to begin in attempting to answer this question appears to be the scattered remarks about protests against the modern pathologies of the lifeworld to which attention has already been drawn at several points. If we accept Habermas's claim that the pathologies most symptomatic of the current evolutionary tendencies bearing on the lifeworld include quality of life concerns, equal rights, individual self-realization, social participation, and human rights, then it becomes especially important to focus on those expressions of protest that have emerged most directly in response to these particular pathologies. These encompass a relatively wide range of special interest groups, including environmental movements, peace initiatives, groups oriented toward the entitlements of new minorities such as the elderly and gays, youth sects, feminism, human potential and encounter groups, and religiously oriented efforts to achieve liberation. What sets these movements apart from protests concerned with wages, work rights, status attainment, and political representation is a primary emphasis on the "sensual-aesthetic" maintenance of the natural environment, on the moral and ethical dilemmas raised by increasing technological and political complexity, or on the revitalization of personalistic and ascriptive dimensions of the everyday lifeworld. All three can be understood best in relation to the advances of technology, capital accumulation, institutional differentiation, and bureaucratization, although the third — revitalization — perhaps encompasses a more historically diverse set of responses. It is for this reason that Habermas seems intent on emphasizing the role of overloads in the communication system as a source of current revitalization movements. He writes: "The revaluation of the particular, the natural, the provincial, of social spaces that are small enough to be familiar, of decentralized forms of commerce and despecialized activities, of segmented pubs, simple interactions and dedifferentiated public spheres — all this is meant to foster the revitalization of possibilities for expression and communication that have been buried alive."[16]

It is also important that the specific variants of these movements that have caught Habermas's attention have not been the more politicized efforts to mobilize legislative or bureaucratic action on behalf of environmental or human rights concerns, but movements that have in a sense opted out of the politico-bureaucratic avenues of mobilization, preferring instead to effect what he calls "alternative practice" and "counterinstitutions." These counterinstitutions have in fact been efforts to carve out arenas of action that negate, and are protected against, the increasing penetration of system rationality into the lifeworld. They have, for instance, rejected the increasing instrumentalization of the workplace, including competitive standards of performance, opting instead for cooperative forms of labor organization, greater emphasis on personal fulfillment and expression, and a more fluid and diverse definition of role expectations. Similar tendencies have appeared in "home schooling" rejections of the competitive, technology-centered emphasis of public education and in efforts to resist clientage-oriented public welfare services in favor of greater self-help and participation among the needy.

As we have already noted, Habermas insists on defining such activities as protests. They arise spontaneously in reaction to pressures from the colonization of the lifeworld, they assume a relatively limited understanding of the broader cultural forces at work, and they attract few participants. Habermas categorically labels them "unrealistic." And on grounds of rationality, technical accomplishment, and bureaucratic efficiency, this judgment is probably accurate.

It is, however, precisely these criteria that such movements — and Habermas's own critique — have sought to resist. Indeed, Habermas seems to recognize this when he concedes that the new resistance and withdrawal movements are important for their "polemical significance." This, it would seem, is precisely their significance, and yet one that does not find full theoretical expression anywhere in Habermas's framework. To say that such movements have polemical significance is, by a limited definition, to concede only that they represent, as suggested earlier, a form of cultural negation. It is simply another way of saying that protest movements are engaged in protest. But in a broader sense, polemics implies discourse, and discourse raises larger questions about the linguistic or symbolic role that such movements may play within the realm of communicative action.

Certainly it is an understatement to say that protest movements of these kinds represent nothing more than a negation of dominant social system imperatives. They have also been concerned to elaborate, both in theory and in practice, their own visions of cultural alternatives. And, however unrealistic these alternatives may be, they nevertheless — sometimes by virtue of their very lack of conventional realism — supply images of nonrational and transrational possibilities to the public sphere. More than anything they may have accomplished as workable models for the entire society, they symbolize possibility: open cultural horizons, a place for keeping imagination and creativity alive, and tangible expressions of nonrationalized action such as love, hope, forgiveness, and trust.

NOTES

1. Jürgen Habermas, *The Theory of Communicative Action*, vol. 1: *Reason and the Rationalization of Society* (Boston: Beacon Press, 1984), and vol. 2: *Lifeworld and System: A Critique of Functionalist Reason* (Boston: Beacon Press, 1987).

2. See, for example, Peter L. Berger, *The Capitalist Revolution* (New York: Basic Books, 1986), and Michael Novak, *The Spirit of Democratic Capitalism* (New York: Simon and Schuster, 1982).

3. Habermas, *Theory of Communicative Action*, 2:382.

4. Ibid., 403.

5. Ibid., 1:44.

6. Ibid., 2:383.

7. Ibid., 1:1.

8. See, for example, the discussion of debunking in Peter L. Berger, *Invitation to Sociology* (Garden City, N.Y.: Doubleday, 1969).

9. Habermas, *Theory of Communicative Action*, 1:10.

10. Ibid., 1:15.

11. Ibid., 1:17.

12. Ibid., 1:8.

13. Ibid., 1:9.

14. Ibid.

15. Jürgen Habermas, *Communication and the Evolution of Society* (Boston: Beacon Press, 1979), chapter 1; see also Robert Wuthnow et al., *Cultural Analysis* (Boston: Routledge and Kegan, 1984), chap. 4.

16. Ibid., 2:395.

9

Transcendence from Within,
Transcendence in this World

Jürgen Habermas

Allow me to make a personal remark to facilitate the start of a difficult discussion. I have continually responded to objections from my colleagues in philosophy and sociology.[1] Here, I again gladly respond to the criticism of Fred Dallmayr and Robert Wuthnow. Up until now, I have held back from a discussion with theologians; I would also prefer to continue to remain silent. A silence on the grounds of embarrassment would also be justified, for I am not really familiar with the theological discussion, and only reluctantly move about in an insufficiently reconnoitered terrain. On the other hand, for decades theologians both in Germany and in the United States have included me in their discussions. They have referred in general to the tradition of critical theory,[2] and have reacted to my writings.[3] In this situation, silence would be a false response: the person who is addressed and remains silent, clothes himself or herself in an aura of indeterminate significance and imposes silence. For this, Heidegger is one example among many. Because of this authoritarian character, Sartre has rightly called silence "reactionary."

I will start by first ascertaining a few premises under which theologians and philosophers today speak to one another, insofar as they share a self-critical assessment of modernity. Then, I will make an attempt to understand the status and truth claim of theological discourse. Following this, I will take up the most important objections from the theological side and, at the end, take a position on the criticism of the nontheologians in this volume.

COMMON PREMISES

From a distance, it is easier to speak about one another than with one another. For sociologists, it is easier to explain religious traditions and their roles from the perspective of an observer than to approach them in a performative stance. For sociologists, as long as they do not step out of their professional role, the change to the stance of an actual participant in religious discourse can only have the methodological sense of a hermeneutical intermediary step. A slightly different situation results for philosophers, at least for one who has grown up at German universities with Fichte, Schelling, and Hegel, including the latter's Marxist legacy. For, from this perspective, there is excluded from the start an approach that would merely objectify Jewish and Christian traditions, especially the speculatively fruitful Jewish and Protestant mysticism of the early modern period as mediated through the Swabian pietism of Bengel and Oetinger. Just as German Idealism with the concept of the Absolute appropriated theoretically the God of creation and of gracious love, it also with a logical reconstruction of the process of the world as a whole appropriated theoretically the traces of salvation history. Also, Kant cannot be understood without recognizing the motive of conceiving the essentially practical contents of the Christian tradition in such a way that these could perdure before the forum of reason. But contemporaries were fully aware of the ambiguity of these attempts at transformation. With the concept of "sublation" [*Aufhebung*] Hegel included this ambiguity in the dialectical method itself. The sublation of the world of religious representation in the philosophical concept enabled the saving of its essential contents only by casting off the substance of its piety. Certainly, the atheistic core, enveloped in esoteric insight, was reserved for the philosophers. Thus the later Hegel trusted philosophical reason only with the power of *partial* reconciliation. He had given up his hope in the concrete universality of that public religion which — according to the "Oldest System Program" — was to make the people rational and the philosophers sensible. The people are abandoned by their priests, now become philosophers.[4]

The *methodical* atheism of Hegelian philosophy and of all philosophical appropriation of essentially religious contents (which does not assert anything about the personal self-understanding of the philosophical author) became an open scandal only after Hegel's death as the "process of decay of the absolute spirit" (Marx) set in. The right-Hegelians, who to this day have reacted only defensively to this scandal, have yet to furnish a convincing response. For under the conditions of postmetaphysical thinking, it is not enough to take shelter behind a concept of the Absolute which can neither be freed from the concepts of the Hegelian "logic," nor be defended without a reconstruction of Hegelian dialectic that would be insightful *today* and would be joined to our philosophical discourses.[5] Clearly, the Young Hegelians did not recognize with equal acuity that along with fundamental metaphysical concepts, a metaphysically affirmed atheism is also no longer tenable. In whatever form materialism may appear, within the horizon of a scientific, fallibilistic mode of thinking it is a hypothesis which at best can claim plausibility for the present moment.

In our parts of the world, the grounds for a politically motivated atheism or, better, for a militant *laicism* have also, by and large, fallen away. During my time as a student, it was, above all, theologians such as Gollwitzer and Iwand who had given morally responsible answers to the political questions that challenged us after the war. It was the Confessing Church which at that time with its acknowledgment of guilt at least attempted a new beginning. In both confessions, leftist associations were formed, by lay people as well as theologians, who sought to free the church from its comfortable alliances with the power of the state and the existing social conditions. They sought renewal instead of restoration and to establish universal standards of judgment in the public political realm. With this exemplary witness and widely effective change of mentality there arose the model of a religious engagement which broke away from the conventionality and interiority of a merely private confession. With an undogmatic understanding of transcendence and faith, this engagement took seriously this-worldly goals of human dignity and social emancipation. It joined in a multivoiced arena with other forces pressing for radical democratization.

Against the background of a praxis which all would respect, we encounter a critical theology that interprets the self-understanding of this praxis in such a way that it helps express our best moral intuitions without tearing down the bridges to secular languages and cultures. Schüssler Fiorenza's fundamental theology offers a good example of a political theology that is in touch with contemporary investigations in morality and in social theory.[6] He first characterizes in a threefold manner the transformations that both religion and theology undergo under the conditions of postmetaphysical thinking, conditions that have become inescapable in modernity.[7] He emphasizes the uncoupling of a religion which is both interiorized and at the same time open to the secularized world from the explanatory claims of cosmological world views. The *Glaubenslehre* [*The Christian Faith*] in Schleiermacher's sense casts off the character of a cosmological world view. As a consequence of the recognition of the pluralism of religious forces, there ensues a reflective relationship to the particularity of one's own faith within the horizon of the universality of the religious as such. Joined with this is the insight that the ethical approaches which have emerged from the contexts of various world religions agree in the basic principles of a universalist morality. In a further step, Schüssler Fiorenza expounds the limits of a philosophical theory of morality which confines itself to the explanation and the grounding of the moral standpoint. He also discusses subsequent problems which arise from the abstractions of such an ethics of justice.

Since a philosophy which has become self-critical does not trust itself any longer to offer universal assertions about the concrete whole of exemplary forms of life, it must refer those affected to discourses in which they answer their substantial questions themselves. The parties should examine in moral argumentation what is equally good for all. But first they must become clear about what the good is for themselves in their respective contexts. These ethical questions in a stricter sense, concerning a life that is worthwhile [*nicht-verfehlten*] or is preferable, can find an answer only in context-dependent discourses of self-understanding. These answers will be more differentiated and more appropriate depending upon how rich the identity-building traditions are that support self-reassurance [*Selbstvergewisserung*]. As Schüssler Fiorenza states using the words of Rawls, the question about one's own identity — who we are and desire to be — requires a "thick concept of the good." Thus each party must bring into the discussion his or her conceptions of the good and preferable life in order to find out with other parties what they all might desire. He suggests a "dialectic between universalizable principles of justice and the reconstructive hermeneutic of normative tradition" and attributes to the churches in modern society the role of being "communities of interpretation in which issues of justice and conceptions of goodness are publicly discussed" (86). Today the ecclesial communities are in competition with other communities of interpretation that are rooted in secular traditions. Even viewed from outside, it could turn out that monotheistic traditions have at their disposal a language whose semantic potential is not yet exhausted [*unabgegoltenen*], that shows itself to be superior in its power to disclose the world and to form identity, in its capability for renewal, its differentiation, and its range.

What I find interesting to observe in this example is that where theological argumentation is pushed so far into the neighborhood of other discourses, the perspectives from within and without meet without restraint. In this sense, I also understand those "correlational methods," which David Tracy employs for the "public theologies"

widespread in the United States. These methods have the goal of
placing in a relation of mutual critique interpretations of modernity proceeding from philosophical and social-theoretical approaches
with theological interpretations of the Christian tradition. Thus,
their goal is to bring these interpretations into a relation where arguments are used. This intention is facilitated when the projects of
Enlightenment and of theology that Helmut Peukert discusses are
described in similar ways from both sides: "The thesis seems plausible to me that the unsolved problem of advanced civilizations is that
of mastering the tendency toward power accumulation."[8] Matthew
Lamb observes how this tendency becomes critical in modernity and
brings forth two false reactions, a romantic one and a historicist one.
He pleads for a self-reassurance of modernity which breaks out of the
cycle of a pernicious back and forth between nihilistic condemnation
and dogmatic self-assertion: "Modern dogmatic self-assertion is profoundly nihilistic, just as modern nihilism is irresponsibly dogmatic."[9]
Tracy specifies the concept of reason which guides a diagnosis of this
kind. The dual failure of positivism and of the philosophy of consciousness confirms the pragmatic turn that took place from Peirce
through Dewey toward a non-fundamentalist concept of communicative reason. At the same time, this concept opposes the conclusions
that Rorty and Derrida draw from this failure, whether in the form
of a radical contextualism or by way of an aesthetization of theory.
Just as strongly, Tracy objects to selective modes of reading that leave
out the ambivalent sense of modernization and perceive it merely as
the history of the decay of a subject-centered reason that progresses
forward in a linear manner and inflates itself up to be the totality.
Even in modernity, reason has not withered into instrumental reason: "If understanding is dialogical, it is also...both historical and
contextual. But...[a]ny act of understanding implicitly puts forward
a claim to more than subjective understanding. Any act of understanding addresses all others with a claim to its validity — a validity
that, in principle, the inquirer is obliged to redeem if challenged."[10]

Tracy draws from this pragmatic insight consequences also for the
activity of theology itself which would be disciplined [*wissenschaftliche*]
work and in no way simply a gift of faith. Peukert understands the
work of theology as a methodically controlled form of religion. Gary
Simpson compares the lifeworld, which reproduces itself through
communicative action and validity claims that are open to critique,
with a "forensically fraught world" and suggests that on the cross
even God submits to this forum. Hence, none of the lifeworld's
segments can immunize themselves against the demands for an argumentative justification, not even — as I understand the sentence —
theology.[11] If this, however, is the *common ground* of theology, sci-

ence, and philosophy, what then still constitutes the distinctiveness of theological discourse? What separates the internal perspective of theology from the external perspective of those who enter into a dialogue with theology? It cannot be the relation to religious discourses in general, but only the nature of the reference to the discourse conducted within each particular religious community.

THE TRUTH CLAIM OF THEOLOGICAL DISCOURSE

Schüssler Fiorenza appeals to the line of tradition from Schleiermacher down to Bultmann and Niebuhr when he distinguishes a critical theology from neo-Aristotelian and neo-Thomist theologies. The great example of Karl Barth demonstrates, indeed, that the consistent unburdening of theology from metaphysical-cosmological explanatory claims does not mean *eo ipso* the willingness to assert that theological arguments have the power to convince in the debate with scientific discourses. From the Barthian viewpoint, the biblically witnessed event of revelation in its historical facticity rejects a mode of argumentation based on reason alone.[12] In the Protestant-shaped milieu of German universities, theological faculties have always enjoyed a special status. The young history of the University of Frankfurt dramatically shows this tension. When in the 1920s theological lectureships were to be introduced there, controversies broke out which could then only be settled by refusing to recognize the Catholic, Protestant, and Jewish subjects of study as specifically *theological* teaching. At this university, which grew out of a business college, it is interesting that in its social science atmosphere personalities such as Steinbüchel, Buber, and Tillich were able to establish themselves. It was thus political theologians in the broadest sense who could move about with ease in the discourses of the humanities and the social sciences.[13] In the Federal Republic of Germany, if I am right, it was primarily a group of Catholic theologians who, having always maintained a less troubled relation to the *lumen naturale*, were able to draw upon this tradition. Yet, the more that theology opens itself in general to the discourses of the human sciences, the greater is the danger that its own status will be lost in the network of alternating takeover attempts.

The *religious* discourse conducted within the communities of the faithful takes place in the context of a specific tradition with substantive norms and an elaborated dogmatics. It refers to a common ritual praxis and bases itself on the specifically religious experiences of the individual. It is, however, more than the non-objectifying, hermeneutically understanding reference to religious discourse and to the experiences underlying this discourse that characterizes theology. For the same would hold for a philosophy which understands itself as the critical appropriation and transformation, as the retrieval, of essential religious contents in the universe of argumentative discourse. This Hegelian self-understanding of philosophy has also not been abandoned by the materialistic students of Hegel. It lives on especially in Bloch, Benjamin, and in critical theory. True, Hegel was the last in an idealistic tradition that upheld the claim of metaphysics in a transformed shape, and completed the philosophical appropriation of the Judeo-Christian tradition as much as was possible under the conditions of metaphysical thinking. Hegel's philosophy is the result of that great experiment, crucially defining European intellectual history, which sought to produce a synthesis between the faith of Israel and the Greek spirit — a synthesis that, on the one side, lead to the Hellenization of Christianity and, on the other, to the ambiguous Christianization of Greek metaphysics. The dialectical God of the philosophers allows the alter ego of prayer to fade away into anonymous thoughts of the Absolute. At least since Kierkegaard, this synthesis has become fragile, because it has been put into question from *both* sides.

In the same way as Adorno's philosophical critique, the theological protest of Johann Baptist Metz is directed against the fundamental concepts of a metaphysics which, even when they have been dialectically set in motion, remain too rigid to be able to retrieve rationally those experiences of redemption, universal alliance, and irreplaceable individuality which have been articulated in the language of the Judeo-Christian history of salvation without truncating them and reducing the fullness of their specific meanings. Metz insists with Benjamin upon the anamnestic constitution of reason and wants to understand the faith of Israel also from its own historical spirit.[14] Adorno circumscribes the non-identical and seeks to think with the aid of concepts beyond all objectifying concepts, because he follows the same impulse: to save intuitions that have not been exhausted in philosophy. Here it is the experience of an equality that does not level out difference and of a togetherness that individualizes. It is the experience of a closeness across distance to an other acknowledged in his or her difference. It is the experience of a combination of autonomy and self-surrender, a reconciliation which does not extinguish the differences, a future-oriented justice that is in solidarity with the unreconciled suffering of past generations. It is the experience of the reciprocity of freely granted acknowledgment, of a relationship in which a subject is associated to another without being submitted to the degrading violence of exchange — a derisive violence that allows for the happiness and power of the one only at the price of the unhappiness and powerlessness of the other.

If, however, this *anti-Platonic turn* takes place on both sides, then it cannot be the postmetaphysical kind of reference to religious discourse that today separates philosophy from a theology open to conversation. Rather, under the conditions of postmetaphysical thought another difference, which was surrounded by ambiguities up until Hegel, clearly emerges: methodical atheism in the manner of the philosophical reference to the contents of religious experience. Philosophy cannot appropriate what is talked about in religious discourse *as* religious experiences. These experiences could only be added to the fund of philosophy's resources, recognized as philosophy's own basis of experience, if philosophy identifies these experiences using a description that is no longer borrowed from the language of a specific religious tradition, but from the universe of argumentative discourse that is uncoupled from the event of revelation. At those fracture points where a neutralizing translation of this type can no longer succeed, philosophical discourse must confess its failure. The metaphorical use of words such as "redemption," "messianic light," "restoration of nature," etc., makes religious experience a mere citation. In these moments of its powerlessness, argumentative speech passes over beyond religion and science into literature, into a mode of presentation that is no longer directly measured by truth claims. In an analogical way, theology also loses its identity if it only cites religious experiences, and under the descriptions of religious discourse no longer acknowledges them as its own basis. Therefore, I hold that a conversation cannot succeed between a theology and a philosophy which use the language of religious authorship and which meet on the bridge of religious experiences that have become literary expressions.

Admittedly, theology which wants to subject itself without reservation to scientific argumentation, as Tracy and Peukert emphasize, will not be satisfied with the limiting criterion that I have proposed. What does "methodical atheism" really mean? To answer this question, I would like to digress a moment.

Religious discourse is closely joined to a ritual praxis that, in comparison with profane everyday praxis, is limited in the degree of its freedom of communication in a specific way. If a functionalist description is permitted, then it could be said that faith is protected against a radical problematization by its being rooted in cult. This problematization unavoidably occurs when the ontic, normative, and expressive aspects of validity, which must remain fused together in the conception of the creator and redeemer God, of theodicy, and of the event of salvation, are separated analytically from one another.[15]

Theological discourse, however, distinguishes itself from religious by separating itself from ritual praxis in the act of explaining it, for example that it *interprets* sacraments such as baptism or the eucharist. Theology for its assertions also aspires to a truth claim that is differentiated from the spectrum of the other validity claims. Yet, beyond the measure of uncertainty that all reflection brings as it intrudes upon practical knowledge, theology did not present a danger to the faith of the community as long as it used the basic concepts of metaphysics. Indeed, these metaphysical concepts were immune to a differentiation of the aspects of validity in a fashion similar to the basic religious concepts. This situation only changed with the collapse of metaphysics. Under the conditions of postmetaphysical thinking, whoever puts forth a truth claim today must, nevertheless, translate experiences that have their home in religious discourse into the language of a scientific expert culture — and from this language retranslate them back into praxis.

This task of translation demanded by critical theology can be formally compared with that which modern philosophy also has to undertake. For philosophy stands in a similarly intimate relationship to common sense which it reconstructs and at the same time undermines. In the opposite direction, philosophy functions in the role of an interpreter that should carry essential contents of the expert culture back into everyday praxis. This task of mediation is not free of a certain paradox, because in the expert cultures knowledge is treated under respectively separate aspects of validity, whereas in everyday praxis *all* linguistic functions and aspects of validity are interwoven and form a syndrome.[16] Nevertheless, philosophy, in a way, has an easier task dealing with common sense, from which it lives and which it at the same time reforms, than does theology with the religious discourses given to it. Today, between these discourses and profane everyday praxis, there is certainly no longer the same distance that once existed between the sacred and the profane spheres of life — and this distance even continues to decrease as the ideas of a "public theology" gain acceptance. But against the reform to which common sense is subject in modern societies, whether with the assistance of philosophers or not, that syndrome of revelation faith, held together in ritualized praxis, still forms a specific barrier. For religious discourses would lose their identity if they were to open themselves up to a type of interpretation which no longer allows the religious experiences to be valid *as* religious.

One must expect, after all, such a far-reaching problematization if theological discourse no longer chooses either of the two premises that are characteristic of modern theology. After Kierkegaard, theology has either taken the "Protestant path" and appealed to the

kerygma and faith as a source of religious insight absolutely independent of reason, or has chosen the path of "enlightened Catholicism"
in the sense that it relinquishes the status of a special discourse and
exposes its assertions to the whole range of scientific discussion. Admittedly, it does this without renouncing the acknowledgment of
the experiences articulated in the language of the Judeo-Christian
tradition as its *own* base of experience. It is this reservation alone
which permits a distanciation from the language game of religious
discourses without invalidating it. It leaves the religious language
game intact. The third way, however, is characterized by what I have
called "methodical atheism." It is this way that leads to a program
of demythologization that is tantamount to an experiment. Without
reservation it is left to the realization of this program to see whether
the theological (not just a history of religions) interpretation of the
religious discourses by virtue of its argumentation alone permits a
joining to the scientific discussion in such a manner that the religious language game remains intact, or collapses. I see the "political
dogmatics" of the Copenhagen theologian Jens Glebe-Möller as an
example of such an experiment.

Building upon the theoretical approaches of Apel, Döbert, and
myself and supported by a discourse ethics, Glebe-Möller subjects the
Christian dogmas to a demythologizing interpretation, which recalls
for me a saying of Hugo Ball: God is the freedom of the lowliest in
the spiritual communication of all. Glebe-Möller interprets baptism,
the eucharist, the imitation of Christ, the role of the church, and
eschatology in the sense of a theology of liberation based on a theory
of communication, which opens up the Bible in a fascinating (for
me, also convincing) way, even in those passages that have become
foreign to modern ears. But I ask myself *who* recognizes himself or
herself in this interpretation.

Does the Christian language game remain intact if one understands the idea of God in the way that Glebe-Möller proposes it?
"The thought of a personified divine power necessarily involves heteronomy, and this is an idea that goes directly against the modern
concept of human autonomy. A political dogmatic in the modern
context must therefore be atheistic. But this does not mean that
there is no thinking about God or that the thought of God is emptied of all content."[17] Taking up a reflection of Peukert's, he explains
this as follows: "If we desire to hold on to solidarity with everyone
else in the communicative fellowship, even the dead... then we must
claim a reality that can reach beyond the here and now, or that can
connect our selves beyond our own death with those who went innocently to their destruction before us. And it is this reality that
the Christian tradition calls God" (110). But in contrast to Peukert,

Glebe-Möller insist on an *atheistic version* of this idea in that he poses
the question:

But are we not then back at the point where only faith in a divine deliverance
can rescue us — where, with Peukert, we have to reintroduce the thought
of God? I continue to be convinced that we are today unable to think that
thought. This means that the guilt remains in effect. Instead of resigning
ourselves to it, however, we must make the consciousness of guilt into something positive, something that spurs us to fight against the conditions that
have produced the guilt. That can happen when we hold fast to our solidarity with all who have suffered and died, now and before. This solidarity
or fellowship contains within itself a "messianic" power that transforms any
passive consciousness of guilt into an active struggle against the conditions
for guilt — just as it was when Jesus, who two thousand years ago, forgave
sinners and set people free to continue that struggle.

But *can* we be in solidarity? In the last analysis, we can be nothing else,
for solidarity — the ideal communicative fellowship — is presupposed in
everything we say and do! (112)

THEOLOGICAL OBJECTIONS

The theologians who in this volume have entered into a dialogue
with me would hardly want to be bound to one of the three alternatives that I have named. They want to follow the path of radical
demythologization as little as they want to follow the classical Protestant path which in our century led to Karl Barth. Yet these same
theologians may not consider valid for themselves the reservation
that I associated with the characterization and the name of "enlightened Catholicism." For settling on a basis of experience which
remains bound a priori to the language of a specific tradition signifies a particularistic limitation of the truth claims of theology. Yet, as
truth claims they extend beyond all merely local contexts — and for
David Tracy this is not open to negotiation. Consistent with this, my
theological dialogue partners therefore choose the indirect procedure of apologetic argumentation and attempt to force the secular
opponent into a corner by way of an immanent critique such that
the opponent can find a way out of the aporias demonstrated only
by conceding the theologically defended affirmations.

Helmut Peukert masterfully employs this technique in his major
investigation, *Science, Action, and Fundamental Theology*.[18] He first of
all criticizes, as does David Tracy, the one-sided, functionalist description that I gave of religion in *The Theory of Communicative Action*. Even
in traditional societies, the world religions do *not* function *exclusively*
as a legitimation of governmental authority: "in their origin and in
their core, they are often protest movements against the basic trend

of a society's development and attempt to ground other ways for human beings to relate to one another and to reality as a whole."[19] I will not dispute this. I would also admit that I subsumed rather too hastily the development of religion in modernity with Max Weber under the "privatization of the powers of faith" and suggested too quickly an affirmative answer to the question as to "whether then from religious truths, after the religious world views have collapsed, nothing more and nothing other than the secular principles of a universalist ethics of responsibility can be salvaged, and this means: can be accepted for good reasons, on the basis of insight."[20] This question has to *remain open* from the view of the social scientist who proceeds reconstructively and who is careful not simply to project developing trends forward in a straight line. It must also remain open from the viewpoint of the philosopher who appropriates tradition and who in a performative stance has the experience that intuitions which had long been articulated in religious language can neither be rejected nor simply retrieved rationally — as I have shown with the example of the concept of individuality.[21] The process of a critical appropriation of the essential contents of religious tradition is still underway and the outcome is difficult to predict. I willingly repeat my position: "As long as religious language bears with itself inspiring, indeed, unrelinquishable semantic contents which elude (for the moment?) the expressive power of a philosophical language and still await translation into a discourse that gives reasons for its positions, philosophy, even in its postmetaphysical form, will neither be able to replace nor to repress religion."[22]

This still does not imply any agreement with Peukert's thesis that the discourse theory of morality and ethics gets so entangled in limit questions that it finds itself in need of a theological foundation. Of course, effective socializing or pedagogical praxis, which under the aegis of an anticipated autonomy [*Mündigkeit*] seeks to provoke freedom in the other, must take into account the appearance of circumstances and spontaneous forces that it cannot at the same time control. And, with an orientation toward unconditional moral expectations, the subject increases the degree of his or her vulnerability. This then makes the subject especially dependent upon a considerate moral treatment from other persons. Yet, the risk of failure, indeed, of the annihilation of freedom precisely in the processes that should promote and realize freedom, only attests to the constitution of our finite existence. I refer to the necessity, which Peirce emphasized again and again, of a self-relinquishing, transcending anticipation of an unlimited community of communication. This anticipation is simultaneously conceded to us and demanded of us. In communicative action, we orient ourselves toward validity claims that, practically, we can raise only in the context of *our* languages and of our forms of life, even if the convertibility [*Einlösbarkeit*] that we implicitly co-posit *points beyond* the provinciality of our respective historical standpoints. We are exposed to the movement of a transcendence from within, which is just as little at our disposal as the actuality of the spoken word turns us into masters of the structure of language (or of the Logos). The anamnestically constituted reason, which Metz and Peukert, rightly, continually advocate in opposition to a Platonically reduced communicative reason that is insensitive to the temporal dimension, confronts us with the conscientious question about deliverance for the annihilated victims. In this way we become aware of the limits of that transcendence from within which is directed to this world. But this does not enable us to ascertain the *countermovement* of a compensating transcendence from beyond.

That the universal covenant of fellowship would be able to be effective retroactively, toward the past, only in the weak medium of our memory, of the remembrance of the living generations, and of the anamnestic witnesses handed down falls short of our moral need. But the painful experience of a deficit is still not a sufficient argument for the assumption of an "absolute freedom which saves in death."[23] The postulate of a God "which is outlined in temporal, finite, self-transcending intersubjective action in the form of a hopeful expectation [*Erwartung*]"[24] relies upon an experience that is either recognized as such in the language of religious discourse — or loses its evidence. Peukert himself resorts to an experience *accessible only in the language of the Christian tradition*, interwoven inseparably with religious discourse: that with the death on the cross, the disastrous web of evil has been broken. Without this "anticipatory" [*zuvorkommende*] goodness of God, a solidarity among human beings who acknowledge one another unconditionally remains without the guarantee of an outcome that extends beyond the individual act and the moment of illumination this ignites in the eye of the other. It is, indeed, true that whatever human beings succeed in doing they owe to those rare constellations in which their own powers are able to be joined with the favorableness of the historical moment. But the experience that we are dependent upon this favorableness is still no license for the assumption of a divine promise of salvation.

Charles Davis takes up the same apologetic figure of thought when he wants to show that the moral viewpoint implied in the structure of a praxis directed toward reaching agreement, as well as the perspective of living together in solidarity and justice, remain ungrounded without a foundation in Christian hope: "A secular hope without religion cannot affirm with certainty...a future fulfillment."[25] Once again I do not see why a *superadditum* is indispensable in order that we would endeavor to act according to moral commands and ethical insights as long as these require something that is objectively possible. It is true that a philosophy that thinks postmetaphysically cannot answer the question that Tracy also calls attention to: why be moral at all? At the same time, however, this philosophy can show why this question does not arise meaningfully for communicatively socialized individuals. We acquire our moral intuitions in our parents' home, not in school. And moral insights tell us that we do not have any good reasons for behaving otherwise: for this, no self-surpassing of morality is necessary. It is true that we often behave otherwise, but we do so with a bad conscience. The first half of the sentence attests to the weakness of the motivational power of good reasons; the second half attests that rational motivation by reasons is more than nothing [*auch nicht nichts ist*] — moral convictions do not allow themselves to be overridden without resistance.

All of this does yet not treat that struggle against the conditions that have caused us to fail again and again. Glebe-Möller, Davis, Peukert, and others have in view not only the observance of concrete obligations. They seek also a far-reaching engagement for the abolition of unjust conditions and the promotion of forms of life that would not only make solidary action more likely but first make it possible for this action to be reasonably expected. Who or what gives us the courage for such a total engagement that in situations of deprivation and degradation is already being expressed when the destitute and deprived summon the energy each morning to carry on anew? The question about the meaning of life is not meaningless. Nevertheless, the circumstance that penultimate arguments inspire no great confidence is not enough for the grounding of a hope that can be kept alive only in a religious language. The thoughts and expectations directed toward the common good have, after metaphysics has collapsed, only an unstable status. In the place of an Aristotelian politics and a Hegelian philosophy of history, a post-Marxist social theory that has become more humble has appeared. This social theory attempts to exhaust the potential for argumentation in the human sciences in order to contribute to assertions about the genesis, constitution, and ambivalent development of modernity. These diagnoses, even if they are somewhat reliably grounded, remain controversial. Above all they perform a critical service. They can take apart the mutual prejudices of affirmative theories of progress and of negativist theories of decline, of patchwork ideologies and premature totalizations. But, in the passage through the discursive universes of science and philosophy, not even the Peircean hope in a fallible theory of the development of being as a whole, including that of the *summum bonum*, will be able to be realized. Kant already had answered the question "What may we hope for?" with a *postulate* of practical reason, not with a premodern certainty that could inspire us with *confidence*.

I believe to have shown that in communicative action we have no choice but to presuppose the idea of an undistorted intersubjectivity. This, again, can be understood as the formal characterization of the necessary conditions for the forms, not able to be anticipated, of a worthwhile life. There is no theory for these totalities themselves. Certainly, praxis requires encouragement; it is inspired by intuitive anticipations of the whole. There is an intuition that impresses me deeply which I have occasionally formulated: If historical progress consists in lessening, abolishing, or preventing the suffering of vulnerable creatures, and if historical experience teaches that on the heels of advances finally achieved, consuming disaster closely follows, then there are grounds for supposing that the balance of what can be endured remains intact only if we give our utmost for the sake of the possible advances.[26] Perhaps it is such assumptions which, indeed, can give no confidence for a praxis whose certainties have been taken away, yet can still leave it some hope.

To reject apologetic figures of thought is one thing; it is another thing to learn from the worthy objections of my theological colleagues. I leave aside here the reservations that David Tracy brings forth against approaches based on an evolutionary theory and shall concentrate on his thesis that dialogue, and not argumentation, offers the more encompassing approach for the investigation of communicative action.

Argumentative discourse is certainly the more specialized form of communication. In it validity claims which previously remained implicit because they arose performatively are expressly thematized. Therefore, they have a reflexive character that requires the more exacting presuppositions of communication. The presuppositions of action oriented toward reaching understanding are more easily accessible in argumentation. This preference as part of a research strategy does not imply an ontological distinction, as if argumentation would be more important or even more fundamental than conversation or the communicative everyday praxis constituted in the lifeworld. This everyday praxis forms the most encompassing horizon. In this sense, even the analysis of speech acts enjoys only a heuristic preference. This analysis of speech acts forms the key for a pragmatic analysis which, as Tracy rightly insists, must comprise the entire spectrum of the world of symbolic forms: symbols and images, indicators and expressive gestures, as well as relations of similarity. Thus, it must extend to all signs that lie beneath the level of propositionally differentiated speech, signs that can represent semantic contents even if they have no author who bestows meaning upon them. The semiotics of Charles S. Peirce has made accessible this archaeology of signs. The richness of this theory is far from being exhausted; this is also true for an aesthetics that points out the world-disclosing function of works of art in their speechless materiality.

Tracy repeats the criticism concerning the reductions of an expressivistic aesthetics which *The Theory of Communicative Action* at least suggested. In the meantime, in response to the works of Albrecht Wellmer and Martin Seel,[27] I have corrected this.[28] Although an innovative world-disclosing power belongs to both prophetic speech as well as to art that has become autonomous, I would hesitate to name religious and aesthetic symbols in the same breath. I am certain that David Tracy in no way wants to suggest an aesthetic understanding of the religious. Aesthetic experience has become an integral component of the modern world in that it has become independent as a cultural sphere of value. Religion would be stabilized by a similar differentiation into a social subsystem specialized, as Niklas Luhmann holds, in coping with contingency, but only at the price of the complete neutralization of its experiential content. In opposition to this, political theology also fights for a public role for religion and precisely in modern societies. Yet then religious symbolism should not conform to the aesthetic, that is, to the forms of expression of an expert culture, but must maintain its *holistic* position in the lifeworld.

Furthermore, I take very seriously Peukert's warning to take into account the temporal dimensions of action that is oriented toward reaching understanding. Nevertheless, phenomenological analyses in the style of *Being and Time* cannot simply be transplanted into a theory of communication. Possibly, Peirce's semiotics offers a better and, until now, unused entry point. Karl-Otto Apel and I have, up to now, appropriated only the fundamental insight of his theory of truth, that a transcending power dwells within validity claims which assures a relation to the future for every speech act: "Thus thought is rational only so far as it recommends itself to a possible future thought. Or in other words the rationality of thought lies in its reference to a possible future."[29] But the young Peirce had already given an interesting reference to the ability of the sign process to establish continuity. In epistemological contexts, he ascribes to the individual symbol the power to produce that continuity in the flow of our experiences that Kant wanted to ascertain through the accompanying "I-think" of transcendental apperception. Because the individual experience itself assumes the threefold structure of a sign that refers simultaneously to a past object and to a future interpretant, this experience can come into a semantic relation to other experiences across temporal distances and thus establish a temporal connection upon a diversity which otherwise, as in a kaleidoscope, would fall apart.[30] In this way, Peirce explains temporal relations that are only first produced through the structure of signs. The medium of language could borrow from this semiotic structure its dynamic of temporalization that is unfolded in the continuities of tradition.

Finally, I respond to the objections that are not motivated by specifically theological considerations.

RESPONSE TO THE NONTHEOLOGIANS

1. Sheila Briggs makes distinctions within the paradigm of praxis philosophy that I find plausible.*However, I still do not quite see how under her premises one can reach the type of dialogical ethics that will ground the universal accountability and the integrity of the particular identity of each person without claiming the universalist viewpoints of equality and justice. Seyla Benhabib, on whose works Briggs supports her feminist critique, also remains faithful to the universalist intentions of Kant and Hegel. Benhabib develops her conception thoroughly in agreement with me:

While agreeing that normative disputes can be rationally settled, and that fairness, reciprocity, and some procedure of universalizability are constituents, that is necessary conditions of the moral standpoint, interactive universalism regards difference as a starting point for reflection and action. In this sense "universality" is a regulative ideal that does not deny our embodied and embedded identity, but aims at developing moral attitudes and encouraging political transformations that can yield a view acceptable to all. Universality is not the ideal consensus of fictitiously defined selves, but the concrete process in politics and morals of the struggle of concrete, embodied selves, striving for autonomy.[31]

Nevertheless, Benhabib questions the limitation of moral argumentation to problems of justice, because she believes that the logical distinction between questions of justice and questions about the good life is based on or, at least, corresponds to the sociological distinction between the public and private spheres. A morality curtailed legalistically, so she thinks, would have to restrict itself to questions of political justice. All private relations and personal spheres of life, which a patriarchal society leaves principally to women, are then excluded *per definitionem* from the sphere of responsibility of morality. This assumption, however, is not correct. For the logical distinction between problems of justice and of the good life is independent from

---

*For this reference to Sheila Briggs, see the introduction to this volume, p. 10.

the sociological distinction between spheres of life. We make a *moral* use of practical reason when we ask what is equally good for everyone; we make an *ethical* use when we ask what is respectively good for me or for us. Questions of justice permit under the moral viewpoint what all could will: answers that in principle are universally valid. Ethical questions, on the other hand, can be rationally clarified only in the context of a specific life-history or a particular form of life. For these questions are perspectively focused on the individual or on a specific collective who want to know who they are and, at the same time, who they want to be. Such processes of self-understanding distinguish themselves from moral argumentation in the way they pose the question, not however, in the gender-specific location of their themes.

That certainly does not mean that in moral questions we have to abstract from the concrete other. Briggs and Benhabib distinguish between two perspectives according to whether we respectively consider all those concerned in their entirety, or the particular individual in his or her situation. In moral argumentation, both perspectives must come into play. But they have to be intertwined. In *justification discourses [Begründungsdiskursen]*, practical reason becomes effective through a principle of universalization, while individual cases are considered only as illustrative examples. Justified norms, admittedly, can claim only prima facie validity. Which norm in the individual case is held to be the most appropriate and, to that extent, has precedence over other, likewise prima facie valid norms cannot be decided in the same way. This application of norms requires instead a discourse of another type. Such *application discourses [Anwendungsdiskurse]* follow a logic different than that for justification discourses. Here, in fact, it is a question of the concrete other in the context of the respective given circumstances, the particular social relationships, the unique identity and life-history. Which norm is respectively the *appropriate* one can only be judged in the light of a description of all the relevant features that is as complete as possible.[32] If there is anything to hold against Lawrence Kohlberg, against whom Benhabib advances considerations from Carol Gilligan, then it is not his explanation of the moral principle on the basis of the process of the ideal role-taking, an explanation based upon George Herbert Mead, but his neglect of the problem of application.

2. At this point I can react only with a few remarks to the very thoughtful, but rather allusively presented criticism of Robert Wuthnow. A great deal of hermeneutical preparatory work would probably be necessary on both sides. Wuthnow is uneasy about the whole undertaking of a critical theory of society that reflexively retrieves, in a way, its context of origin, and which relies upon a

rational potential found in the linguistic medium of socialization itself.[33] He does not keep separate the different analytical levels and does not bear in mind the methodical difference between a formal-pragmatically performed theory of language, of argumentation, and of action, on the one hand, and a sociological theory of action and of systems, on the other hand. He does not distinguish between the concept of the lifeworld employed formal-pragmatically or sociologically. He also does not distinguish between a discourse theory of truth, of morality, and of justice which proceeds normatively, on the one hand, empirically substantive attempts at reconstruction that have a descriptive claim, on the other hand. This theoretical framework is certainly not unproblematic. But I don't see how his ad hoc objections can be properly discussed if there is not a closer understanding of the architectural plan.

For example, it is not the case that I oppose a radiant future to a devalued past. The proceduralist concept of rationality that I propose cannot sustain utopian projects for concrete forms of life as a whole. The theory of society within which my analyses take place can at best lead to diagnostic descriptions which allow the ambivalence of contrary tendencies of development to emerge more clearly. It is not a case of idealizing the future; if anything, in *The Structural Transformation of the Public Sphere*, there was on my part an idealization of the past.

It is correct that I advocate a pragmatic theory of meaning according to which a hearer understands an expression when he or she knows the conditions under which it can be accepted as valid. The basic idea is simple: one understands an expression only if one knows how one could utilize it in order to come to an understanding with anyone about something in the world. This internal relation between the process of reaching agreement and rationality is inferred from the methodically assumed attitude of a virtual participant. But from here there is no direct path that leads to a social-scientific rationalism which remains deaf to "personal freedom, willful violations of established norms, pluralism, and nonreductive modes of expressivity." [34] Wuthnow can recognize in communicative rationality, which is inherent in the medium of language, only an extension of instrumental rationality. In doing this, he is relying upon the analyses that were put forth at the beginning of the first volume of *The Theory of Communicative Action*, namely, that of the use of propositional knowledge in affirmations, on the one hand, and purposive-rational actions, on the other hand. He does not take into consideration that these two model cases form merely the starting point for a progressively expanded analysis. By the way, I consider information [*Mitteilung*] and norm-regulated action (as also expressive self-presentation) only as limit cases of communicative action. The contrast between an innovative and idiosyncratic use of language serves only the explanation of the use of evaluative expressions.

All these things must first be set right before Wuthnow's interesting remark concerning a resacralization of the lifeworld could be discussed. That is probably the real point of dispute: whether the liberation of everyday praxis from alienation and colonialization is to be described more in the sense that I hold, as a rationalization of the lifeworld, or in the sense of Odo Marquard as a "re-enchantment."[35]

3. Fred Dallmayr's paper on "Critical Theory and Reconciliation" presents me with some difficulties. With great understanding Dallmayr traces important religious background motifs in Horkheimer and Adorno's *Dialectic of Enlightenment* as well as in Adorno's later philosophy. He analyses in a manner similar to my own the aporias in which critical theory gets entangled. Against this background, he then subjects *The Theory of Communicative Action* to an astonishingly prejudiced critique. It is astonishing for the reason that Dallmayr is thoroughly acquainted with my writings. For decades, he has commented upon my publications not uncritically, but rather with great sensitivity and a comprehensive knowledge of the German discussion and its context.[36]

Dallmayr has set the course for the present dispute in an interesting essay on the question: "Is Critical Theory a Humanism?" In it the expression "humanism" is used pejoratively as with Heidegger and means as much as anthropocentrism. Dallmayr thinks that I merely exchange the transcendental subject for a quasi-transcendental intersubjectivity. To him, the linguistic turn of critical theory only veils the fact that beyond language subjectivity is reinstated in its Cartesian rights: "Habermas's outlook...can with some legitimacy be described as a 'humanism' — where this term stands for a more or less man- or subject-focused orientation. The distinctions between empiricism and hermeneutics, system and lifeworld and propositional and reflexive speech can, without undue violence, be reconciled with the Cartesian and Kantian subject-object bifurcation (and thus with the basic framework of metaphysics."[37] This focus, naturally, must surprise an author who, in his own understanding, has pursued the pragmatic-linguistic turn as the critique of any form of a philosophy of the subject — certainly with enough caution as not to fall from the frying pan of subject-centered reason into the fire of a history of Being circumscribed by a negative metaphysics. Precisely this anti-Heideggerian accent to the paradigm shift might provoke Dallmayr into disavowing the paradigm shift itself.

This is especially difficult for me to understand in view of a book like *The Philosophical Discourse of Modernity*, in which I develop the new paradigm of the process of understanding from its context in the history of philosophy. My intention is to show how one can avoid the traps of the philosophy of the subject without entangling oneself at the same time in the aporias of a self-referential and totalizing critique of reason — neither in the deconstructionist version of the late Heideggerians nor in the contextualistic version of the late Wittgensteinians.[38] Since the argumentative substance of the third, critical part of Dallmayr's contribution is not sufficient for an extensive debate, I limit myself to a few cursory remarks.

a. Dallmayr supports his assertion of a "continuity" between the paradigm of the process of understanding and that of the subject-object relation with the point that speech acts demonstrate the same teleological structure as do purposive activities (see p. 141 of this volume). Yet, as I have argued elsewhere, the teleological language game has a different meaning in the theory of language than in the theory of action.[39] The same fundamental concepts are respectively interpreted in each case in a different sense — and, indeed, interpreted differently in a sense that is relevant for our question. In contrast to teleological actions, speech acts are directed toward illocutionary goals, which do not have the status of a purpose that is to be realized *innerworldly*. These goals also cannot be realized without the *uncoerced* cooperation and agreement of the one addressed and, finally, can be explained only through recourse to the concept of reaching agreement that is *inherent* in the medium of language itself. As opposed to teleological actions, speech acts in addition interpret themselves on the basis of their twofold illocutionary-propositional structure itself: by performing speech acts, one states at the same time what one does.

b. Dallmayr believes further that the theory of speech acts privileges the role of the speaker and does not take into account the accomplishments of the hearer (see p. 143). The opposite is the case for an analysis which insists (against Searle) that every action of speech remains incomplete without the "Yes" or "No" response of a potential hearer. The hearer must take the position of a second person, give up the perspective of an observer in favor of that of a participant, and enter into a lifeworld that is intersubjectively shared by a linguistic community if he or she wants to take advantage of the characteristic reflexivity of natural language. This thoroughly hermeneutical conception of language is directed against the theoreticism of the causalistic model of linguistic understanding shared by Quine, Davidson, and others.

c. Dallmayr then emphasizes the complementarity of speaking and silence: "language...reverberates with its own silence" (143). This reference to the ontological "unfathomability" of language clearly remains in needs of further elaboration beyond the mystical language allusions of the later Heidegger. If Dallmayr does not want to withdraw from the start the phenomenon of silence from an analysis of language, he can make use of my theory of communication: nonauratic silence draws from the specific context a more or less unmistakable meaning. Moreover, every speech act is, of course, situated, and every speech situation is embedded in an intersubjectively shared lifeworld context, which silently wreathes what is spoken in a mute presence.[40]

d. Furthermore, Dallmayr accuses me of having an instrumentalist conception of language (142ff.). This linguistic empiricism has already been overcome by Hamann and Humboldt. I, too, do not develop my theory of communication from Locke, but from hermeneutics and from American pragmatism. Clearly, the act of naming, which from the Romantic philosophy of language up to Benjamin has played a paradigmatic role (a role rich in associations with respect to Christian speculations about the Logos), has proved to be a rather one-sided model for the explanation of linguistically creative powers. In a strict interpretation, it leads to a conception of language based upon a semantics of reference. According to it, expressions should represent states of affairs in the same way that a name stands for an object — which is false. Just as incorrect is the speculative interpretation of the model of naming, which hypostatizes the constitutive, i.e., world-disclosing power of language and thereby neglects the relevance of the validity of language-enabled practices in the world (the confrontation with whatever is encountered in the world).

e. Finally, Dallmayr blames me for the restoration of a "shallow" (as it was called in Germany until 1945) Enlightenment Rationalism (132ff.). The shallow and the profound have their own pitfalls. I have always attempted to steer between the Scylla of a leveling, transcendence-less empiricism and the Charybdis of a high-flying idealism that glorifies transcendence. I hope to have learned much from Kant, and still I have not become a Dallmayrian Kantian because the theory of communicative action *integrates* the transcendental tension between the intelligible and the world of appearances in communicative everyday praxis, yet does not thereby *level* it out. The Logos of language founds the intersubjectivity of the lifeworld, in which we find ourselves already preunderstood, in order that we can encounter one another face to face as subjects. Indeed, we meet as subjects who impute to each other accountability, that is, the capability to guide our actions according to transcending validity claims. At the same time, the lifeworld reproduces itself through the medium of our communicative actions which are to be accounted for by us. Yet, this does not mean that the lifeworld would be at our disposal. As agents of communicative action, we are exposed to a transcendence that is integrated in the linguistic conditions of reproduction without being *delivered up* to it. This conception can hardly be identified with the productivist illusion of a species that generates itself and which puts itself in the place of a disavowed Absolute. Linguistic intersubjectivity goes beyond the subjects without putting them *in bondage* [*hörig*]. It is not a higher-level subjectivity and therefore, without sacrificing a transcendence from within, it can do without the concept of an Absolute. We can dispense with this legacy of Hellenized Christianity as well as with any subsequent right-Hegelian constructions, upon which Dallmayr still seems to rely.

Translated by Eric Crump and Peter P. Kenny

NOTES

1. See my "A Postscript to *Knowledge and Human Interests*," in *Philosophy of the Social Sciences* 3 (1975): 157–89, as well as my replies in John B. Thompson and David Held, eds., *Habermas: Critical Debates* (Cambridge, Mass.: MIT Press, 1982); Richard J. Bernstein, ed., *Habermas and Modernity* (Cambridge, Mass.: MIT Press, 1985); and Axel Honneth and Hans Joas, eds., *Kommunikatives Handeln* (Frankfurt am Main: Suhrkamp, 1986) [ET: Axel Honneth and Hans Joas, eds., *Communicative Action* (Cambridge, Mass.: MIT Press, 1990)].

2. Hans-Georg Geyer, Hans-Norbert Janowski, and Alfred Schmidt, *Theologie und Soziologie* (Stuttgart: Kohlhammer, 1970); Rudolf J. Siebert, *The Critical Theory of Religion: The Frankfurt School* (Berlin /New York /Amsterdam: Mouton, 1985).

3. See the impressive bibliography compiled by Edmund Arens in *Habermas und die Theologie. Beiträge zur theologischen Rezeption, Diskussion und Kritik der Theorie kommunikativen Handelns*, ed. Edmund Arens (Düsseldorf: Patmos, 1989), 9–38.

4. Jürgen Habermas, *The Philosophical Discourse of Modernity*, trans. Frederick Lawrence (Cambridge, Mass.: MIT Press, 1987), 35–41; see also Karl Löwith, "Hegels Aufhebung der christlichen Religion," in Karl Löwith, *Vorträge und Abhandlungen. Zur Kritik der christlichen Überlieferung* (Stuttgart: Kohlhammer, 1966), 54–96.

5. This appears to me to be the awkward situation in which Fred Dallmayr finds himself.

6. Francis Schüssler Fiorenza, *Foundational Theology: Jesus and the Church* (New York: Crossroad, 1984).

7. Francis Schüssler Fiorenza, "The Church as a Community of Interpretation: Political Theology between Discourse Ethics and Hermeneutical Reconstruction," in this volume, 66–91. The page numbers in the text refer to this essay.

8. Helmut Peukert, "Enlightenment and Theology as Unfinished Projects," 44 in this volume.

9. Matthew Lamb, "Communicative Praxis and Theology: Beyond Modern Nihilism and Dogmatism," in this volume, 95.

10. David Tracy, "Theology, Critical Social Theory, and the Public Realm," in this volume, 23–24.

11. Gary M. Simpson, "Die Versprachlichung (und Verflüssigung?) des Sakralen," in *Habermas und die Theologie*, 158 f.; also as "The Linguistification (and Liquefaction?) of the Sacred: A Theological Consideration of Jürgen Habermas's Theory of Religion," *Exploration* 7:21–35.

12. See Peter Eicher, "Die Botschaft von der Versöhnung und die Theorie des kommunikativen Handelns," in *Habermas und die Theologie*, 199f.

13. Paul Kluke, *Die Stiftunguniversität Frankfurt am Main 1914–1932* (Frankfurt am Main, 1972); Notker Hammerstein, *Die Johann-Wolfgang-Goethe-Universität*, vol. 1 (Frankfurt am Main: Luchterhand, 1989).

14. Johann Baptist Metz, "Erinnerung," in Hermann Krings et al., eds., *Handbuch philosophischer Grundbegriffe* (München: Kösel, 1973) 2:386–96; Metz, "Anamnetische Vernunft," in Axel Honneth, Thomas McCarthy, Claus Offe, and Albrecht Wellmer, eds., *Zwischenbetrachtungen* (Frankfurt am Main: Suhrkamp 1989), 733f.

15. Jürgen Habermas, *The Theory of Communicative Action* (Boston: Beacon Press, 1984, 1987), 2:281ff.

16. Habermas, *The Philosophical Discourse of Modernity*, 245 f.; See also my article "Die Philosophie als Platzhalter und Interpret," in Habermas, *Moralbewußtsein und kommunikatives Handeln* (Frankfurt am Main: Suhrkamp, 1983), 9–28 [ET *Moral Consciousness and Communicative Action* (Cambridge, Mass.: MIT Press, 1990)].

17. Jens Glebe-Möller, *A Political Dogmatic* (Philadelphia: Fortress, 1987), 102. The page numbers in the text refer to this book.

18. Trans. James Bohman (Cambridge, Mass: MIT Press, 1986) [ET of *Wissenschaftstheorie — Handlungstheorie — Fundamentale Theologie* (Düsseldorf: Patmos, 1976, Frankfurt am Main: Suhrkamp, 1978].

19. Peukert, "Enlightenment and Theology," in this volume, 56.

20. Jürgen Habermas, *Die neue Unübersichtlichkeit* (Frankfurt am Main: Suhrkamp, 1985), 52.

21. Jürgen Habermas, "Individuierung durch Vergesellschaftung," in *Nachmetaphysisches Denken* (Frankfurt am Main: Suhrkamp, 1988), 187–241, esp. 192ff.

22. Habermas, *Nachmetaphysisches Denken*, 60.

23. For a more extensive treatment of this argument, see Thomas McCarthy, "Philosophical Foundations of Political Theology: Kant, Peukert and the Frankfurt School," in Leroy S. Rouner, ed., *Civil Religion and Political Theology* (Notre Dame, Ind.: University of Notre Dame Press, 1986), 23–40.

24. Peukert, "Enlightenment and Theology," 60.

25. Charles Davis, "Kommunikative Rationalität und die Grundlegung christlicher Hoffnung," in *Habermas und die Theologie*, 111.

26. Jürgen Habermas, *Eine Art Schadensabwicklung* (Frankfurt am Main: Suhrkamp, 1987), 146.

27. Albrecht Wellmer, "Wahrheit, Schein, Versöhnung. Adornos ästhetische Rettung der Modernität," in Albrecht Wellmer, *Zur Dialetik von Moderne und Postmoderne* (Frankfurt am Main: Suhrkamp, 1985), 9–47; Martin Seel, *Die Kunst der Entzweiung* (Frankfurt am Main: Suhrkamp, 1986).

28. J. Habermas, "Questions and Counterquestions," in *Habermas and Modernity*, 192ff., here 202f.; further, Habermas, *The Philosophical Discourse of Modernity*, 204ff.

29. Charles S. Peirce, *Writings of Charles S. Peirce: A Chronological Edition, Vol. 3: 1872–1878*, ed. Max H. Fisch et al. (Bloomington, Ind.: University of Indiana Press, 1986), 3:108.

30. Ibid., 3:68–71.

31. Seyla Benhabib, "The Generalized and the Concrete Other," *Praxis International* 5 (1986), 406.

32. Klaus Günther, *Der Sinn für Angemessenheit. Anwendungsdiskurse in Moral und Recht* (Frankfurt am Main: Suhrkamp, 1988).

33. See the Introduction to my *Theory and Practice*, trans. John Viertel (Boston: Beacon Press, 1973), 1–40.

34. Robert Wuthnow, "Rationality and the Limits of Rational Theory," in this volume, 216.

35. Odo Marquard, *Abschied vom Prinzipiellen: Philosophische Studien* (Stuttgart: Reclam, 1981).

36. Fred Dallmayr, *Beyond Dogma and Despair* (Notre Dame, Ind.: University of Notre Dame Press, 1981), 220ff. and 246ff.; Dallmayr, *Twilight of Subjectivity* (Amherst: University of Massachusetts Press, 1981), 179ff. and 279ff.

37. Fred Dallmayr, *Polis and Praxis* (Cambridge, Mass.: MIT Press, 1984), 158.

38. See Fred Dallmayr, "The Discourse of Modernity: Hegel, Nietzsche, Heidegger (and Habermas)," *Praxis International* 8 (1989): 377–406; see also the discussion about *Theorie des kommunikativen Handelns* in Fred Dallmayr, *Polis and Praxis*, 224–53. Dallmayr is similarly prejudicial in "Habermas and Rationality," *Political Theory* 16 (1988), 553–79. In his response, Richard J. Bernstein remarks about Dallmayr: "Considering his hermeneutical sensitivity, his most recent discussion of Habermas comes a bit as a shock. For although he makes use of extensive citations to create the impression that the 'author' is speaking for himself, the result is a distortion of Habermas' views" (ibid., 580).

39. Habermas, *Nachmetaphysisches Denken*, 64ff.

40. See my analysis of the lifeworld in *Nachmetaphysisches Denken*, 82–104.

A Select Annotated Bibliography

Francis Schüssler Fiorenza

HABERMAS'S WRITINGS

The Structural Transformation of the Public Sphere: An Inquiry into a Category of Bourgeois Society. Cambridge, Mass.: MIT Press, 1989. Habermas traces the development and eclipse of the public sphere within modern society. Written as his "habilitation" (a dissertation qualifying someone to become a professor), this work displays the roots of Habermas's concern with discourse ethics and communicative action, even though his later writings provide a much more complex and less optimistic view of the public sphere.

On the Logic of the Social Sciences. Cambridge, Mass.: MIT Press, 1988. This volume is basically a bibliographical survey. Habermas compares and analyzes functional, positivistic, and behaviorist approaches to the study of society, on the one hand, and historical, narrative, and hermeneutical approaches on the other. He demonstrates the limitations and inadequacy of the respective approaches.

Theory and Praxis. Boston: Beacon Press, 1973. A collection of early essays that elaborates the relation between theory and practice by criticizing positivistic and instrumental conceptions, reason, philosophy, and politics.

Knowledge and Interest. Boston: Beacon Press, 1971. In this early and first systematic development of his ideas, Habermas formulates the thesis of three distinct cognitive interests, the technical interest of the empirical analytical sciences, the practical interest of the historical-hermeneutic sciences, and the emancipatory interest of critical social sciences. Although Habermas has subsequently reformulated and revised many of his theses, this book remains a pivotal work.

Toward a Rational Society: Student Protest, Science and Politics. Boston: Beacon Press, 1970. In addition to essays more directly on the student protests and the democratization of the German university, Habermas analyzes the role of technology and science as ideology and points to the scientization of politics and public opinion.

Legitimation Crisis. Boston: Beacon Press, 1971. Deals with the diverse crises of economic life, motivation, rationality, and legitimacy within advanced capitalism.

Philosophical-Political Profiles. Cambridge, Mass.: MIT Press, 1983. Habermas provides brief sketches of select twentieth-century German thinkers, including Heidegger, Jaspers, Adorno, Bloch, Benjamin, Scholem, Arendt, Gadamer, and others.

Communication and the Evolution of Society. Boston: Beacon Press, 1979. Important for his revision of the Marxist theory of history in view of his own development of a theory of communicative action.

The Theory of Communicative Action. 2 vols. Boston: Beacon Press, 1984, 1987. These two volumes constitute Habermas's interpretation of a theory of communicative action and of modernity by setting his systematic conception in the context of an analysis of modern classic positions: Marx, Durkheim, Weber, Mead, and Parsons.

The Philosophical Discourse of Modernity: Twelve Lectures. Cambridge, Mass.: MIT Press, 1987. Habermas enters into the current debates about modernity versus postmodernity with these lectures dealing with Hegel, Nietzsche, Foucault, Derrida, and others.

The New Conservatism: Cultural Criticism and the Historians' Debate. Cambridge, Mass.: MIT Press, 1989. Selected essays of cultural criticism that focus on contemporary neoconservatism and recent German debate about its past during the Nazi period.

Moral Consciousness and Communicative Action. Cambridge, Mass.: MIT Press, 1990. This volume contains Habermas's latest essays on discourse ethics and communicative action.

GENERAL INTRODUCTIONS TO CRITICAL THEORY

Benhabib, Seyla. *Critique, Norm, and Utopia: A Study of the Foundations of Critical Theory*. New York: Columbia University Press, 1986. An important and influential analysis of the Frankfurt School. Benhabib carefully traces the origins of critical theory back to Hegel and Marx. Her analysis of autonomy as mimetic reconciliation and her argument for the relation between human autonomy and the utopian dimension of human experience bring critical reflections to Habermas's notion of discourse ethics.

Dews, Peter. *Logics of Disintegration: Post-Structuralist Thought and the Claims of Critical Theory*. London: Verso, 1987. Although it is primarily a study of French poststructural thought, it offers a comparison of Habermas and Foucault.

Guess, Raymond. *The Idea of Critical Theory*. Cambridge: Cambridge University Press, 1981. A critical analysis of the Frankfurt School that focuses on the adequacy of its idea of ideology.

Held, David. *Introduction to Critical Theory*. Berkeley: University of California Press, 1980. A careful analysis. Part 1 deals with the origin of critical theory in the early writings on the family and the individual, and with the philosophy of history of the *Dialectic of Enlightenment*. It discusses the basic concepts of Horkheimer, Adorno, and Marcuse. Part 2 deals with the work of Habermas up until his formulation of a universal pragmatism and the crises of capitalism. Part 3 attempts an assessment of the limit and potential of critical theory.

Jay, Martin. *The Dialectical Imagination: A History of the Frankfurt School and the Institute for Social Research, 1923–1950.* Boston: Little, Brown, & Co., 1973. An excellent historical survey of the origins of the Frankfurt School, its transition to United States during World War II, and its postwar return to Germany.

———. *Marxisms and Totality: The Adventures of a Concept from Lukács to Habermas.* Berkeley: University of California Press, 1984. A broad survey of leading Marxist theorists (French, Italian, and German) with concise treatments of Adorno, Horkheimer, and Habermas.

Wellmer, Albrecht. *Critical Theory of Society.* New York: Seabury, 1971. An early work on critical theory that focuses on its critique of instrumental reason and the latent positivism of Marxist theory.

GENERAL INTRODUCTIONS TO HABERMAS

Dews, Peter, ed. *Autonomy and Solidarity: Interviews with Jürgen Habermas.* London: Verso, 1986. A set of interviews that enable Habermas to clarify important diverse aspects of his work and writings.

Ferry, Jean-Marc. *Habermas: L'éthique de la communication.* Paris: Presses Universitaires de France, 1987. An important French study of Habermas's ideas in the context of his confrontation with other thinkers on the relation between understanding and politics, critique and domination, and legitimacy and democracy.

McCarthy, Thomas. *The Critical Theory of Jürgen Habermas.* Cambridge, Mass.: MIT Press, 1978. A clear, concise, and competent introduction to Habermas's work by a philosopher who has translated the majority of his writings. Discussing his diverse writings, it traces the development of Habermas's ideas from his early critique of positivism and instrumental rationality to development of a theory of communicative action. It remains the best single introduction to the whole corpus of Habermas's work.

White, Stephen. *The Recent Work of Jürgen Habermas.* Cambridge: Cambridge University Press, 1988. A discussion primarily of Habermas's theory of discourse ethics and communicative action that relates his ideas to Anglo-Saxon theories of justice.

ANALYSES OF HABERMAS'S
THEORY OF COMMUNICATIVE ACTION

Brand, Arie. *The Force of Reason: An Introduction to Habermas's Theory of Communicative Action.* Boston: Allen & Unwin, 1990. Brand introduces Habermas's two-volume *Theory of Communicative Action* by analyzing first Habermas's key concepts and then his positions on the social theorists and their specific theses.

Honneth, Axel, and Hans Joas, eds. *Communicative Action.* Cambridge, Mass.: MIT Press, 1990. A collection of essays by students and associates of Habermas critically analyzing the major themes and categories of Habermas's theory of communicative action.

Ingram, David. *Habermas and the Dialectic of Reason*. New Haven: Yale University Press, 1987. An analysis primarily of Habermas's volumes on communicative action. It explains Habermas's position vis-à-vis Weber's theory of rationalization, the notion of rationalization as reification in Lukács and Adorno, the social theories of Mead and Durkheim, and the systems theory of Parsons. Ingram reviews Habermas's revision of the theory practice problem.

Rassmussen, David M. *Reading Habermas*. Cambridge: Basil Blackwell, 1990. Written from a phenomenological perspective, Rassmussen discusses Habermas's position within the modernity/postmodernity debate and the relationship between a discourse ethics and law.

Rockmore, Tom. *Habermas on Historical Materialism*. Bloomington: Indiana University Press, 1989. Rockmore traces the development of Habermas's views on Marxism and argues that Habermas moves further away from Marxism in his reconstruction of Marxism so that Marxism remains more of a goal than a means.

HABERMAS, MODERNITY, AND PUBLIC THEORY

Baynes, Kenneth, *The Normative Grounds of Social Criticism: Kant, Rawls, Habermas*. Albany: State University of New York Press, 1992. Baynes examines the differences between Habermas's discourse ethics and John Rawls's conception of justice against the background of their common roots in Kant's conception of justice and moral autonomy.

Benhabib, Seyla, and Fred Dallmayr, eds. *The Communicative Ethics Controversy*. Cambridge, Mass.: MIT 1990. A collection of essays dealing with the recent debates about Habermas's communicative ethics. Since most of the essays are translations of German essays, they reflect the German discussion. The exception is Benhabib's own contribution, which deals with North American feminist theory and communitarian ethics.

Bernstein, Richard J., ed. *Habermas and Modernity*. Cambridge, Mass.: MIT Press, 1985. A selection of essays originally published in the journal *Praxis International* that deal with the Enlightenment, modernity, and postmodernity.

Braaten, Jane. *Habermas's Critical Theory of Society*. Albany: State University of New York Press, 1991. Braaten analyzes the notions of truth and consensus underlying Habermas's theory of communicative competence. She concretely relates critical theory to recent discussions of social psychology and of a politics of need interpretation.

Forester, John, ed. *Critical Theory and Public Life*. Cambridge, Mass.: MIT, 1985. This collection of essays relates critical theory to public policy in education, information, ecology, consumerism, and social choice.

Kelly, Michael, ed. *Hermeneutics and Critical Theory in Ethics and Politics*. Cambridge, Mass.: MIT Press, 1990. A discussion of Habermas's discourse ethics in relation to current positions in practical philosophy, such as those of MacIntyre, Walzer, Derrida, and Kohlberg, as well as in relation to the classic positions of Aristotle, Kant, and Hegel.

Smith, Tony. *The Role of Ethics in Social Theory: Essays from a Habermasian Perspective*. Albany: State University of New York Press, 1991. Smith examines capitalism as well as historical materialism with the analytical tools and normative models of Habermas's political philosophy and conception of justice.

Thompson, John, and David Held, eds. *Habermas: Critical Debates*. Cambridge, Mass.: MIT Press, 1982. An important collection of essays that examine Habermas's writings on rationality, pragmatics, social evolution, Marxism, and the crises of late capitalism. Habermas's extended response clarifies several major issues of his work.

White, Stephen K. *Political Theory and Postmodernism*. New York: Cambridge University Press, 1991. Dealing with the issues raised by postmodernism for contemporary political theory, White shows the contribution of Habermas's conception of justice and philosophical social ethics and surveys the issues raised by feminist political theorists in relation to Habermas's interpretation of modern society.

HABERMAS AND THEOLOGY

Arens, Edmund. *Habermas und die Theologie*. Düsseldorf: Patmos Verlag, 1989. A collection of essays from diverse theological perspectives that deal with the significance and relevance of Habermas's work for theology. It contains German versions of three of the essays (Peukert's, Fiorenza's, and Lamb's) that were given at the University of Chicago Divinity School conference on critical theory (1988).

Bauer, Karl. *Der Denkweg von Jürgen Habermas zur Theorie des kommunikativen Handelns*. Regensburg: S. Roderer Verlag, 1987. Bauer traces the development of Habermas's thought from his dissertation on Schelling to his theory of communicative action. He offers proposals of fundamental theology based on Habermas's response to the rationality of modernity and the challenge of nihilism.

Davis, Charles. *Theology and Political Society*. New York: Cambridge, 1980. An important exposition of critical theory and especially Habermas's early work that explores its potential for political theology.

Lakeland, Paul. *Theology and Critical Theory: The Discourse of the Church*. Nashville: Abingdon Press, 1990. Lakeland profiles Habermas's work in relation to Roman Catholic social ethics and theory and shows the distinctive contribution that his communicative theory can make.

Peukert, Helmut. *Science, Action, and Fundamental Theology*. Cambridge, Mass.: MIT Press, 1986. Peukert provides an extensive survey of the development of the philosophy of science. His survey displays the importance of Habermas's work in overcoming the impasses of positivism as well as the relevance of a universal solidarity within the religious tradition.

Siebert, Rudolf J. *The Critical Theory of Religion: From Universal Pragmatic to Political Theology*. New York and Amsterdam: Mouton, 1985. A wide-ranging discussion of critical theory with special emphasis on Hegel's philosophy and political theology.

Contributors

Don Browning is Alexander Campbell Professor of Religion and Psychological Studies at the Divinity School of the University of Chicago. Among his many books are *Religious Ethics and Pastoral Care; Religious Thought and the Modern Psychologies: A Critical Conversation in the Theology of Culture;* and *A Fundamental Practical Theology: Descriptive and Strategic Proposals.* He has also edited many books dealing with practical theology, among them: *Practical Theology* and *Religious and Ethical Factors in Psychiatric Practice.*

Fred R. Dallmayr is Professor Packey J. Dee Professor of Political Theory at the University of Notre Dame. Among his recent books are *Twilight of Subjectivity: Contributions to a Post-Individualist Theory of Politics; Polis and Praxis: Exercises in Contemporary Political Theory; Language and Politics: Why Does Language Matter to Political Philosophy?* and *Critical Encounters between Philosophy and Politics.*

Charles Davis is professor of religious studies at Concordia University, Montreal. Among his recent books are *Theology and Political Society* and *What Is Living, What Is Dead in Christianity Today? Breaking the Liberal-Conservative Deadlock.*

Francis Schüssler Fiorenza is Charles Chauncey Stillman Professor of Roman Catholic Theology at the Divinity School of Harvard University. He is the author of *L'assenza di dio come problema teologico* and *Foundational Theology: Jesus and the Church;* translator and editor of Friedrich Schleiermacher's *On the Glaubenslehre: Two Letters to Dr. Lücke;* and co-editor, with John Galvin, of the recently published *Systematic Theology: Roman Catholic Perspectives* (2 volumes).

Jürgen Habermas is professor of philosophy at the University of Frankfurt. Among the works for which he is most noted are *Knowledge and Interest; Legitimation Crisis;* and *The Theory of Communicative Action* (2 volumes).

Matthew Lamb is professor of theology at Boston College. He is the author of *History, Method, and Theology: A Dialectical Comparison of*

Wilhelm Dilthey's Critique of Historical Reason and Bernard Lonergan's Meta-methodology and *Solidarity with Victims: Toward a Theology of Social Transformation.*

Helmut Peukert is a professor at the Pedagogical Institute of the University of Hamburg. He is the author of *Science, Action, and Fundamental Theology: Toward a Theology of Communicative Action* and *Wilhelm Flitner und die Frage nach einer allgeminen Erziehungswissenschaft im 20. Jahrhundert.*

Gary M. Simpson is associate professor of systematic theology at Luther Northwestern Theological Seminary in St. Paul, Minnesota. Articles of his on political theology have appeared in the *Journal of Religion,* the *Journal of the American Academy of Religion, Currents in Religion and Intellectual Life,* and in *Habermas und die Theologie,* edited by Edmund Arens.

David Tracy is Andrew Thomas Greeley and Grace McNichols Greeley Distinguished Service Professor of Catholic Studies at the Divinity School of the University of Chicago. His books include: *Blessed Rage for Order; The Analogical Imagination; Plurality and Ambiguity;* and *Dialogue with the Other.*

Robert Wuthnow is professor of sociology at Princeton University and the author of *The Consciousness Reformation; Experimentation in American Religion: The New Mysticisms and Their Implication for the Churches; Meaning and Moral Order: Explorations in Cultural Analysis; The Restructuring of American Religion: Society and Faith Since World War II; Communities of Discourse: Ideology and Social Structure in the Reformation, the Enlightenment, and European Socialism,* and *Acts of Compassion: Caring for Others and Helping Ourselves.*